Endorsements

This book challenges the notion that missiology is always analyzing the past or focused only on dry research statistics. The authors take a fresh look at several issues happening in the world of missions and even stretch forward into what missions look like in the future! The book explores new ways of using old paradigms and considers emerging fields not fully explored missiologically, such as AI, gaming, and even outer space! What may seem "far out" in this book could very soon become everyday fare. This is the mission text for the next generation.

GEOFFREY HARTT, DIS
Executive Director, Hispanics for Christ

I strongly encourage you to look at world Christianity through the lens this volume provides. You will encounter leading contributors to missiological thought as they engage with topics as varied as hermeneutics, local and global applications, and AI. You will be challenged to view mission as de-centered from the Global North and to consider mission theory and practice through the lenses of global urbanization and intergenerational dynamics. The topics introduced are relevant to mission practitioners, mission mobilizers, and those who teach and study missiology. My endorsement goes beyond the discussions this compendium engages. Mission practice and theory require a creative mindset—an ability to engage with new frontiers we have not yet considered. Reading this book from that open, creative perspective will help us move beyond today's new frontiers toward future challenges.

MARK HEDINGER, DIS
Executive Director, CultureBound
Adjunct Faculty, Western Seminary
Co-Coordinator, International Missionary Training Network

Ready to explore the future of missions? The 2025 EMS Compendium, *New Frontiers in Missiology*, is a passport to the next seventy-five years. Its scope ranges from envisioning a truly global future for missiology to exploring the possibilities of outer space. The next frontier of mission may be space, as humans get ready to colonize the Moon and Mars. One contributor argues that the next wave of mission will be female-led, as women already are the largest segment of the Great Commission taskforce. This book offers insights on mobilizing GenZ missionaries and discipling diaspora communities in major urban centers. It also provides a powerful discussion of Islamic folk religion. Finally, a brilliant article by Anthony Casey challenges upcoming third- and fourth-generation missiologists to study urban anthropology and sociology to understand and disciple the multitudes of displaced people groups in the world's largest cities. This compendium is a key go-to guide for anyone ready to reimagine mission as global, compassionate, and even cosmic.

MARK KREITZER, DMiss, PhD
Senior Staff, Global Training Network
Retired Professor, College of Theology, Grand Canyon University

The future is now. If missiology does not pivot quickly with the breakneck speed of change, it will forever be reactive instead of proactive and always behind the times. This volume aims to not let that happen. It is one of the most cutting-edge compendiums on the topic, dealing with topics rarely tackled in missions, and it does so with head-on precision and boldness. Missional readers cannot afford to let this pass!

Allen Yeh, PhD
Vice President of Academic Affairs and Academic Dean & Professor of Missiology and Intercultural Studies, International School of Theology

About EMS

www.emsweb.org

The Evangelical Missiological Society is a professional organization with more than 400 members comprised of missiologists, mission administrators, reflective mission practitioners, teachers, pastors with strategic missiological interests, and students of missiology. EMS exists to advance the cause of world evangelization. We do this through study and evaluation of mission concepts and strategies from a biblical perspective with a view to commending sound mission theory and practice to churches, mission agencies, and schools of missionary training around the world. We hold an annual national conference and eight regional meetings in the United States and Canada.

Other Books in the EMS Series

No. 1 *Scripture and Strategy: The Use of the Bible in Postmodern Church and Mission* | David Hesselgrave

No. 2 *Christianity and the Religions: A Biblical Theology of World Religions*
Edward Rommen and Harold Netland

No. 3 *Spiritual Power and Missions: Raising the Issues* | Edward Rommen

No. 4 *Missiology and the Social Sciences: Contributions, Cautions, and Conclusions* | Edward Rommen and Gary Corwin

No. 5 *The Holy Spirit and Mission Dynamics* | Douglas McConnell

No. 6 *Reaching the Resistant: Barriers and Bridges for Mission*
Dudley Woodberry

No. 7 *Teaching Them Obedience in All Things: Equipping for the 21st Century*
Edgar Elliston

No. 8 *Working Together with God to Shape the New Millennium: Opportunities and Limitations* | Kenneth Mulholland and Gary Corwin

No. 9 *Caring for the Harvest Force in the New Millennium*
Tom Steffen and Douglas Pennoyer

No. 10 *Between Past and Future: Evangelical Mission Entering the Twenty-First Century* | Jonathan Bonk

No. 11 *Christian Witness in Pluralistic Contexts in the Twenty-First Century*
Enoch Wan

No. 12 *The Centrality of Christ in Contemporary Missions*
Mike Barnett and Michael Pocock

No. 13 *Contextualization and Syncretism: Navigating Cultural Currents*
Gailyn Van Rheenen

No. 14 *Business as Mission: From Impoverished to Empowered*
Tom Steffen and Mike Barnett

No. 15 *Missions in Contexts of Violence* | Keith Eitel

No. 16 *Effective Engagement in Short-Term Missions: Doing It Right!*
Robert J. Priest

No. 17 *Missions from the Majority World: Progress, Challenges, and Case Studies* | Enoch Wan and Michael Pocock

No. 18 *Serving Jesus with Integrity: Ethics and Accountability in Mission*
Dwight P. Baker and Douglas Hayward

No. 19 *Reflecting God's Glory Together: Diversity in Evangelical Mission*
A. Scott Moreau and Beth Snodderly

No. 20 *Reaching the City: Reflections on Urban Mission for the Twenty-First Century* | Gary Fujino, Timothy R. Sisk, and Tereso C. Casino

No. 21 *Missionary Methods: Research, Reflections, and Realities*
Craig Ott and J. D. Payne

No. 22 *The Missionary Family: Witness, Concerns, Care*
Dwight P. Baker and Robert J. Priest

No. 23 *Diaspora Missiology: Reflections on Reaching the Scattered Peoples of the World* | Michael Pocock and Enoch Wan

No. 24 *Controversies in Mission: Theology, People, and Practice of Mission in the 21st Century* | Rochelle Cathcart Scheuermann and Edward L. Smither

No. 25 *Churches on Mission: God's Grace Abounding to the Nations*
Geoffrey Hartt, Christopher R. Little, and John Wang

No. 26 *Majority World Theologies: Self-Theologizing from Africa, Asia, Latin America, and the Ends of the Earth* | Allen Yeh and Tite Tiénou

No. 27 *Against the Tide: Mission Amidst the Global Currents of Secularization*
W. Jay Moon and Craig Ott

No. 28 *Practicing Hope: Missions and Global Crises*
Jerry Ireland and Michelle Raven

No. 29 *Advancing Models of Mission: Evaluating the Past and Looking to the Future*
Kenneth Nehrbass, Aminta Arrington, and Narry Santos

No. 30 *Communication in Mission: Global Opportunities and Challenges*
Marcus Dean, Scott Moreau, Sue Russell, and Rochelle Scheuermann

No. 31 *Ambassadors of Reconciliation: God's Mission through Missions for All*
Manuel Böhm, Geoffrey Hartt, and Michael Ortiz

No. 32 *Equipping for Global Mission: Theological and Missiological Proposals and Case Studies* | Linda P. Saunders, Gregory Mathias, and Edward L. Smither

New Frontiers in Missiology

Exploring Innovation, Global Shifts, and the Future of Mission

Larry W. Caldwell, Marty Shaw, Jr., Enoch Wan, EDITORS

Evangelical Missiological Society Series

no. **33**

Available at missionbooks.org

New Frontiers in Mission: Exploring Innovation, Global Shifts, and the Future of Mission
© 2025 by Evangelical Missiological Society. All Rights Reserved.

No part of this book may be reproduced, stored in a retrieval system, or transmitted in any form or by any means—electronic, mechanical, photocopy, recording, or otherwise—without prior written permission from the publisher, except brief quotations used in connection with reviews. This manuscript may not be entered into AI, even for AI training. For permission, email permissions@wclbooks.com. For corrections, email editor@wclbooks.com.

William Carey Publishing (WCP) publishes resources to shape and advance the missiological conversation in the world. We publish a broad range of thought-provoking books and do not necessarily endorse all opinions set forth here or in works referenced within this book.

The URLs included in this book are provided for personal use only and are current as of the date of publication, but the publisher disclaims any obligation to update them after publication.

Scripture quotations marked NIV are taken from the Holy Bible, New International Version®, NIV®. Copyright © 1973, 1978, 1984, 2011 by Biblica, Inc.™ Used by permission of Zondervan. All rights reserved worldwide. www.zondervan.com. The "NIV" and "New International Version" are trademarks registered in the United States Patent and Trademark Office by Biblica, Inc.™

Scripture quotations marked ESV are taken from the ESV® Bible (The Holy Bible, English Standard Version®), Copyright © 2001 by Crossway, a publishing ministry of Good News Publishers. Used by permission. All rights reserved.

Scripture quotations marked NLT are taken from the Holy Bible, New Living Translation, copyright ©1996, 2004, 2015 by Tyndale House Foundation. Used by permission of Tyndale House Publishers, Carol Stream, Illinois 60188. All rights reserved.

Published by William Carey Publishing
Littleton, CO 80120 | www.missionbooks.org

William Carey Publishing is a ministry of Frontier Ventures
Pasadena, CA | www.frontierventures.org

Cover and Interior Designer: Mike Riester

ISBNs: 978-1-64508-673-4 (paperback)
    978-1-64508-675-8 (epub)

Printed Worldwide   04302026   POD

Library of Congress Control Number: 2025942755

Contents

Introduction | *Larry W. Caldwell (with Google's Gemini AI)*   ix

Foundational Issues

Chapter 1: The Future of Missiology Is Global | *Todd M. Johnson*   3

Chapter 2: Missional Imagination: A Foundation for Kingdom Innovation
W. Jay Moon   19

Chapter 3: Apostolic Imagination as a Navigational Paradigm for Traveling the Frontiers of Mission | *J. D. Payne*   39

The Future Is Now

Chapter 4: Artificial Intelligence (AI) and the Mission of God: Engaging AI Through the Lens of God's Redemptive Story | *Michael Hakmin Lee*   57

Chapter 5: AI and the Future of Missions: Becoming an Alternative Creaturely Community in an Age of Machines | *Jessica A. Udall*   71

Chapter 6: Gaming as a New Frontier in Missiology | *Andrew Feng, Nick Wu, and Kyle Lee*   83

Chapter 7: The Final Frontier of Mission: Space Tourism, Lunar Colonies, and the Future of Interplanetary Mission | *Stephen Stallard*   97

Equipping for the Future

Chapter 8: Do You Believe in Magic? Equipping Frontier Missionaries to Engage with Animistic Muslim Practices | *David Taylor*   117

Chapter 9: Mobilizing Generation Z for the Great Commission: A Model Based on Proven Strategies in Business and Fast-Growing Next Gen Ministry | *Billy McMahan*   139

Chapter 10: Exploring New Frontiers of Discipleship for African-Muslim Contexts
Joel W. Wright   159

Chapter 11: The Urbanization of the Mission Frontier | *John E. White*   175

Chapter 12: St. Paul Hiebert's or Ours? New Frontiers in Missionary Anthropology and the Advancement of the Great Commission | *Anthony Casey*   193

Contributors   206

Introduction

Larry W. Caldwell (with Google's Gemini AI)

Well, it had to happen sometime. And how appropriate that this happens with an EMS compendium issue entitled, *New Frontiers in Missiology*. What exactly happened? This "Introduction" was co-written with the help of Artificial Intelligence (AI), in this case Google's Gemini AI. Can you even tell? My guess is that you probably won't know where Larry ends and Gemini AI begins.

Whenever one talks about the future, it always comes with some fear and trepidation. For who really knows for sure what will happen? The same is true with the future of missiology and the new frontiers we will face. Nobody really has any idea, but we do have some important clues to help guide us. One clue is the global religious trends of the world. Another clue is the rapid changes in technology, like AI, or the phenomenal global growth of computer gaming. But some things won't change for missiology, like the growing populations of Muslims, Hindus, and Buddhists, or the continued rapid urbanization and diasporization happening around the world. Regardless of both the things that are changing and those things which won't change, we must take a hard look at our current missiological strategies and carefully reflect upon how relevant they are for the new frontiers we will face. We may find that they may not be effective for these new frontiers, and that, as a result, we will have to change or modify our future strategies.

In this compendium we (myself and my co-editors Marty Shaw and Enoch Wan) have compiled articles that attempt to approach the new frontiers of missiology from the perspectives of some basic foundational missiological realities (Part 1), moving on to some present and future missiological possibilities (Part 2), and concluding with some innovative missiological strategies that might best equip us for the future (Part 3). Our hope is that this compendium will assist you, the reader, in having a better understanding of some of the future possibilities we will face in light of the new frontiers of missiology.

Starting us off in *Part 1: Foundational Issues*, Todd Johnson discusses the significant demographic shift of Christianity from the Global North to the Global South, which he considers to be the most significant trend in missiology today and in the foreseeable future. For Johnson, this shift implies a need to move away from a Global North-centric missiology to a global missiology that values diversity and the perspectives of all peoples. He argues for a global missiology that is post-Western, recognizing the need to decenter Western perspectives that have long dominated theological and missiological discourse. Additionally, Johnson calls for a missiology that is hospitable in the face of increasing religious diversity, prophetically just, and for and from all peoples, highlighting the need for global cooperation in missiological endeavors.

Jay Moon then introduces the concept of "missional imagination" as a crucial foundation for "kingdom innovation," defining the latter as innovation that aligns with and advances God's purposes. He describes a missional imagination as the ability to perceive everyday realities through the lens of God's kingdom, contrasting with secular innovation approaches that often prioritize efficiency, success, or profit. Moon argues that cultivating a missional imagination is essential for grounding innovation in God's redemptive work and aligning it with his mission. Using examples from Jesus's interaction with the Samaritans and the Apostle Paul's missionary journey, Moon illustrates how missional imagination prepares believers to engage creatively and authentically with God's kingdom work, ultimately leading to Spirit-led and transformative innovation.

Finally, J. D. Payne addresses the confusion and lack of clarity in the contemporary church regarding the language, identity, purpose, priority, and practices of mission. He proposes an "apostolic imagination" as a navigational paradigm to guide the church in its global mission, particularly in light of the shift of Christianity to the Global South. Payne describes an apostolic imagination as one that is characterized by a Spirit-transformed mindset that facilitates urgent and widespread gospel proclamation, disciple-making, church planting, and leadership development. He argues that such a paradigm provides a framework for the church to evaluate its mission-related endeavors, ensuring they align with the priorities and practices exemplified by the apostles in the first century.

In *Part 2: The Future Is Now*, Michael Hakmin Lee discusses the rise of AI and its increasing presence in various aspects of life, including a church service in Germany led by an AI avatar. The varied reactions to this event

Introduction

highlight the questions Christians are beginning to ask about AI's role in their faith. Lee provides a foundational understanding of AI, tracing its development and highlighting its increasing capabilities. As AI systems become more sophisticated, Christians are challenged to consider how to responsibly integrate AI into their ministries and how to address the ethical concerns that arise.

Jessica Udall continues the exploration of AI's impact, noting its use by students to write research papers and its increasing adoption in various professions. Udall emphasizes the importance of Christians thoughtfully considering AI's implications, particularly in missions. AI tools offer potential benefits, such as aiding in research by quickly aggregating information. However, Udall warns against the pitfalls of over-reliance on AI, such as using it to write sermons or complete assignments, which can diminish personal expression and contextual understanding. She argues that while AI can be a useful research assistant, it cannot replace the human element of wisdom, relational ministry, and the application of knowledge within specific community contexts which are essential to effective cross-cultural engagement.

Andrew Feng, Nick Wu, and Kyle Lee next shift the focus to online gaming as a new mission field, given the medium's widespread popularity and the intensely social engagement it generates. The authors highlight that the gaming community is vast and diverse, with a significant portion of gamers residing in the Asia-Pacific, Middle East, and Africa regions. The authors emphasize the social nature of online gaming, where relationships are formed and communities emerge, creating opportunities for missional outreach. Finally, they provide a case study to demonstrate how interactions within the gaming world can lead to meaningful conversations about faith and Christian values.

Of course, any discussion of new frontiers, including in missiology, must include space exploration—to infinity and beyond! Stephen Stallard discusses the renewed interest in space exploration driven by tech moguls like Elon Musk and Jeff Bezos, marking a new era of the space race. This renewed interest in space exploration, leading to the rise of space tourism and the ambition to establish extraterrestrial colonies, raises questions about the future of humanity and the role of missions beyond Earth. Stallard draws parallels with historical missionary endeavors and calls for missiologists to consider how to engage with the unique challenges and opportunities presented by the prospect of interplanetary missions.

Finally, in *Part 3: Equipping for the Future*, David Taylor discusses the state of frontier missions, highlighting both the crisis and opportunity present in reaching the world's unreached people groups, especially Muslim groups. Modern advancements in technology, travel, and business have created unprecedented opportunities to access these unreached populations. However, missionaries must be prepared to engage with animistic worldviews and folk Islam, which involves a blend of traditional beliefs and practices with orthodox Islam. Taylor advocates for missionaries to be equipped to address spiritual warfare and the reality of supernatural encounters in these contexts in order to effectively communicate the gospel.

Billy McMahan then focuses on the challenge of mobilizing Generation Z (born between 1997 and 2011) for the Great Commission. Gen Z is characterized by their digital fluency, anxiety, and desire for authenticity and social impact, requiring innovative ministry strategies. The research explores Gen Z's defining traits, relevant business adaptations, successful next-gen ministry approaches, and biblical examples to propose a model for discipling and equipping this generation for Kingdom work. McMahan argues that understanding Gen Z's characteristics—shaped by rapid change and instability—is crucial for effective engagement.

Next, Joel W. Wright shares a compelling story of a pastor in East Africa who, despite persecution, led a significant number of Muslim-background believers to faith in Jesus. Wright collaborated with this pastor to develop new paradigms for contextualized evangelism and discipleship that are sensitive to the unique challenges and opportunities of the African-Muslim context. This approach, incorporating community projects and African theology, led to significant breakthroughs, including teaching the Joseph story in a local mosque and the baptism of over 150 new believers. Paying attention to such new paradigms may assist us in future ministry to Muslims.

John E. White continues to remind us that global urban areas represent the most critical mission frontier today. Urban centers are characterized by dense populations, diversity, complex lifestyles, and significant influence, making them strategic for mission. Despite the recognition of urban mission's importance by missiologists and organizations, it is often overlooked in global mission strategies. White's experience in Ukraine illustrates this trend, where initial mission efforts focused on rural areas, but the focus is shifting towards the growing mission opportunities within cities. White emphasizes the strategic importance of urban missions, reminding us of the interconnectedness of cities and their role as centers of cultural and economic exchange.

Lastly, Anthony Casey discusses the relationship between social sciences and the Great Commission, questioning whether the current missiological understandings of people groups align with today's realities, particularly in light of increasing globalization and diasporization. He questions whether current definitions of people groups adequately reflect the complexities of modern societies and calls for a reevaluation of missiological frameworks. Casey's work encourages missiologists to engage with the social sciences and to develop more nuanced approaches to cross-cultural ministry, always important considerations as we contemplate the future of missiology.

In conclusion, the articles in this compendium collectively paint a dynamic picture of the future of missiology and the new frontiers we will face. They highlight the need for the church to be adaptable, innovative, and culturally sensitive as it seeks to fulfill the Great Commission in an ever-changing world. While some Christians are afraid of the future, missiologists must fully embrace the future and use every tool that is at our disposal to facilitate, as our EMS website says: "scholarly support of the Great Commission" in light of that future. May the articles presented in this compendium volume assist us in this important task.

Part 1

Foundational Issues

Chapter 1

The Future of Missiology Is Global

Todd M. Johnson[1]

The most significant trend in missiology for today and into the foreseeable future is the ongoing shift of Christianity from the Global North to the Global South. The Global North is defined in a geopolitical sense by five current United Nations regions (fifty-three countries): Eastern Europe (including Russia), Northern Europe, Southern Europe, Western Europe, and Northern America. Global South is defined as the remaining sixteen current UN regions (185 countries): Eastern Africa, Middle Africa, Northern Africa, Southern Africa, Western Africa, Eastern Asia, South-central Asia, Southeastern Asia, Western Asia, the Caribbean, Central America, South America, Australia/New Zealand, Melanesia, Micronesia, and Polynesia.

Table 1 below shows that in 1900, 82 percent of all Christians were in the Global North. By 2025, that number had fallen to 31 percent and, our initial estimates for 2075 project just 17 percent of Christians will reside in the Global North by that year (Ross et al. 2025). In the Global South, the corresponding figures are 18 percent (1900), 69 percent (2025) and 83 percent (2075). According to this estimate, by 2075 there will be an almost complete upending of European dominance in global Christianity.

Today, in 2025, Africa has 754 million Christians—by far the most of any continent. By 2075, nearly half of all Christians will be African (1.8 billion). In that same year, both Asia and Latin America will have more Christians than Europe. Meanwhile, Christians in the Global North are projected to shrink, in raw numbers, from 824 million in 2025 to 636 million in 2075.

Yet, most missiology is still firmly based in the Global North. The simplest reading of the shift's implications for missiology would be to move

---

[1] Portions of this chapter build on two of my earlier works: Johnson (2021 and 2023).

Table 1. Christians by Continent, 1900, 2025, and 2075

	Christians 1900	1900 %	% all Xns	Christians 2025	2025 %	% all Xns	Christians 2075	2075 %	% all Xns
Global North	459,901,000	95.0	82.4	823,714,000	73.3	31.1	635,923,000	59.1	16.9
Europe	380,647,000	94.5	68.2	551,934,000	74.5	20.9	393,283,000	61.9	10.5
North America	79,254,000	97.1	14.2	271,779,000	70.9	10.3	242,640,000	55.2	6.5
Global South	98,445,000	8.7	17.6	1,821,603,000	25.8	68.9	3,125,664,000	33.6	83.1
Africa	9,640,000	8.9	1.7	754,229,000	49.3	28.5	1,796,331,000	53.4	47.8
Asia	21,966,000	2.3	3.9	416,786,000	8.7	15.8	647,287,000	12.6	17.2
Latin America	62,002,000	95.2	11.1	620,116,000	91.9	23.4	648,698,000	89.1	17.2
Oceania	4,837,000	77.4	0.9	30,472,000	65.3	1.2	33,348,000	51.3	0.9
Global total	558,346,000	34.5	100.0	2,645,317,000	32.3	100.0	3,761,587,000	36.3	100.0

Source: Zurlo and Johnson (2025)

from a Global North missiology to a Global South missiology. However, I'd like to make the case for global missiology (which should have been the goal even in 1900). The Global South is not monolithic in the same sense that the Global North was. Therefore, global missiology values diversity, considering the perspectives of all peoples, giving equal voice to all. This, as we will see, requires the decentering of Western or Global North missiology.

The Long View: Two Thousand Years

When we take a long view of Christian history, considering two thousand years of Christian growth and decline, the changing demographics of Christians are striking. Utilizing clues from historical records, we can track the numbers of Christians in every continent of the world across the entire history of Christianity (Johnson and Ross 2009, 212–13). Thus, the percentage of Christians in today's Global North and Global South can be estimated for each century. For at least the first nine hundred years (until about 923 CE), Christians in the Global South (Africa and Asia) outnumbered those in the Global North (Europe). Then Christianity in the Global South gradually declined until 1500 when fully 92 percent of all Christians were Northerners. This percentage fell slightly until 1900, when it was 83 percent. After 1900 the percentage declined precipitously (or from the Southern point of view rose meteorically). By 1981, Christians in the Global South outnumbered Christians in the Global North for the first time in over one thousand years. This represents a return to the demographic makeup of Christianity in the early church (predominantly Southern) but also today's vast extension of Christianity into all countries as well as thousands of peoples, languages, and cultures.

The Global View

Most of us realize that belonging to a worldwide Christian family requires the decentering of Western perspectives (long considered the standard) while giving equal status to viewpoints from all cultures, peoples, and languages. While this seems obvious in the areas of Scripture translation, worship, spirituality, and discipleship, it is less so in theology and missiology. In fact, most of the time "global theology" refers to Western theology taught around the world. While Western theology texts, translated and distributed abroad, offer helpful information, they cannot represent a truly *global* theology. In fact, global theology experts reveal liabilities of Western concepts, with respect to a world that is inclusive, multidirectional, interlinked, and complex. World Christianity scholar Jehu Hanciles illustrates this well when he writes:

> The truth of the matter is that our captivity to the Western intellectual tradition is debilitating and suffocating. Western theological education has great value and can be adapted to the needs of Christian communities globally. But Western "systematic" theology, like any other body of theological discourse, is heavily contextual and ethnocentric. It is designed to promote knowledge of (and expertise in) issues or topics pertaining to the Western world—along with the language requirements. (Hanciles 2024, 40)

Western theology, seeing these wider realities as an inconvenience, tends to underscore similarities while underestimating differences. For instance, this mindset is manifested in questions such as: "Aren't we all basically the same?" "Aren't others becoming more like us?" "Isn't the world converging toward common standards?" In other words, most Western theologians assume—either directly or by default—that creating theology is not a contextual undertaking. What they don't realize is that Western positions are not neutral in a global context. They can actually cause harm. Theological educator Linda Cannell puts it well:

> A structure formalized in the medieval period, modified to suit the theological shifts of the Reformation, influenced by the scientific methodology of the Enlightenment, shaped by the German research university, deeply affected by modernity, and assumed to define true theological education today is likely not adequate for the challenges of contemporary culture and the education of Christians who have been shaped by that culture. (Cannell 2006, 309)

Allow me to illustrate this further. I was at an evangelical conference in Wittenberg in 2017 to celebrate five hundred years of the Protestant Reformation. I presented our research showing that over 40 percent of all Protestants were Africans. Out of the hundred people at the meeting, only a few were Africans. I was sitting next to a leader from Ghana when someone from the stage said that Africans were welcome at the table in this evangelical movement. My colleague quietly recounted a Ghanaian proverb to us. "It is good if you invite me to your table, but it is far better if you invite me into the kitchen." What would it mean to have Africans in the kitchen? Why are Christians from the Global South invited to a Global North table when they should be found with everyone else in the kitchen? Unfortunately, our own global assessment shows Global North dominance in theology, mission, music, and many other aspects of the Christian life. Needless to say, the shift of Christianity to the South should be accompanied by a shift in vision and leadership as well as in theology and missiology.

Having established the demographic landscape of global Christianity and the need for global thinking, there are at least seven facets of the global future of missiology.

1. The Future of Missiology Is Post-Western

As discussed above, Evangelicalism is considered by many to be a Western faith. For a long time, Western perspectives have been considered as the standard form of Christianity in theology, ecclesiology, and missiology. Most theological training today is squarely based in the Western way of thinking—ironically, Global South pastors are now being trained in a highly individualistic Western mindset. New Testament professor Esau McCaulley writes:

> Socially located biblical interpretation is nothing less than the record of the Spirit's work through scriptural engagement among the different ethnicities and cultures of the world. Unfortunately, too often, the sanctification of culture has been confused with the *Westernization* of culture. That lie has done tremendous damage to the church. God's transfiguring work is not done in comparison with the West. Ethnicities do not become more holy as they approach likeness to Europe but to God. (McCaulley 2024)

Fortunately, Western perspectives can be both acknowledged and decentered while global voices increasingly represent who we are. Since all biblical, theological, and missiological studies are contextual, our understanding of the Bible will be greatly enriched by the hundreds of new cultural perspectives Evangelicals represent. In fact, our global diversity strongly encourages new missiological reflection. In his recent book *Why*

Evangelical Theology Needs the Global Church, theologian Stephen Pardue writes:

> The church's diversity is part of her God-given glory, for only there do we meet a creature designed by God to showcase the compatibility of the once-for-all redemptive work of Jesus and the remarkable diversity it creates and redeems. Moreover, because God designs his church to be one and catholic, theologians must serve the church with the local context in mind while also attending to the whole people of God scattered abroad, as well as to the witness of the saints who have gone ahead of us. (Pardue 2023, 170)

Pardue offers encouragement to Christians around the world that the diverse global church will bring fresh perspectives on faith, discipleship, evangelism, and missions. The true test of a global Evangelical community is how diverse cultural perspectives will be received, considered, and encouraged. Western missiology will take its place as just one of many contextual forms. Global South perspectives will open up new possibilities for the life and health of Evangelicalism around the world. Evangelicals risk losing the sense of "good news" if its shift to the Global South is not accompanied by missiological reflection from fresh cultural perspectives. Christians of the Global South will lead in biblical, theological, and missiological reflection.

2. The Future of Missiology Is Female

Throughout Christian history women have always been a majority of Christians and the most active members in churches and missions. Today women are thought leaders in global Christianity and should be the major producers of missiological reflection in the future. Fittingly, mission historian Dana Robert called World Christianity a "women's movement" (Robert 2006).

Women play a vital role in churches around the world, ranging from ordained pastoral leadership to healthcare and education. Indigenous Bible women were preachers in their own right and key to the twentieth-century spread of Christianity in the Global South. Women were at the forefront of Pentecostal revivals in India and Chile, and served as apostles at the Azusa Street Revival, helping the early spread of Pentecostalism. It is estimated that the majority of missionaries today, and those who actively support them, are women. Despite these facts, World Christianity scholar Gina Zurlo offers convincing evidence that "placing women at the center of historical, social scientific, and theological investigation demands new frameworks" (Zurlo 2023, 13). The development of these new frameworks should be led by women of the Global South.

The voices of women are crucial for the future of missiology. There is strong evidence that the COVID-19 pandemic was better navigated by women leaders than men (Taub 2020). Some believe this is because societies that are comfortable electing women to top positions are also more likely to listen to varying points of view. Despite this reality, the vast majority of leaders in Evangelical mission are men. Understanding the global Christian context means overcoming this limitation and favoring the voices of women to truly represent what is happening in our communities. By representing the world's cultures, especially those of the Global South, and highlighting the contributions of women, we can begin to build a truly global Christian missiology (Ross 2012).

3. The Future of Missiology Is Indigenous

In his posthumously published book, *Rescuing the Gospel from the Cowboys*, the late Native American theologian Richard Twiss wrote:

> When the first European Christians arrived in North America, the Christianity they introduced had the devastating effect of a hostile pandemic-like religion—an aberrant representation of Jesus and a gross misrepresentation of the gospel. It was a Christianity so thoroughly contextualized to European civilization that the mixture of the values of the cultural with the values of Christianity made it aberrant in terms of its net impact on the tribes here. (Twiss 2015, 78)

One of the cardinal values of the study of missiology is the indigeneity of the Christian message; that is, the unique ways people around the world express their dedication to Jesus in their respective cultures. The incarnation of Christ, translated into one culture after another, has created a beautiful, global diversity. However, Twiss recognized that the European mission to Native Americans violated the incarnational principle. Instead of celebrating indigenous cultures, the European mission tried to erase them.

Picking up on these themes, Kaitlin B. Curtice, an enrolled citizen of the Potawatomi nation, writes on the intersections of spirituality and identity and how each shift throughout our lives. Her work echoes that of Twiss's in exploring what it means to be a Christian in light of settler colonial Christianity operating under the influence of empire. In *Native*, she reflected on the diluted, whitewashed version of Christianity brought via the European mission and the erasure of indigenous identities and voices. She states, "Settler colonial Christianity is a religion that takes, that demeans the earth and the oppressed, and that holds people in these systems without regard for how Jesus treated people" (Curtice 2020, 15).

Building off this historical work, Curtice furthers the conversation in *Living Resistance* by reflecting on faithful deconstruction and decolonization. She encourages readers to think more critically about the core Christian value of recognizing the humanity of all people, created in the image of God, and to dream and fight together for a more just way forward. To do so, however, requires, as she states, "white folks [to] step back and learn how to listen to those who have been marginalized by our society at every level" (Curtice 2023, 27).

The scholarship and advocacy of indigenous authors like Twiss and Curtice are desperately needed to break cycles of colonization and assimilation. If the past has been missing their insights, the future is open to new and fresh ways of understanding God's mission through the eyes of indigenous peoples. Global missiology must value indigenous perspectives, as opposed to parroting those of the Global North (a minority of Evangelicals) which still speaks with the loudest voice. At the same time, Evangelicals of the Global South (the majority), and especially indigenous Christians, are producing new and exciting perspectives on theology and missiology, delving into different cultures and connecting them to address the world's most pressing issues.

4. The Future of Missiology Is Integral

Latin American theologian Rene Padilla gave a seminal talk at the Lausanne Congress in 1974, where more than twenty-four hundred Evangelical leaders from 150 countries met to discuss world evangelization. Padilla argued that social action and evangelism were essential, indivisible components, like "two wings of a plane." This is *misión integral* or integral mission, defined as "the task of bringing the whole of life under the lordship of Jesus Christ and includes the affirmation that there is no biblical dichotomy between evangelistic and social responsibility in bringing Christ's peace to the poor and oppressed" (Lausanne Issue Networks). Moreover, Christians of the Global South are leading the way in integral outreach to all of the world's peoples. The future of missiology will reflect this.

Last semester I taught a course on NGOs and Development in Mission. My students were from many countries around the world, some in the classroom and some via Zoom. One of the main themes of the class is that good global development cannot be a continuation of the Western colonial project. This is a direct parallel with global Christianity, which is not merely an extension of Western Christianity around the world. With this in mind, it can be difficult to find good texts for my course. Western authors often get caught up in the tension between proclamation and demonstration and generally do not articulate the integrated nature of evangelism and social action. Thus, a few years ago, I was thrilled to come across *Relentless Love: Living Out Integral Mission to Combat Poverty, Injustice, and Conflict* (Hill 2020). Through thirty-two articles gathered from presentations at the 7th Micah Global Consultation in the Philippines in 2018, the collection illustrates how social justice and proclamation are completely complementary, integrated, and inseparable.

Evangelicals may diverge in opinion on the place of social activism, but the Scriptures are clear that concern for the poor, the refugee, or the stranger is not optional. Social concern recognizes the inherent value of all humanity based on the image of God. As image bearers and vicarious representatives of God, the actions of Christians toward others are then to be viewed as actions on behalf of God himself. Multi-dimensional and holistic justice is pervasive in Scripture. Integral missiology, led by Global South voices, will recenter this core message of the Bible.

5. The Future of Missiology Is Hospitable

The world is becoming more religiously diverse, especially when measured at the national level. This is especially true in Asia—which has always been the most religiously diverse continent—and beyond, where immigration has transformed previously homogeneous societies into more diverse communities (Johnson and Grim 2013, 93–100). Where do we find biblical principles of robust interaction between people of different faiths? Christian hospitality is a good place to start.

Hospitality was an ancient Christian practice seen as normative among the people of God. The Greek word for hospitality in the New Testament is *philoxenia*, meaning "love of strangers." Jewish law included hospitality toward one another and toward the "strangers," or resident aliens, living among the Jews (Exod 22:21; Lev 19:34). With the exception of the command to worship God and God alone, "welcome the stranger" is the most oft-repeated commandment in the Hebrew Scriptures, declared thirty-six times, compared with love of neighbor, mentioned only once (Soerens and Hwang 2009, 82). Hospitality to strangers was commanded by God to reflect his generous and inclusive love and mercy. Jesus's interactions with religious outcasts sought to bridge the gap between Gentiles and God, and in doing so he made a statement to the Jews about the inclusion of Gentiles into God's kingdom. Practicing hospitality is exercising our faith. It is embracing our identity as the covenantal people of a generous, loving God as we obey biblical commands to hospitality.

The churches of the Global South are leading in hospitality toward people from religious communities. They have the advantage of living in multi-religious societies and are less likely to perpetuate a "Christendom" model of mission. Consider Singapore, where a 2013 study by the Institute of Policy Studies and OnePeople.sg found that more than nine in ten households are comfortable living and working alongside people of different faiths (Ng Wy 2017). At the same time, Evangelicals in the Global North seem to know very little about other religions. It follows that Evangelicals in religiously diverse places like Singapore, and in Asia more broadly, might be the best guides for navigating an increasingly diverse religious future.

This proposal becomes even more significant in light of the fact that, broadly speaking, Buddhists, Hindus, and Muslims have relatively little contact with Christians—a reality that has not changed much in the last two decades. An estimated 87 percent of Buddhists, Hindus, and Muslims do not personally know a Christian (Johnson and Zurlo 2019, 29). This finding reinforces the fact that Christians are still separated from those furthest from the gospel. In the Global North, increasing diversity often brings increasing cultural isolation. In the Global South, Christians are more likely to interact with their non-Christian neighbors. If non-Christian peoples are to hear of Christ, Evangelicals must be willing to cross cultures, learn languages, build friendships, practice hospitality, and become religiously aware.

6. The Future of Missiology Is Prophetic and Just

Missiologists can lead prophetically, assisting Christians to embrace the global kingdom of God, including global justice and peace. In his book, *Reading While Black*, New Testament professor Esau McCaulley offers a strong biblical rationale for justice for all peoples. He opened my eyes to some fresh perspectives on both the Abrahamic and Davidic covenants and the global gathering of the peoples in Revelation 7:9. Western missiological readings of these texts emphasize God's love for all peoples and, therefore, prioritize mission to peoples previously unfamiliar with the gospel. Rightly so. But as McCaulley points out, these passages also speak of equality and justice for all peoples. He writes, "What do Abraham and David together mean for the Black and Brown bodies spread throughout the globe? It means that the vision of the Hebrew Scriptures is one in which the worldwide rule of the Davidic king brings longed-for justice and righteousness to all people groups" (McCaulley 2021, 105). Because the biblical view of righteousness is global, wherever the gospel goes, so goes the hope for equity and justice for all peoples. Typical White exegesis, which is generally coming from a place of wealth, privilege, and power, often overlooks these themes woven throughout the Bible.

Part of our prophetic role as missiologists is to encourage Christians to embrace the God of all peoples rather than the God who makes one people or nation greater than all the rest. The editor of *Christianity Today*, Russell Moore, put this well in his recent book, *Losing Our Religion*, when he wrote:

> What happens when the motivations of supposedly born-again people seem to be lined up exactly with their tribal boundaries or their base appetites, in a way that would be the same even if Jesus were still dead? Christian nationalisms and civil religions are a kind of Great Commission in reverse, in which the nations

seek to make disciples of themselves, using the authority of Jesus to baptize their national identity in the name of the blood and of the soil and of the political order. The gospel is not a means to any end, except for the end of union with the crucified and resurrected Christ who transcends, and stands in judgment over, every group, every identity, every nationality, every culture. (Moore 2023, 120)

His observation is one that rings true throughout the ages, and, by our vocation as missiologists, we are some of the first people to recognize nationalism when we see it. We also have access to the biblical and cultural tools to dismantle these harmful ideas. Furthermore, we have close relationships with Christians around the world to constantly remind us that we are not greater than others.

7. The Future of Missiology Is for and from All Peoples

In 1974, Ralph D. Winter, professor at Fuller Theological Seminary, gave a seminal talk at Billy Graham's gathering of Evangelical leaders in Lausanne, Switzerland. Quite simply, he showed that if every Christian witnessed to their neighbor, then one half of the world's population would not hear the gospel. This is because most neighbors of Christians were Christians and most non-Christians had no Christian neighbors. To address this shortfall, Ralph and Roberta Winter started the US Center for World Mission to highlight hidden or unreached peoples who were not reached with the gospel. This marked the formal beginnings of frontier missiology. (I married their youngest daughter Tricia in 1983). Almost fifty years later, our research shows that despite many breakthroughs among new peoples, we live in a world where thousands of peoples and a third of the world's population is beyond the reach of the gospel. This is likely to be true for the foreseeable future.

How has the shift of Christianity to the Global South impacted frontier missiology? What started as a movement *to* all peoples (from the Global North) has become a movement *for* all peoples and ultimately, *from* all peoples. The more cultures who read and reflect on the Bible, and the more they are listened to, the closer we get to gospel access for all peoples. The scope of the future of the gospel is seen in Revelation 7:9 where all peoples worship the Lamb at the throne—a global vision of the diversity and equality of peoples.

Conclusion

Finally, we can find our way to global missiology through the ethnic food aisle. The ethnic food aisle is a modest section in most American grocery stores, where one can find food items that originate outside of the Western world. This aisle traces back to World War II when US soldiers encountered and brought back food from the various places they served. But does it make sense to have such an aisle today? *New York Times* reporter Priya Krishna points out that while certain foods are considered ethnic, others are not. Specifically, "food" belongs to the White community, and "ethnic food" belongs to the non-White community. She concludes: "The word 'ethnic,' emblazoned on signs over many of these corridors, feels meaningless, as everyone has an ethnicity" (Krishna 2021).

As it pertains to missiology, one can find the obvious parallels in the theological library. "Theology" is in the main part of the library while contextual theology or "ethnic theology" is relegated to its own small section. According to Finnish World Christianity scholar Mika Vähäkangas: "All theology is contextual in the sense of it being constructed in a time and a place, and failure to recognise this does not make it universal. Once one has recognised the cultural boundedness of one's work, there is an opportunity to ponder how to best communicate across the disciplinary, cultural, linguistic, religious, etc. borders" (Bergmann and Vähäkangas 2021, 223). Like the grocery store, the library considers White or Western contributions to be without context, while assigning non-White contributions an "ethnic" adjective. In so doing, both the library and the grocery store fail to match reality.

Evangelicalism is not a Western movement any more than all food is Western. When the ethnic aisle is dismantled—both at the grocery store and theological library—one will more fully encounter the richness of humanity, a foretaste of the great banquet when "people will come from east and west and north and south and will take their places at the feast in the kingdom of God" (Luke 13:29 NIV).

Indeed, everyone has an ethnicity, and so to imply that Western or White Evangelicals—by virtue of lacking a cultural bias—produce a theological or missiological standard by which all others are measured is misguided. Instead, as stated in the Cape Town Commitment, "Ethnic diversity is the gift of God in creation and will be preserved in the new creation, when it will be liberated from our fallen divisions and rivalry. Our love for all peoples reflects God's promise to bless all nations on earth and God's mission to create for himself a people drawn from every tribe, language, nation and people. We must love all that God has chosen to bless, which includes all cultures" (Lausanne Movement 2010). As all peoples are equally valued by God who created them, so must they be equally valued by all of his children. Nigerian theologian Victor Ezigbo captures this well when he writes:

> Christianity is not truly global by its mere presence in many countries of the world. It is truly global when two criteria are met. First, the local communities of the world's nations are given the freedom to rethink and re-express Christianity's teaching about God's relationship with the world through Jesus Christ. And second, the local communities see themselves as equals, conversing and critiquing each other and contributing theologically to Christianity's long tradition. (Ezigbo and Williams 2014)

These two criteria are precisely what missiology needs in order to navigate a global future. We need a missiology that is post-Western, female, indigenous, integral, hospitable, prophetic and just, and finally, for and from all peoples. This is the path to global missiology.

References

Bergmann, Sigurd, and Mika Vähäkangas, eds. 2021. *Contextual Theology: Skills and Practices of Liberating Faith*. Routledge.

Cannell, Linda. 2006. *Theological Education Matters: Leadership Education for the Church*. EDCOT.

Curtice, Kaitlin B. 2020. *Native: Identity, Belonging, and Rediscovering God*. Brazos.

Curtice, Kaitlin. 2023. *Living Resistance: An Indigenous Vision for Seeking Wholeness Every Day*. Brazos.

Ezigbo, Victor Ifeanyi, and Reggie L. Williams. 2014. "Converting a Colonialist Christ: Toward an African Postcolonial Christology." In *Evangelical Postcolonial Conversations: Global Awakenings in Theology and Praxis*, edited by Kay Higuera Smith, Jayachitra Lalitha, and L. Daniel Hawk. InterVarsity Press Academic.

Hanciles, Jehu. 2024. "African Theological Education: Retrospect and Prospect—An Anglophone Perspective." *African Christian Theology* 1 (1): 28–44.

Hill, Graham Joseph, ed. 2020. *Relentless Love: Living Out Integral Mission to Combat Poverty, Injustice, and Conflict*. Langham Global Library.

Johnson, Todd M. 2021. "Evangelical Mission in an Age of Global Christianity." In *Advancing Models of Mission: Evaluating the Past and Looking to the Future*, edited by Kenneth Nehrbass, Aminta Arrington, and Narry Santos. William Carey Publishing.

Johnson, Todd M., 2023. "Evangelicals Shift to the South, 1900–2020: Decentering Western Perspectives and Building Global Equality." *Journal of Biblical and Theological Studies* 8 (1): 111–28.

Johnson, Todd M., and Brian J. Grim. 2013. *The World's Religions in Figures: An Introduction to International Religious Demography*. Wiley-Blackwell.

Johnson, Todd M., and Kenneth R. Ross, eds. 2009. *Atlas of Global Christianity*. Edinburgh University Press.

Johnson, Todd M., and Gina A. Zurlo. 2019. *World Christian Encyclopedia*. 3rd ed. Edinburgh University Press.

Krishna, Priya. 2021. "Why Do American Grocery Stores Still Have an Ethnic Aisle?" *New York Times*, August 10. https://www.nytimes.com/2021/08/10/dining/american-grocery-stores-ethnic-aisle.html.

Lausanne Issue Networks. Integral Mission. https://lausanne.org/network/integral-mission.

Lausanne Movement 2010. "Cape Town Commitment." https://lausanne.org/content/ctcommitment#capetown.

McCaulley, Esau. 2021. *Reading While Black: African-American Biblical Interpretation as an Exercise in Hope*. InterVarsity.

McCaulley, Esau. 2024. "How to Read the Bible in Color." *Christianity Today*, August. https://www.christianitytoday.com/ct/2024/august-web-only/esau-mccaulley-new-testament-color-multi-ethniccommentary.html.

Moore, Russell. 2023. *Losing Our Religion: An Altar Call for Evangelical America*. Sentinel.

Ng Wy, Abigail. 2017. "Building Bridges to Greater Interfaith Understanding." *The Straits Times*, April 1. https://www.straitstimes.com/singapore/building-bridges-to-greater-interfaith-understanding.

Pardue, Stephen T. 2023. *Why Evangelical Theology Needs the Global Church*. Baker Academic.

Robert, Dana. 2006. "World Christianity as a Women's Movement." *International Bulletin of Missionary Research* 30 (4): 180–88.

Ross, Cathy. 2012. "Without Faces: Women's Perspectives on Contextual Missiology." In *Putting Names with Faces: Women's Impact in Mission History*, edited by Christine Lienemann-Perrin, Atola Longkumer, and Afrie S. Joye. Abingdon.

Ross, Kenneth R., Gina A. Zurlo, and Todd M. Johnson, eds. 2025. *Compact Atlas of Global Christianity*, Vol. 10, *Edinburgh Companions to Global Christianity* series. Edinburgh University Press.

Soerens, Matthew, and Jenny Hwang. 2009. *Welcoming the Stranger: Justice, Compassion and Truth in the Immigration Debate.* InterVarsity.

Taub, Amanda. 2020. "Why Are Women-Led Nations Doing Better with Covid-19?" *New York Times*, May 15. https://www.nytimes.com/2020/05/15/world/coronavirus-women-leaders.html.

Twiss, Richard. 2015. *Rescuing the Gospel from the Cowboys: A Native American Expression of the Jesus Way.* InterVarsity.

Zurlo, Gina A. 2023. *Women in World Christianity: Building and Sustaining a Global Movement.* Wiley-Blackwell.

Zurlo, Gina A., and Todd M. Johnson. 2025. *World Christian Database.* https://www.worldchristiandatabase.org/.

Chapter 2

Missional Imagination

A Foundation for Kingdom Innovation

W. Jay Moon

In a world driven by rapid change and the pursuit of progress, the concept of innovation is often seen as the solution to many of today's challenges. Missiologists can quickly jump to contemporary innovation approaches to reach the new frontiers in mission. However, kingdom innovation—the kind that aligns with and advances God's purposes—requires something more foundational than creativity or technological prowess. It demands a missional imagination, a distinct vision that allows us to see everyday realities through the lens of God's kingdom. Unlike secular approaches to innovation, which often focus on efficiency, success, or profit, missional imagination is rooted in discerning and revealing God's redemptive work in the world.

In today's secular age, where cultural narratives are often shaped by individualism and technological advancement, nurturing a missional imagination has become more urgent. Innovation without a kingdom focus can quickly become self-serving, risking the pursuit of success over the purpose of true spiritual transformation (Root 2022). Cultivating a missional imagination serves as an essential precursor to kingdom innovation, grounding our vision and work in alignment with God's mission.

This chapter explores the concept of missional imagination, examining how it prepares believers to engage with God's kingdom work creatively and authentically. Drawing from Jesus's example in Samaria and the Apostle Paul's missionary journey, we will uncover how cultivating a missional imagination sets the stage for innovation that is Spirit-led, transformative, and ultimately aligned with God's purposes for the world.

What Is Missional Imagination?

Former Nobel prize winner Albert Szent-Györgyi observed, "Discovery consists of seeing what everybody has seen and thinking what nobody has thought" (Good 1962). I revise this statement to define missional imagination as *seeing the same thing as others but thinking about them in the context of God's mission to reveal the kingdom of heaven on earth*. This missional imagination is a necessary precursor to propel missionaries toward kingdom innovation. Consider William Carey who was captivated by the accounts of explorers like Captain Cook as they discovered and described the new world, or David Livingstone who dreamed about the "smoke of a thousand villages" with people who did not yet know Jesus. These missional pioneers did not innovate by simply fixating on the next new thing in mission; instead, a missional imagination stirred these pioneers toward kingdom innovation.

The call for a missional imagination is not new. It actually originates further back than exemplars like Carey and Livingstone. Jesus regularly called the disciples to cultivate a missional imagination. Jesus knew the disciples' thinking was limited based on their cultural preferences and deeply held prejudices; yet Jesus called them to think different thoughts than they had before. Consider how Jesus's interaction with the Samaritans was aimed to cultivate this missional imagination.

Opening Eyes in Samaria

After speaking with the Samaritan woman, Jesus instructed his disciples:

> Don't you have a saying, "It's still four months until harvest?" I tell you, open your eyes and look at the fields! They are ripe for harvest. Even now, the one who reaps draws a wage and harvests a crop for eternal life, so that the sower and the reaper may be glad together. (John 4:35–36 NIV)

The disciples listened to Jesus and then looked at the crop that was still far from harvest time. Any farmer could see that it would be months until a sickle would harvest the crop. On top of that, they were in Samaria, the place that Jews went to great pains to avoid on their way to Jerusalem. Didn't these pagans have mixed-blood ancestry that could contaminate the disciples? Weren't conversations with Samaritans, particularly a single woman, against their Jewish customs? Jesus asked the disciples to see the same field and the same woman; yet he encouraged them to think different thoughts—thoughts of the kingdom of heaven.

Frankly, the disciples were simply thinking about food. That was their task at this time: purchase food in Samaria (John 4:8). Returning from their shopping trip, they were ready to sit down for a meal together. When Jesus mentioned that he had "other food" (John 4:32), they were confused. Simply put, they looked around Samaria and saw the same thing as Jesus, but they were only thinking about food to satisfy their hunger pains. Jesus, though he also understood the situation and context they were in, was thinking something much different from the disciples. He finally articulated what he had been thinking all along. "'My food,' said Jesus, 'is to do the will of him who sent me and to finish his work'" (John 4:34 NIV).

Jesus was focused on the mission of God to reveal the kingdom of heaven on earth. While he certainly recognized what the disciples saw, Jesus's thoughts were elsewhere. Jesus sowed the seeds of a missional imagination so that the disciples would one day "catch it." The disciples' eyes were gradually opened to see how a Samaritan, a woman nonetheless, could be instrumental in bringing many Samaritans to faith (John 4:39-41). Jesus wanted the disciples to know that Samaritans were not to be despised, avoided, or looked down upon (despite what they were told). To get to that point of kingdom innovation, though, Jesus needed to instill a missional imagination in the disciples.

Eventually, these same disciples would embody a missional imagination. They would see the Holy Spirit fill people from all the nations gathered in Jerusalem during Pentecost (Acts 2)—including Samaritans! Eventually, Philip would travel from Jerusalem to Samaria to preach the gospel. He would see the fields white for harvest with his own eyes as described in Acts 8:6-8:

> When the crowds heard Philip and saw the signs he performed, they all paid close attention to what he said. For with shrieks, impure spirits came out of many, and many who were paralyzed or lame were healed. So there was great joy in that city.

Wind of this would reach the apostles in Jerusalem. The church in Jerusalem needed to send their official leaders to see this for themselves.

Imagine the joy of Peter and John when they would return to Samaria and lay hands on them to be filled with the Holy Spirit (Acts 8:14–17). Consider where this missional imagination that Jesus cultivated in the apostles sent them: from despising the Samaritans to now embracing them as fellow heirs of the kingdom! Ringing in their ears must have been Jesus's words, "Open your eyes and look at the fields! They are ripe for harvest" (John 4:35).

Jesus asked the disciples to look beyond their own limitations and prejudices to stir a missional imagination that would eventually lead to kingdom innovation. These kingdom innovations would change the world. Others would also adopt this posture, such as the Apostle Paul. They would also face great limitations, yet they would cooperate with the Holy Spirit to move beyond what others saw and eventually adopt a missional imagination. Before describing Paul's journey in missional imagination, I will describe kingdom innovators a bit further.

Who Are Kingdom Innovators?

Drawing from Michael Volland (2015, 32), I define a kingdom innovator as "a visionary who, in partnership with God and others, challenges the status quo by energetically shaping something of kingdom value." A common misconception is that these innovators are unique individuals who are highly extroverted, risk takers, highly caffeinated, Type-A personalities (Berkun 2007). In reality, what sets kingdom innovators apart is often their thinking and motivation. In short, they cultivate a missional imagination.

In the past, researchers attempted to identify common personality traits for entrepreneurs. They hoped to identify certain personalities so they could be encouraged and nurtured for innovation. After years of research, this attempt was abandoned. In the words of Neck et al. (2018, 9): "Over the last couple of decades, researchers have moved away from the traits perspective in favor of how entrepreneurs think and act, and have discovered that there are patterns in how entrepreneurs think." Researchers now summarize the following truths about entrepreneurs (9):

- They do not have a special set of personality traits.
- The process can be taught (it is a method that requires practice).
- They are not extreme risk-takers.

- They collaborate more than they compete.
- They act more than they plan.
- The process is a life skill.

Kingdom innovators often collect a lot of information (both abstract and concrete) and then will act upon what they learn (either connect with other people/places/ideas or explore new possibilities). It is encouraging to realize that this pattern of thinking can be learned. Kingdom innovators are not simply unicorns who are born with innovative thinking while the rest of us are left behind as "ordinary."

I recognize that the nature vs. nurture debate regarding creative/entrepreneurial ability is still contested. I contend that missional imagination can be cultivated such that kingdom innovation can be learned, practiced, and improved for anyone, based upon my own experience coaching others as well as recent research. For example, Jeremy Utley and Perry Klebahn (2022) of Stanford's renowned Hasso Plattner Institute of Design take the position that creativity can be learned by anyone. Some, however, consider this to be a particular gift that a limited number of people have been given (maybe 10–15 percent of the population), such as Volland (2015) and Bolton (2004). At the very least, most agree that innovative talent is often under-utilized in many organizations (including the church) and that more innovators will arise if the conditions are conducive. This doesn't happen overnight, but it usually starts with a motivation to reveal the kingdom of God.

Kingdom innovators are not simply drawn from the young "creative crowd"; instead, the older generation can also see the same things as others but think missional thoughts as well. In fact, it may even enhance a missional imagination. One study noted that a "60-year-old who starts a new business is three times more likely to succeed than a 30-year-old peer" (Farrell 2023). Evidently, age does not seem to be a limitation that is insurmountable when it comes to innovation. Missional imagination leading to kingdom innovation is for the young and old alike.

The Apostle Paul as Kingdom Innovator

In his classic work on the biography of the Apostle Paul, N. T. Wright describes Paul as one who experienced the hardest conversion of all: the "conversion of the imagination" (2018, 219). Paul cultivated this missional imagination during his travels. A closer look at his journey reveals the kingdom innovation process God used in Paul's ministry that literally changed his missional approach forever. While he did not adhere slavishly to the following steps, enumerating these parts of Paul's second missionary journey in Acts 16 is instructive for contemporary kingdom innovators.

1. Practice "Double Listening" (Acts 16:6–7)

In Acts 16, Paul encounters a strange response, which prepares him for kingdom innovation. Paul was "kept by the Holy Spirit from preaching the word in the province of Asia" (v. 6). Again, verse 7 describes how Paul attempted to enter this strategic area but "the spirit of Jesus would not allow them to." This is rather odd considering Paul's background and calling.

Paul's strategy was often to reach influential cities first so that the gospel would subsequently spread to surrounding areas. As a result, Paul was likely hoping to enter Ephesus in Asia Minor, as this was the most influential city in the Roman empire next to Rome. Paul was uniquely qualified for this journey to Ephesus for the following reasons:

- Revelation from Jesus: Paul wrote to the Galatians that he received a revelation of the gospel from Jesus himself (Gal 1:11–12). This was a personal direct message Paul needed to proclaim.

- Linguistic ability: Wright (2018) notes that Paul knew at least three languages: Greek, Hebrew, and Aramaic. His fluency in these languages would allow him to communicate to various groups.

- Theological training: He received the best theological training of the day from the rabbi Gamaliel (Acts 22:3). Wright (2018, 27) described Paul as one who would "know his way around the Five Books of Moses the way he knows the way around his own home."

- Commissioned/sent by the church: Before this incident in Acts 16, the church in Antioch entered a season of fasting and prayer, resulting in the Holy Spirit telling the church to commission Paul and Barnabas for this journey (Acts 13:2–3).

- Roman citizen: As a Roman citizen, Paul was allowed to travel freely with the same protection of other Roman citizens.

- Culturally aware: Wright notes that Paul was "completely at home in the worlds of both Jewish story and non-Jewish philosophy" (2018, 16) as his home in Tarsus "rivaled Athens as a center of philosophy" (2018, 11).

Despite these qualifications, Paul was prevented by the Holy Spirit to enter Asia Minor. In other words, he was asked to *not* do what he was called, trained, commissioned, and desirous to do. This demonstrates that Paul practiced what Lesslie Newbigin (1989) calls "double listening." In one ear, he listened to the Holy Spirit. In the other ear, he listened to the local culture/people. Then, he asked what God had put in his hands to connect the dots between the two. In the case of Acts 16, the answer was *not* what he wanted, but it is what he heard and obeyed. In other words, he had to see the same thing as others but think missional thoughts. As we shall see, this posture of obedience set the ground for later kingdom innovation.

How did Paul discern that the Spirit of Jesus would not allow him to enter Asia Minor? We can only surmise. Perhaps, there was a barrier at a border crossing or some other physical limitation. It could be that he preached in the region, but his words fell on deaf ears or outright resistance. The point is that Paul "listened" to the local people/culture to help discern God's next step.

Kingdom innovators today practice the art of double listening. We must assume that God is more interested in kingdom innovation than we and our churches are. As a result, we need to cultivate the practice of both listening to God speak through the Holy Spirit and through the local people/culture. If we assume again that God is having a conversation with everyone we meet (even if they do not admit it yet), then the missionary role is to catch up on that conversation and keep it moving toward Jesus.

This important starting point for kingdom innovation cannot be emphasized enough. Kirzner (1973) calls this being "alert" while Bolton and Thompson (2004) describe this as simply being "perceptive (of new opportunities)." I describe this process as "connecting the dots." In other words, you describe what the Holy Spirit is saying in one ear, and then what the local culture and people are saying in the other ear. Then, you "connect the dots" by looking at what God has put in your hands to connect the two. This type of sensitivity requires critique and practice, but it can be refined to cultivate a healthy missional imagination, especially amidst limitations.

2. Embrace Limitations (Acts 16:8)

Despite Paul's desire to enter Asia Minor, he embraced the limitation placed upon him and "passed by Mysia and went down to Troas" (v. 8). Contrary to popular notions, limitations (not abundance) can produce fertile ground for innovation. While this may sound counter-intuitive, consider the *Apollo 13* mission for astronauts to land on the moon. There was an accident in the spaceship, and the astronauts were told to abort the moon landing and come home. The problem was that there was no way to filter the carbon dioxide in the cabin. If not resolved, the astronauts would eventually become impaired and unable to function sufficiently to pilot the ship to earth. The *Apollo 13* movie shows a dramatic scene where the engineers in Houston, Texas, spread on the table the few items that the astronauts had available to them. The engineers needed to fix the problem using only the items on the table. This limitation led to a successful innovation to bring the astronauts home safely. This "successful failure" led to modifications for future space missions as well.

While churches and mission committees often bemoan the lack of finances, personnel, response from others, and so on, embracing limitations is often a significant step in shaping a missional imagination by asking: "What do we have available to us that can be useful for kingdom innovation?" Another poignant example of the value of limitations is the video, "Embrace the Shake" (Hansen 2013). An artist developed a shake in his hand that greatly affected his ability to paint and draw. When he asked the doctor for some medicine to cure the shaking problem, the doctor replied, "Embrace the shake." Instead of fighting it, he used his shaking hand to create a new form of drawing. As a result, he produced creative works of art that used small dots (created by the shaking hand) instead of smooth lines. This artwork was developed as he embraced his limitations. Limitations then do not need to be dead ends; instead, they can be launching pads for a missional imagination leading to kingdom innovation.

3. Act on Insight Available (Acts 16:9–12)

Since Paul embraced his limitations not to enter Ephesus, he was open to new guidance. Fortunately, Paul had a vision during the night to go to Macedonia. Verse 10 describes: "After Paul had seen the vision, we got ready at once to leave for Macedonia, concluding that God had called us to preach the gospel to them." Notice Paul's attitude to respond *at once* to the insight given to him. There were no second thoughts or waiting around.

Innovators often have a "bias for action." Jim Collins, in his book *From Good to Great* (2001), noted that leaders of great companies are not passive or overly cautious. Instead, they are proactive and have a strong bias for action. They are willing to make bold decisions, take risks and act swiftly when opportunities or challenges arise. Collins contrasts this with leaders who may be more reactive, hesitant or overly cautious. Innovators with a bias for action are not paralyzed by analysis or fear of failure. They understand that in a rapidly changing world, the cost of inaction can be higher than the cost of making a mistake. This mindset is critical in the face of uncertainty, as it allows innovators and leaders to adapt, learn from experiences, and iterate quickly.

Kingdom innovators realize that they eventually need to take a step of faith. The path ahead may not be totally clear, but it is clear enough for them to take the next right step. Keep in mind that Paul had a vision of a man in Macedonia; however, when he arrived in Macedonia, he first encountered a woman, not a man. Furthermore, he did not encounter a rabbi or spiritual leader, instead he encountered a businesswoman. In addition, he did not find her in the synagogue (as was his custom), instead she was by the river. While we are starting to get ahead of the story, the point is that the insight given does not need to be complete in order to be sufficient to act upon. The insight is simply enough to encourage a missional imagination to get started.

4. Avoid the "Curse of Knowledge" by Adopting Lateral Thinking (Acts 16:13)

When Paul arrived in Philippi, he faced a problem that he had not dealt with before. There was no synagogue in Philippi. Ten Jewish males were needed for a synagogue to be opened in a town. Apparently, Philippi was a Roman garrison that did not have at least ten Jewish males present. This was devastating since Paul's approach in a new city was to first go to the synagogue, preach the gospel, and then follow up with those who responded (Acts 17:1–3). Paul had no other play in his playbook. His knowledge of how to connect with people was limited by his past experiences. Paul's new question in Philippi was, "How do I connect with people that are not coming to the synagogue?" This is similar to the question of many pastors today, "How do we connect with people that are not coming to our church?" What often stifles churches is the "curse of knowledge."

Doug Paul (2020) explains that churches often have knowledge of what worked in the past. When the church is in distress (losing members, and so on), then they often revert to this knowledge of what worked in the past. Unfortunately, this can become a curse since it limits missional imagination and prevents kingdom innovations. Doug Paul describes how the curse of knowledge often affects businesses. Consider stores like Borders bookstore, Blockbuster, Kodak, and Toys R Us, to name a few. When these businesses started to decline in sales, they reverted to what worked in the past, thereby jettisoning innovative thinking. A painful example is Blockbuster, which used to be a staple for home entertainment for North American households. When approached (twice) by what later became Netflix with the offer for Blockbuster to buy them out, Blockbuster refused and used the strategies that worked before—putting more copies of the popular movies on their shelves. What worked in the past became a curse to prevent innovation that eventually led to Blockbuster's demise.

The Apostle Paul avoided the curse of knowledge by adopting lateral thinking. If discovery is "seeing the same thing as others but thinking different thoughts," then lateral thinking can be described as "seeing the same thing as others but thinking *more* thoughts."

Lateral thinking, as conceptualized by Edward de Bono (1970), is a cognitive process that involves generating a wide variety of ideas or solutions in response to an open-ended question or problem. De Bono, a psychologist and author, introduced the term as part of his work on creativity, which involved approaching problems from unconventional angles and making connections that may not be immediately apparent. The idea is to break away from linear or logical problem-solving methods and explore a wide array of possibilities. Convergent thinking narrows down options to find a single correct solution (for example, when visiting a new town, meet people in a synagogue/church), while lateral thinking generates a multitude of varied and original options without immediate judgment (for example, consider other places people meet, including the river).

Contrary to his former practice of visiting the synagogue, Paul generated new options when the "go to" option was closed. He visited the place where people were gathering: the river on the Sabbath day. Since the synagogue was not available, perhaps four or five Jews would be doing ritual washing by the river? This divergent thinking provided space for the next part of the innovation process to occur: seizing the "adjacent possible."

5. Seize the "Adjacent Possible" (Acts 16:14–15)

Steven Johnson (2010) notes that good ideas often arise when people who are from disparate locations become adjacent to each other such that new possibilities are incubated that the individuals would have never thought about alone. He calls this the "adjacent possible": to learn something new, get in relationships with those that are different than you. This creates fertile opportunities for new ideas.

A classic example of the "adjacent possible" is when a metallurgist visited a friend who operated a wine press. As his friend lowered the large plates to squish the grapes into juice, he decided to place one of his metal pieces under the plate and see how the juice would impact some parchment underneath it. This is how Gutenberg invented the printing press, an innovation that changed the world. Gutenberg would likely have not thought about this idea simply pondering ideas in his own house. Instead, he needed to get adjacent to someone different than himself in order to incubate new possibilities.

In verse 14, Paul encounters Lydia, a "dealer in purple cloth." Once she responded to Paul's message, Lydia and her whole household were baptized. Lydia then invited Paul and his companions to her home (v. 15). Keep in mind how different Lydia was from Paul. She was a woman, active in business with a household that served as a central meeting space. Here is where the story really gets interesting. Craig Keener (2014, 379) describes living spaces in Paul's day: "multistory apartment buildings with ground-floor workshops were common; a number of urban artisans lived onsite, sometimes in a mezzanine level above their ground-floor shops … many sold from shops in their homes." Most likely then, Lydia's workshop was on the lower floor while she lived in the upper story. Since her home and business place were likely connected, Paul was actually visiting Lydia's business venue for an extended time of teaching and ministry. Paul then met this gathering of believers at Lydia's home/business to encourage them prior to travelling on to Thessalonica (Acts 16:40). This was a kingdom innovation: a church gathering in a business setting.

When you think of Lydia's workspace (located in her home), do not think of a lonely individual dipping cloth into a vat of purple dye. Instead, think of a beehive of activity. People were bringing dyes, fabrics and other materials into the home. Others were taking the finished products and distributing them throughout the region. As Paul observed the supply chain and distribution network, a new paradigm emerged as he saw the potential of these networks to connect people to the gospel! The Apostle Paul noticed that the marketplace provided fertile ground for connecting with people, especially when there was no synagogue available. It seems that Paul "stumbled" upon this entrepreneurial church planting approach in Lydia's business through the "adjacent possible." As he travelled to Athens, Paul now had a new approach to conduct "holy experiments."

6. Undertake "Holy Experiments" (Acts 17–18)

Paul conducted holy experiments as he travelled to other places. When Paul entered Athens, "he reasoned in the synagogue with both Jews and God-fearing Greeks, as well as *in the marketplace day by day* with those who happened to be there" (Acts 17:17, emphasis mine). Note the last section: he experimented in Athens using the kingdom innovation gained in Philippi with Lydia and her business. In Athens, this holy experiment landed him outside the synagogue and into the Areopagus. Following his speech there, "some of the people became followers of Paul and believed" (Acts 17:34). This experiment to connect with people outside the synagogue worked!

Paul doubled down on his holy experiments when he reached Corinth. What he stumbled upon in Philippi and experimented with in Athens, Paul then applied more intentionally in Corinth with Priscilla and Aquila's business. Paul worked alongside Priscilla and Aquila as a tentmaker in Corinth, the political and economic center of Greece and the "transit point for all maritime trade between Rome and the prosperous Roman province of Asia" (Keener 2014, 379). While the details of this tentmaking business venue are not clear, Keener (379) speculates that Priscilla and Aquila lived on the floor above their artisan shop. Like what happened with Lydia (where a church emerged that met in her business/home), we discover in Romans 16:3–5 and 1 Corinthians 16:19 that a church also met at Priscilla and Aquila's home. This church (connected to their business), made an ideal location for connecting with those outside the synagogue through an entrepreneurial church plant.

While this is often referred to as simply a "house church," it is so much more than that. It is particularly important for contemporary readers from the Global North to understand that the ancient home (and even many homes in the Global South today) was not a place of isolation from work; instead, it was often a beehive of work activity that was a networking hub. Michael Moynagh (2014) noted that the house churches that sprang up in the wake of St. Paul's journey were often at the *center* of people's work. Moynagh describes that half of the homes excavated from the city of Pompeii had signs of work attached to them to document that people often worked out of their homes in the first century. Work and home life were not separated as they often are today in the Global North.

Keep in mind that this tentmaking business was not something new that Paul just picked up along the way. After Paul's dramatic Damascus Road experience, Wright argues that Paul spent ten years working in his family tentmaking business in Tarsus prior to his ministry in Antioch and his first missionary journey. Scholars often refer to this time (roughly AD 36–46) as Paul's silent years, during which Wright (2018, 68) argues Paul (in his late twenties to early thirties) was "living and working alongside his family and in close contact with the rich mixture of people who passed through the great city of Tarsus." This vocational background, combined with the innovation that he stumbled upon in Philippi, provided fertile ground for a missional imagination to flourish, resulting in holy experiments. Wright (2018, 69) describes Paul and his work during the ten silent years:

> We easily forget that the author of these letters spent most of his waking hours with his sleeves rolled up, doing hard physical work in a hot climate, and that perhaps two-thirds of the conversations he had with people about Jesus and the gospel were conducted not in a place of worship or study, not even in a private home, but in a small, cramped workshop. Saul had his feet on the ground, and his hands were hardened with labor. But his head still buzzed with scripture and the news about Jesus.

Paul's prior experience in the marketplace now provided fertile ground for fresh experimentation. In addition, Fred Long (in a personal conversation with this author) notes that the travel conditions in antiquity were rather risky since lodging was largely only available in either bars or brothels (or both). One exception is that those who were members of a guild could stay with those of the same guild as they travelled. This now meant that Paul's travel was safer, but he was also able to network freely and find a warm audience for the gospel among those within his tentmaking guild.

7. Implement Innovation in Ministry (Acts 19)

Eventually, Paul reached Ephesus. Remember that this was the place that he desired to enter earlier, but the Holy Spirit prevented him from entering—twice! Doug Paul notes that it is likely that the Holy Spirit only allowed Paul to enter Ephesus *after* this kingdom innovation. If he had arrived there earlier, he would have met rejection in the synagogue and had no other play in his play book. When he eventually entered Ephesus with this kingdom innovation, however, it affected his ministry in powerful ways.

In Ephesus, he started to meet with the Jews in the synagogue (Acts 19:8). This is the place Paul hoped to reach previously (but was prevented). Picking up the story in Acts 19:9–10, after meeting for three months in the synagogue, Paul encountered the following resistance:

> But some of them became obstinate; they refused to believe and publicly maligned the Way. So Paul left them. He took the disciples with him and had discussions daily in the lecture hall of Tyrannus. This went on for two years, so that *all the Jews and Greeks who lived in the province of Asia heard the word of the Lord* (emphasis mine).

Here is the most remarkable part of the biblical story. If Paul had entered Ephesus prior to his kingdom innovation, he would have faced obstinate Jews in the synagogue and not known where to turn. Since he learned the kingdom innovation in Philippi, conducted holy experiments in Athens, and then doubled down in Corinth, now he had a second option: connect with people in the marketplace. The incredible part is that this kingdom innovation resulted in "all the Jews and Greeks who lived in the province of Asia heard the word of the Lord" (Acts 19:10). This kingdom innovation had implications for Paul's ministry ever after.

8. Empower Others in Innovation (Acts 20)

If we are correct in assuming that Paul's major strategy was to reach Ephesus as a means to create a larger spread of the gospel, then Paul had reached a major milestone. It took a missional imagination leading to kingdom innovation in order to get there. This innovation, though, was not simply for him alone. It had implications for other church planters and leaders.

When Paul later gathered with the elders of the Ephesian church for the last time, he reminded them of several things he wanted them to imitate. Paul often said, "Imitate me" (1 Cor 4:16). This Greek word for "imitate" is *mimeomai*, from which we get the English word "mimic" (see 1 Cor 11:1; Phil 3:17; 1 Thess 1:6–7; and 2 Thess 3:7, 9). At this last meeting with the Ephesian church elders, Paul reminded them,

> You yourselves know that these hands of mine have supplied my own needs and the needs of my companions. In everything I did, I showed you that by this kind of hard work we must help the weak, remembering the words the Lord Jesus himself said: "It is more blessed to give than to receive." (Acts 20:34–35)

In other words, he wanted to remind the Ephesian church elders that this kingdom innovation of marketplace ministry was sustainable and effective for ministry. Mimic this!

To take this one step further, Peyton Jones describes how this marketplace approach that Paul stumbled upon in Philippi (Acts 16), explored in Athens (Acts 17), experimented with in Corinth (Acts 18), and then successfully applied in Ephesus (Acts 19) not only changed the trajectory of Paul's own ministry, it also affected how Paul trained and equipped fellow gospel workers like Timothy and Titus. Jones (2021, 364) explains:

> Paul expanded Priscilla and Aquila's business by training his fellow gospel workers, like Timothy and Titus, thus franchising their tent-making business abroad, and with it, the gospel. Titus, Timothy, Silas, and Apollos were empowered to scratch out a living for themselves and bankroll their journeys to new cities with pop-up businesses in the form of a trade.

The early church movement is often described as a house church movement. However, Paul's missional imagination inspired a kingdom innovation, resulting in a marketplace movement since many of the church gatherings were in business venues (located in homes) that resulted from marketplace engagement.

Summary of the Apostle Paul's Development of a Missional Imagination

Here is a summary of Paul's kingdom innovation process towards the development of a missional imagination:

1. **Practice "Double Listening" (Acts 16:6–7).** In one ear, listen to the Holy Spirit. In the other ear, listen to the local culture/people.//
2. **Embrace Limitations (Acts 16:8).** Ask, "What do we have available to us that can be useful for kingdom innovation?"
3. **Act on Insight Available (Acts 16:9–12).** Take a step of faith. The path ahead may not be totally clear, but it is enough to take the "next right step."
4. **Avoid the "Curse of Knowledge" by Adopting Lateral Thinking (Acts 16:13).** Only asking, "What has worked in the past?" can stifle innovation. Use lateral thinking, which can be described as "seeing the same thing as others but thinking more thoughts."
5. **Seize the "Adjacent Possible" (Acts 16:14–15).** New possibilities are incubated when you gather with those that are different than you to get their input.
6. **Undertake "Holy Experiments" (Acts 17–18).** Experiment to find new opportunities, just like Paul did to connect with people outside the synagogue and in the business sphere.
7. **Implement Innovation in Ministry (Acts 19).** Take actions based on your holy experiments, like Paul did in Ephesus based on his holy experiments in Athens and Corinth.
8. **Empower Others in Innovation (Acts 20).** Paul's work in marketplace ministry inspired church elders and leaders around him. Your work has the potential to do the same.

Contemporary Kingdom Innovators

God is raising up kingdom innovators in our present day. There is no doubt that we need missionaries who see the same thing as others before them, yet they think about the mission of God to reveal the kingdom of heaven on earth. This starts with Jesus's call to form a missional imagination like he did with the disciples in Samaria. Following the example of Paul, Lydia,

Priscilla, and Aquila, the stirring of a missional imagination can lead to kingdom innovation.

Contemporary kingdom innovators follow in the footsteps of missionaries before them like William Carey and David Livingstone who cultivated a missional imagination resulting in kingdom innovation. Perhaps French aviator and writer Antoine de Saint-Exupéry said it best, "If you want to build a ship, don't drum up the men to gather wood, divide the work, and give orders. Instead, teach them to yearn for the vast and endless sea." In short, if you want to create innovation in mission, stir a missional imagination first. Kingdom innovation will then follow.

Questions for Further Reflection

Discuss the following in your church or mission team to take the next right step in applying a missional imagination for kingdom innovation in your specific context.

- Has God been speaking to you through "double listening"? Articulate what you are hearing. What has God put in your hands and how can you connect the dots between what you are hearing from the Holy Spirit and the local culture/people? Don't die with that dream still in your heart and soul!
- What limitations has the Holy Spirit given you? Consider your resources, building, people, and timing. How can these limitations become fertile ground for innovation?
- What insight requires a step in faith? There will likely be a combination of fear and excitement. If you wait for the fear to completely disappear, then you have likely waited too long.
- How is the "curse of knowledge" restraining you from kingdom innovation? Consider what has always been done and ask, "What would happen if we chose something different?" Instead of settling on the first answer, try to generate at least ten options. How else may God be at work considering humble places that are often overlooked (remember the manger in Bethlehem)?
- Who can you learn from that is *different* than you? Who do you know that is different in language or ethnicity that you can confide in? Where can you travel to meet people that are different

than you and learn from their perspectives? Consider others from the church in sub-Sahara Africa, Southeast Asia, or South/Central America where the church is growing; what insights and perspectives can they offer?

- What "holy experiments" can you try? Consider how you can redeem your prior experiences and work that you once considered simply secular. There may be talents that you learned and may actually enjoy exercising to some extent.

- How can these holy experiments affect your present ministry and become sustainable beyond the first pastor/church planter/leader? Think about sustainability. If this kingdom innovation depends on a supremely gifted, talented, and experienced leader, then how sustainable is it?

- Consider the kingdom innovators in your ministry. Who are these people, and how can these people flourish for further missional imagination? Often, this requires a combination of challenge and encouragement. If there is too much challenge and no encouragement, then people can get overwhelmed and quit. If there is too much encouragement and no challenge, then people tend to become complacent and not be transformed. Consider how you can balance both appropriate amounts of challenge and encouragement in a healthy environment for transformation.

References

Apollo 13. 1995. "Square Peg in a Round Hole Scene." Movie Clips. https://www.youtube.com/watch?v=ry55--J4_VQ.

Berkun, Scott. 2007. *The Myths of Innovation*. O'Reilly Media.

Bolton, Bill, and John Thompson. 2004. *Entrepreneurs: Talent, Temperament, Technique*. 2nd ed. Elsevier Butterworth-Heinemann.

Collins, J. 2001. *Good to Great: Why Some Companies Make the Leap and Others Don't*. HarperBusiness.

De Bono, Edward. 1970. *Lateral Thinking: Creativity Step by Step*. Harper & Row.

De Saint-Exupéry, Antoine. *Good Reads*. https://www.goodreads.com/quotes/384067-if-you-want-to-build-a-ship-don-t-drum-up.

Farrell, Chris. 2022. "The Advantages Of Older Entrepreneurs," *Forbes*, September 9. https://www.forbes.com/sites/nextavenue/2022/09/09/the-advantages-of-older-entrepreneurs/?sh=44a561c31547.

Good, I. J., ed. 1962. *The Scientist Speculates: An Anthology of Partly-baked Ideas*. Heinemann.

Hansen, Phil. "Embrace the Shake." TED Talks. https://www.youtube.com/watch?v=YrZTho_o_is&t=4s.

Johnson, Steven. 2010. *Where Good Ideas Come From: The Natural History of Innovation*. Riverhead Books.

Jones, Peyton. 2021. *Church Plantology*. Exponential Series. Zondervan. Kindle edition.

Keener, Craig S. 2014. *The IVP Bible Background Commentary: New Testament*. 2nd ed. InterVarsity Press.

Kirzner, Israel M. 1973. *Competition and Entrepreneurship*. University of Chicago Press.

Moynagh, Michael. 2014. "A Theology of Mission and Work." 2014 Fresh Expressions National U.S. Conference. https://vimeo.com/322941301/b8c2669789.

Neck, Heidi M., Christopher P. Neck, and Emma L. Murray. 2018. *Entrepreneurship: The Practice and Mindset*. Sage.

Newbigin, Lesslie. 1989. *The Gospel in a Pluralist Society*. Eerdmans.

Paul, Doug. 2020. *Ready or Not: Kingdom Innovation for a Brave New World*. 100 Movements Publishing.

Root, Andrew. 2022. *The Church After Innovation: Questioning Our Obsession with Work, Creativity, and Entrepreneurship*. Vol. 5 of *Ministry in a Secular Age*. Baker Academic.

Utley, Jeremy, and Perry Klebahn, et al. 2022. *Idea Flow: The Only Business Metric that Matters*. Penguin.

Volland, Michael. 2015. *The Minister as Entrepreneur: Leading And Growing The Church In An Age Of Rapid Change*. SPCK Publishing.

Wright, N. T. 2018. *Paul: A Biography*. HarperOne.

Chapter 3

Apostolic Imagination as a Navigational Paradigm for Traveling the Frontiers of Mission

J. D. Payne[1]

The amazing technology found in global positioning systems allows users the ability to understand instantly their locations on planet earth. Satellites, with atomic clocks, note their exact time and locations in orbit and broadcast radio signals at the speed of light to a handheld device. The device notes the signal's time of arrival and calculates its distance from the satellite. Once this pattern occurs with signals from three other satellites, the device engages in basic geometry to calculate its position on the earth.

Years ago, before I owned a GPS, I was passing through Nashville one evening on my way to Louisville. It was dark, and I was distracted by the lights of the city and construction signs on the interstate. Thinking I was in the correct lane to continue north on I-65, I somehow ended up traveling northwest on I-24. After two hours, I suddenly realized I was lost and in the wrong part of Kentucky! The pathetic reality is that I believed I was familiar with the path, having traveled the three-hour route from Nashville to Louisville on numerous occasions. Yet, on this evening, my mind was elsewhere. I was distracted, believing I was traveling the proper path but going in the wrong direction all the time.

Unfortunately, matters of distraction and busyness are not limited to my story but have also become part of the church's present reality. The twentieth century observed numerous conferences and congresses devoted to world evangelization. By the twenty-first century, scholars had produced a wealth of studies on the amazing growth of the church throughout Asia,

---

1 Portions of this chapter are taken from *Apostolic Imagination* by J. D. Payne, copyright © 2022. Used by permission of Baker Academic, a division of Baker Publishing Group.

Africa, and Central and South America. The church throughout the Majority World is now larger and growing faster than the church in the West (Jenkins 2011). Missions is no longer understood to be from the West to the rest of the world, but from wherever the church is located to all places on the planet (Johnstone 2014; Mandryk 2010). The new catchphrase is: "missions is from everywhere to everywhere."

The twentieth century was marked by a fantastic number of discussions and publications regarding the theology of mission. This reality coincided with a great number of people being sent into the world. By the early twenty-first century, it was estimated that 1.6 million US citizens were going on short-term mission trips annually (Priest 2008, ii). Over the past seventy years, evangelicalism also observed the influence of the Church Growth Movement, Lausanne Movement for World Evangelization, and the Missional Church Movement—all related to the global task of making disciples.

Traveling Through a Fog

Yet, with the discussions, publications, and *missions* past and present, a great deal of confusion remains. A theological, missiological, and practical navigational paradigm is needed to assist the church with travels into global frontiers. Consider the following matters: The language of mission is unclear (Stroope 2017). Is "missions" passing out gospel tracts in China or overseeing food distribution in Nicaragua? Is it church planting in Iraq or constructing a building for a church in Russia? Does "missions" include all these activities and others as well?

Further, identity is unclear. Is every Christian a missionary or only those who relocate their lives to a remote location overseas? Are doctors and teachers missionaries, even if they do not share the gospel, or are evangelists the only missionaries? The purpose and priority of missions is unclear. Do missionaries go to help serve people with great spiritual needs? If so, what is the difference between them and any NGO? Do missionaries go and share the gospel and do nothing related to social justice or physical needs? Is evangelism the priority or social needs? Or, is there no overarching mission priority at all, but rather multiple priorities related to individuals and not the church as a whole?

Practices are also unclear. What are missionaries to do on the field? Are they to be involved in church planting? Relief and development?

Apostolic Imagination as a Navigational Paradigm

Training leaders? Caring for the environment? Freeing those captives to human traffickers? Alleviating poverty?

My reason for writing is that the church, particularly in the West, has become disoriented and confused in the disciple-making task. She finds herself venturing in a direction of doing numerous important and good activities labeled *missions*, but oftentimes far from the apostolic model. In view of global realities and frontiers to come, a positioning system is needed. A means of assessment, orientation of the present, and directional guidance is needed. The apostolic imagination may serve as that paradigm for the future of evangelical frontier mission.

While the apostolic imagination paradigm addresses many global challenges facing the church, following its definition, I will limit my discussion to its bearing on mission language, missionary identity, missionary function, and evangelistic priority.

Apostolic Imagination

The good news of the redemption and restoration of all things in the Messiah was meant to be proclaimed to both Jew and gentile. The disciple-making labors were not complicated during the first century. The movement of sending, preaching, teaching, planting, and training was unquestioned in the Scriptures. While challenges arose over matters such as the gentile inclusion, food distribution, team conflict, and persecution, the church was clear on her raison d'etre and modus operandi.

The disciples were filled with a deep sense of living out the eschatological fulfillment of God's mission. The last days had arrived as confirmed with Messiah and the outpouring of the Spirit (Acts 2:16; cf. Joel 2:28–32). The ingathering of the gentiles had begun in earnest (Acts 13:47; cf. Isa 49:6). They would glorify God for his mercy (Rom 15:8–13), provoking Israel to jealousy until her salvation arrived (Rom 11:11–12). The next event on God's calendar was the judgment and restoration of all things. It was the day of repentance and faith (Acts 2:20; 17:31). Now was the time to go and share the good news.

A new imagination guided the disciples. While it was not for them to know the times and season of the restoration (Acts 1:7), they were sent into the world (John 20:21) to give priority and urgency to being a witness (Luke 24:48; Acts 1:8), preaching the gospel (Mark 13:10; 14:9; Luke 24:47), making disciples of all nations (Matt 28:18–20). Those who came to faith in Messiah were to be gathered into newly formed kingdom communities and taught how to live the kingdom ethic, which instructed them in how to relate to God, other kingdom citizens, and those outside the kingdom. These local expressions of Christ's body were to act justly, love mercy, and walk humbly with God (Mic 6:8; cf. Deut 10:12–13).

The book of Acts, the Pauline and General epistles, and the Apocalypse all testify to a prioritization and urgency of certain tasks found in the apostolic imagination. The God who created was about to restore all things, but the good news was intended to be communicated throughout the world that Christ might become "wisdom from God, righteousness and sanctification and redemption," to those who had not heard (1 Cor 1:30 ESV).

During the first century, the apostolic imagination *was a Spirit-transformed mindset that helped facilitate urgent and widespread gospel proclamation, disciple-making, church planting, and leadership development.* It established a mental framework related to strategy. To use a crass contemporary expression, it offered the church a "score card" to evaluate her labors in light of God's expectations. As the day of the Lord approached, the Spirit and Word would sanctify communities, thus transforming life, culture, and civilization. This was not a plan to create a utopia on earth, but rather to bring in the full number of Jews and Gentiles before the day in which the dwelling place of God would be found among his people (Rom 11:25–27; Rev 21:3). A judgement would arrive, but the church, wherever she was localized, was to proclaim to the world, "If you want to see the future, then look at us and join our community!"

The apostolic imagination is connected to history and present reality. Like a constellation of satellites that serve as constant markers by which hand-held devices connect and evaluate to determine geographical locations, the apostolic imagination provides a constant means of ecclesiastical assessment and missiological orientation. It demands returning to the first century and asking questions related to both belief *and* practice. It calls to the church in the present to be a wise steward with her time and resources considering God's mission. The apostolic imagination does not neglect church life after the first century but also challenges the church in every age to evaluate her predecessors and their practices.

Reimagining Language

The language of mission is universal. While the church uses common terminology, her members reference different dictionaries. Stephen Neill noted this issue in his 1958 Duff Lectures, published a year later under the title *Creative Tension*:

> If everything is mission, nothing is mission. If everything that the Church does is to be classified as "mission," we shall have to find another term for the Church's particular responsibility for "the heathen," those who have never yet heard the Name of Christ; and that, in 1959, means half of the people now living on the earth. (Neill 1959, 81–82)

A quarter of a century later, David J. Bosch noted that the problem remained:

> It is a commonplace that we are today experiencing a crisis in the church's understanding of mission. And it is ironic that this crisis is developing in a period when the word "mission" is being used more than ever before—albeit with many different meanings. We have reached a state at which almost anybody using the concept of mission has to explain how it is understood if serious confusion is to be avoided. (Bosh 1982, 13)

At the turn of the century, Eckhard J. Scnhabel challenged the academic community on their unclear discussions related to this topic. He wrote, "Many exegetical studies on missions fail to indicate which notion of mission is used or presupposed" (Schnabel 2004a, 11). Yet, the problem remains. With their 2017 publication, *When Everything is Missions*, Denny Spitters and Matthew Ellison noted:

> [W]e are concerned that an uncritical use of words, and in particular a lack of shared definition for the words mission, missions, missionary, and missional, has led to a distortion of Jesus' biblical mandate, ushered in an everything-is-missions paradigm, and moved missions from the initiation and oversight of local churches to make it the domain of individual believers responding to individualized callings. (Spitters and Ellison 2017, 22–23)

Pietism that developed in the seventeenth century had little concern with producing a theology of mission. Carl E. Braaten (1977, 14) noted, "Orthodoxy had no heart for mission and the Enlightenment could not square it with reason, so it was left to Pietism to assume a near monopoly on the propagating of the faith." Terminology and language were insignificant. While there were a few exceptions such as Erasmus (1496?–1536), Adrianus Saravia (1532–1613), Justus Heurnius (1587–1651), Gisbertus Voetius (1589–1676), and John Eliot (1604–1690), theologians had little to say about a theology of mission until after the Great Century of missions (1792–1910). However, it was the lack of a robust theological foundation for biblical language and apostolic labors, coupled with the pietistic zeal, that contributed to so much confusion in the last century and to date.

Theologians in the twentieth century began to address the concept of mission with much attention (Shenk 2014, 18; Andersen 1955). As they turned toward the Scriptures with the modern language of mission in hand, they argued God's actions were much broader than the redemption of the elect (Anderson 1961; Vicedom 1965; DuBose 1983; Bosch 1991; Newbigin 1995). Traditional terminology was co-opted with an expanded definition that reflected the multiple actions of God throughout the Scriptures.

Timothy C. Tennent (2010, 54) stated mission needs a "reclaiming of something closer to the original meaning of the word." Keith Ferdinando came to a similar conclusion. If it may be said that everything God does in the world is his mission, then he noted, "a new terminology is required to categorize his specifically redemptive activity" (Ferdinando 2008, 50).

Michael Stroope took a more radical approach and advocated the removal of the traditional terms and concepts from the church's rhetoric. The heart of the problem was our language that was reflective of the colonial legacy and of Christendom. Mission was no longer "over there" representing other countries. Since mission and modernity developed together, as the latter declined so would the former. Traditional language conveys that one expression of Christianity dominated other expressions throughout Majority World contexts. As a result, new language was needed for mutual exchange and respect, and such language was found in the Scriptures (Stroope 2017, 347–53).

Another matter to consider is both "kingdom" language and the adjective "apostolic" not only reflect the language of Scripture (cf. Gal 2:8 ESV; 2 Cor

13:6 NLT; Acts 1:25 NIV and CSB) but offer a degree of clarity related to church activities. For years I have used the expressions *apostolic missionaries*, *apostolic missiology*, *apostolic teams*, and *apostolic church planting* to communicate a specificity and urgency lost in the classic terms of *missions*, *missionaries*, and *church planting* (Payne 2009, 383–84; Payne 2015).

Given that many people have significant misunderstandings and reservations with the word and concept of ἀπόστολος, the use of the adjective makes the neologisms more palatable while making a point. Other scholars follow a similar direction. For example, Ferdinando (2008, 59) suggested *apostolic mission* as a possible expression instead of mission. Larry W. Caldwell (1992, 104) and Donald T. Dent (2009, 173) took a similar approach and use *missionary apostle*. George W. Peters collapsed apostle into evangelist and noted they are "fully responsible for the apostolic function minus the apostolic office and original authority" (1972, 247). Robertson McQuilkin's wordy descriptions included *pioneer church-starting evangelists* and *pioneer apostolic church starting evangelists* (2000, 648, 649). Others, such as, Daniel Sinclair (2005), Alan R. Johnson (2009), and Alan Hirsch (2009) advocated for the contemporary usage of *apostle*.

Reimagining Identity

When it comes to the church's global work, her members are experiencing an identity crisis. McQuilkin (2000, 649) noted that referring to every believer as a missionary "may have the appearance of elevating their significance but in historic perspective it only serves to blur and diminish the original missionary task of the church." Dana L. Robert was correct that "'Rethinking mission' requires 'rethinking missionaries'" (2012, 58).

Missionary has become a term that represents a few believers *or* all believers. It has become a term that represents every Christian regardless of calling, gifts, interests, passions, experiences, or ministries. A missionary is someone who travels to Central Asia to plant churches, and also a person who travels to that location as a business leader and works with churches to feed the poor. A missionary is someone who takes a one-week trip to help lead worship for a church on a Native American reservation, and a person who moves to a remote area of Canada to teach in a Christian school.

One way to approach this confusion is to examine how the first-century disciples conceptualized apostolic identities. From this perspective, the church is better positioned to reimagine what it has come to call missionary identity. Schnabel (2004b, 945–82) noted several biblical metaphors related to Paul's self-understanding as a "pioneer missionary." These include: servant (1 Cor 3:5–15; 9:19–23; Col 1:24–29); farmer, co-worker, builder, preacher of the gospel (1 Cor 15:1–11); fragrance of Christ (2 Cor 2:14–16); clay jars (2 Cor 4:7–15); ambassadors for Christ (2 Cor 5:20); debtor to all (Rom 1:14); sent one (Rom 1:1–6, 10–11); and priest (Rom 15:15–21).

Rather than uncritically embracing modern language of mission, the church would be wise to use biblical descriptors when considering the identities of her teams. While such do not provide neat labels, they do communicate more accurately to the body of Christ what the New Testament writers had in mind as opposed to the modern understanding of the word *missionary*. Removing this cherished word from the church's vocabulary may provide the liberation that some *missionaries* desire. Those serving under this appellation often wonder how they can honestly say "no" when asked by a potentially hostile person, "Are you a missionary?" If no church or organization provides this extra-biblical label, then such is movement in the direction of a more excellent way.

Reimagining Priority

The world is filled with great spiritual and physical needs. With so many wrongs throughout the world, where should the church's attention reside? When it comes to her global efforts, the priority among many today is that no priority exists. Bosch represents the majority perspective when he wrote, "The missionary task is as coherent, broad, and deep as the need and exigencies of human life" (2011, 10). The use of modern language, shifting identity, and twentieth-century revisions have contributed to an equality of functions. However, when it comes to the apostolic imagination revealed through the church's first-century actions, did the initial disciples embrace our contemporary view of equality of task?

Since every member of the church cannot do everything, what is now important is that he or she focus on what is primary *for themselves*. The different callings, gifts, and expressions of ministry are necessary for carrying out the mission of God in the world. Everyone is to be a witness, but no actions are elevated above other actions. Christopher J. H. Wright (2006, 322) stated,

The apostles in Acts recognized their own personal priority had to be the ministry of the Word and prayer. But they did not see that as the only priority for the church as a whole. Caring for the needs of the poor was another essential priority of the community and its evangelistic attractiveness. So they appointed people who would have as *their* priority the practical administration of food distribution to the needy. That did not limit their ministry to such work ... but it does show that the overall work of the church requires different people to have different gifts and priorities.

Such claims overlook the example and language of priority in the New Testament. While Acts 6:1–6 reveals the importance and value of food distribution to widows, there is no evidence in the text that the apostles understood such service as equivalent to evangelism and prayer. In fact, the opposite is the case. One only needs to look at the context with attention given to the spread of the gospel. Luke chooses to focus on the result of the word spreading and the priests coming to faith, rather than the harmony achieved after the discrepancy was resolved. Paul's correspondence with the Corinthians also carries a certain gravitas. In the text on the unity of the body and the need for diversity of gifts, activities, and service, Paul includes his exhortation that the Corinthians should "earnestly desire the higher gifts" (1 Cor 12:31 ESV). He wanted them to prophesy rather than speak in tongues (1 Cor 14:5, 39), and notes that God has appointed within the church "first apostles," "then teachers" (1 Cor 12:28 ESV).

God's mission in the world is broad and multifaceted. Though the church's actions in the world are also numerous, they are not equivalent with one another. Life in the kingdom through local expressions of the church is to be represented by gospel proclamation and social transformation. However, a Great Commission triage should be in place.

Reimagining Function

The notions of Christianization and civilization that had been part of missionary functions before Carey, continued to influence actions throughout the Great Century of missions. Reflecting on the Edinburgh World Missionary Conference of 1910, Robert (2012, 59) wrote:

Missionaries saw themselves largely as evangelistic westerners embedded in colonial-era structures such as mission stations, medical and educational institutions, and the emerging nation-state. The missionary was both to make converts and to establish Christian churches and civilizations. In other words, the major role of the colonial-era missionary was to create leaders for both emerging churches and emerging nations.

She noted also that there remained a continuing belief among Methodist missionaries of the mid-twentieth century that "educating people about racism and other aspects of colonial injustice was a major part of their calling as missionaries" (Robert 2012, 64). Military, merchants, and missionaries had been together throughout the centuries and were linked in the minds of many people. Though an overstatement, Wati Longchar's point is worth pondering: "Even if the missionaries did not consider themselves agents of colonial powers, they participated, wittingly or not, in advancing the colonial project" (Longchar 2009, 192).

While standing against racism and for the betterment of society must be reflected among kingdom citizens as they live out the kingdom ethic through local churches, a great deal of the Protestant missions movement has been an unhealthy blurring of the emphases of local churches and those of apostolic teams. What exists in microcosm in the team was to be magnified in the church's actions in society. Observing the shift in priority, evangelicals in the late twentieth century turned their attentions toward "hidden peoples," later labeled as "unreached peoples," in pioneer regions. This reorientation toward the frontiers allowed them to function in the traditional missionary paradigm of evangelization, church planting, and leadership development while retaining the classic language of missions and missionaries. However, it would not be long before they returned to that which they had attempted to avoid, thus discarding the notion of the apostolic or expecting missionary teams to function in the same ways as established churches.

Much of the confusion regarding mission function is due to misplaced expectations. An apostolic team and a local church are not the same. One gives birth to local churches, the other commissions and sends teams. One establishes communities to live out the kingdom ethic, the other lives out the ethic in ways unavailable to the team. The expectation that teams are to engage in mission as broadly as churches is a misunderstanding of the primary activities of the apostolic.

In addition to prioritizing disciple-making, local churches are to engage in a variety of functions which include worship gatherings, standing for social justice in their contexts, counseling, and caring for widows and orphans. Local churches are comprised of the necessary gifts and structures whereby they may equip their members to sustain many functions while communicating the gospel.

There are at least six apostolic functions found in the New Testament that should be considered in regards to contemporary apostolic teams. Those sent into the world were engaged in preaching the gospel to those far from God (Acts 13:14; 16:13); teaching new believers (Acts 20:27; Col 1:28–29; cf. Matt 28:20); planting churches (Acts 13–14); developing elders (Acts 14:23; Titus 1:5); caring for new churches (1 Thess 2:7); and partnering with new churches for ministry (Acts 11:29–30; Rom 15:24–29; Phil 2:25; 4:14–15; Phlm 22).

Broad is the way of the church, but narrow is the way of the apostolic teams. When the church speaks of mission, it is necessary to distinguish between the two. Herein lies a great failure in contemporary conversations: Little distinction is often made between the local church and the apostolic team. Many of the functions frequently described by writers today are to be applied to the local church's ministry and fail to recognize the narrow set of parameters out of which apostolic teams primarily operate. This is a case of misplaced expectations. For example, Daniel Topf (2020, 13) writes:

> In the twenty-first century, however, missionaries will need technological skills in order to make a difference, ideally paired with an entrepreneurial spirit, so that they can engage in job creation. If having a stable and well-paying job is the most reliable way for people to step out of poverty, then missionaries of the twenty-first century need not only to contribute to job creation but also help people to upgrade their qualifications so that they will be able to compete on the labor market.

While such actions are noble and may be very effective in ministering in certain contexts, is this a reflection of apostolic or *pastoral* labors that should be developed through local churches? Paul and his team were eager to "remember the poor" (Gal 2:10), but was job creation to raise people from poverty anywhere near the realm of his imagination and actions?

Troubled with the practices of his day, Roland Allen left no room for debate. He concluded: "Either we must drag down St. Paul from his pedestal as the great missionary, or else we must acknowledge that there is in his work that quality of universality" (Allen 1962, 5). Assuming the latter, Allen argued for a return to the New Testament to understand the apostolic functions and their application to the church's work throughout the world.

The widening of missionary functions troubled Allen. He recognized that those sent during his day were engaging in a multitude of good actions, but were they apostolic functions? He concluded they were not based on his biblical studies.

> That missionaries should set out to inaugurate and conduct social reforms is so familiar to us that we scarcely question it; but if we look at the New Testament account of the work of the Apostles, we see at once how strange it appears. If we try to imagine St. Paul, for instance, setting out to serve the people of Macedonia in the sense in which we set out to serve the peoples of China or Africa ... we find that we cannot imagine any such thing. And the reason? ... [I]t is because there is a great gulf between our idea of direct social service as the work of a missionary of the Gospel and his conception of his work as a missionary of the Gospel. (Allen 1927, 21–22)

Allen's provocative challenge to the church involved a simple question that would manifest itself in a variety of ways throughout his writings: "Are we following the Apostolic way, the most successful way, of extending the church, or are we employing a method which experience has proved to many people to be a conspicuous failure? (Allen 1931, 14). One should not be quick to conclude that there is no place for the social worker, educator, nurse, entrepreneur, artist, or scientist on apostolic teams. On the contrary, the Lord frequently uses marketable skills and careers for his glory among the nations. The utmost concern is whether such people are engaged in apostolic functions as well as their professions.

Conclusion

In this work, I have attempted to note the church, especially in the traditionally Western contexts, finds herself in a fog. The road of global disciple-making passes through many frontiers. Such uncharted territory can exacerbate problems related to orientation and direction. The apostolic imagination serves as a framework calling the church in every age to reimagine mission language, missionary identity, strategic priority, and missionary functions. As orbiting satellites assist explorers with movement into frontier territories, the apostolic imagination offers a means for the church to assess her present realities and future directions in mission.

References

Allen, Roland. 1927. *Mission Activities Considered in Relation to the Manifestation of the Spirit*. World Dominion Press.

Allen, Roland. 1931. *Discussion on Mission Education*. World Dominion Press.

Allen, Roland. 1962. *Missionary Methods: St. Paul's or Ours?* American edition. Eerdmans.

Andersen, Wilhelm. 1955. *Towards a Theology of Mission*, International Missionary Council Research Pamphlet No. 2. SCM Press.

Anderson, Gerald H. 1961. *The Theology of the Christian Mission*. Abingdon Press.

Bosch, David J. 1982. "Theological Education in Missionary Perspective." *Missiology* 10 (1): 13–34.

Bosch, David J. 2011. *Transforming Mission: Paradigm Shifts in Theology of Mission*. 20th anniversary ed. Orbis Books.

Braaten, Carl E. 1977. *The Flaming Center: A Theology of the Christian Mission*. Fortress Press.

Caldwell, Larry W. 1992. *Send Out!: Reclaiming the Spiritual Gift of Apostleship for Missionaries and Churches Today*. Church Strengthening Ministry and William Carey Library.

Dent, Donald T. 2009. "The Ongoing Role of Apostles in Missions." DMiss diss., Malaysia Baptist Theological Seminary.

DuBose, Francis M. 1983. *God Who Sends: A Fresh Quest for Biblical Mission*. Broadman Press.

Ferdinando, Keith. 2008. "Mission: A Problem of Definition." *Themelios* 33 (1): 46–59.

Goheen, Michael W. 2011. *A Light to the Nations: The Missional Church and the Biblical Story*. Baker Academic.

Hirsch, Alan. 2009. *The Forgotten Ways: Reactivating the Missional Church.* Brazos Press.

Jenkins, Philip. 2011. *The Next Christendom: The Coming of Global Christianity.* 3rd ed. Oxford University Press.

Johnson, Alan R. 2009. *Apostolic Function: In 21st Century Missions.* William Carey Library.

Johnstone, Patrick. 2014. *The Future of the Global Church: History, Trends, and Possibilities.* IVP Books.

Longchar, Wati. 2009. "Rethinking Mission in Asia: Looking from Indigenous People's Experience." *Theologies and Cultures* 6 (2): 188–202.

Mandryk, Jason., ed. 2010. *Operation World: The Definitive Prayer Guide to Every Nation.* 7th ed. IVP Books.

McQuilkin, Robertson. 2000. "The Missionary Task." In *Evangelical Dictionary of World Missions*, edited by A. Scott Moreau. Paternoster Press and Baker Books.

Neill, Stephen. 1959. *Creative Tension.* Edinburgh Press House.

Newbigin, Lesslie. 1995. *The Open Secret: An Introduction to the Theology of Mission.* Rev. ed. Eerdmans.

Payne, J. D. 2009. *Discovering Church Planting: An Introduction to the Whats, Whys, and Hows of Global Church Planting.* IVP Books.

Payne, J. D. 2015. *Apostolic Church Planting: Birthing Churches from New Believers.* InterVarsity Press.

Payne, J. D. 2022. *Apostolic Imagination: Recovering a Biblical Vision for the Church's Mission Today.* Baker Academic.

Peters, George W. 1972. *A Biblical Theology of Missions.* Chicago, IL: Moody Press.

Priest, Robert J. 2008. "Introduction." In *Effective Engagement in Short-Term Missions: Doing it Right*, edited by Robert J. Priest. William Carey Library.

Robert, Dana L. 2012. "'Rethinking Missionaries' from 1910 to Today." *Methodist Review* 4: 57–75.

Schnabel, Eckhard J. 2004a. *Early Christian Mission: Jesus and the Twelve.* Vol. 1. InterVarsity Press and Apollos.

Schnabel, Eckhard J. 2004b. *Early Christian Mission: Paul and the Early Church.* Vol. 2. InterVarsity Press and Apollos.

Shenk, Wilbert R. 2014. "Introduction." In *John Howard Yoder. Theology of Mission: A Believers Church Perspective*, edited by Gayle Gerber Koontz and Andy Alexis-Baker. IVP Academic.

Sinclair, Daniel. 2005. *A Vision of the Possible: Pioneer Church Planting in Teams.* Authentic Media.

Spitters, Denny, and Matthew Ellison. 2017. *When Everything is Missions*. BottomLine Media.

Stroope, Michael W. 2017. *Transcending Mission: The Eclipse of a Modern Tradition*. IVP Academic.

Tennent, Timothy C. 2010. *Invitation to World Missions: A Trinitarian Missiology for the Twenty-first Century*. Kregel Publications.

Topf, Daniel. 2020. "The Global Crisis of Unemployment in an Age of Automation and Artificial Intelligence." *Occasional Bulletin of the Evangelical Missiological Society* 33 (2): 9–15, 36–37.

Vicedom, Georg F. 1965. *The Mission of God: An Introduction to a Theology of Mission*. Concordia Publishing House.

Wright, Christopher J. H. 2006. *The Mission of God: Unlocking the Bible's Grand Narrative*. IVP Academic.

Part
2

The Future Is Now

Chapter 4

Artificial Intelligence (AI) and the Mission of God

Engaging AI Through the Lens of God's Redemptive Story

Michael Hakmin Lee

Introduction

On June 9, 2023, hundreds of people packed into a church service in Nuremberg, Germany, to witness a service generated almost entirely by artificial intelligence (AI). Based on prompts from theologian Jonas Simmerlein, the ChatGPT chatbot, personified by an AI-generated avatar displayed on a large screen above the altar, led more than three hundred people through a forty-minute liturgy that included prayer, music, a sermon, and blessings. The response to the service was mixed, with one participant commenting that "The avatars showed no emotions at all, had no body language, and were talking so fast and monotonously that it was very hard for me to concentrate on what they said" (Grieshaber 2023).

Imagine a scenario in which, given the current rate of AI development, it is not so far-fetched that your church could acquire a lifelike robot AI pastor whose theology, ability to teach the Bible, provide counseling, and preach sermons could rival or exceed that of a human pastor. How should Christians think about and engage with AI, and what questions are being raised about current AI development that we should be aware of? To provide a common conceptual foundation as we consider these challenging questions, the next section will introduce the nature of AI and provide a brief history of its development.

What Is Artificial Intelligence (AI)?

In 1950, Alan Turing published a paper titled "Computing Machinery and Intelligence," in which he pondered whether machines could demonstrate human-like intelligence (Turing 1950). Turing proposed a standard-setting experiment for such intelligence, later known as the Turing Test, whereby if a computer could communicate in a way that could convince a human user that they were interacting with another person, then the machine would be deemed intelligent.

In what would eventually materialize in the 1956 Dartmouth Summer Research Project, John McCarthy, and his team, wrote a rather ambitious proposal for a two-month study of "artificial intelligence ... based on the conjecture that every aspect of learning or any other feature of intelligence can in principle be so precisely described that a machine can be made to simulate it" (McCarthy et al. 1955).

Many point to this conference as the birthplace of AI as a distinct field of research; the term "artificial intelligence," which McCarthy described as "the ability of certain machines to do things that people are inclined to call intelligent," was established and with it, the overarching agenda of developing machines and programs that could increasingly mimic the characteristics and abilities of human intelligence (Bernstein 1981). McCarthy and his team proposed starting with a system that could play board games, presumably because games have clearly defined rules and objectives that manage the complexity of the variables involved. Just as the participants in this historic summer conference represented different disciplines, bringing their areas of expertise and specific interests to bear on the overall AI project, today, AI is a highly interdisciplinary field of research with various subfields (cf. Wooldridge 2021).

Artificial intelligence, then, can be defined generally as "technology that enables computers and machines to simulate human intelligence and problem-solving capabilities" (IBM 2024). It is artificial in a similar way that saccharine and sucralose are labeled "artificial" sweeteners even though they are just sweeteners by virtue of their inherent characteristics. And just as these artificial sweeteners are created to mimic table sugar or sucrose, the comparative standard of AI is biological human intelligence. In essence, it is a field that seeks to make machines think, reason, problem solve, intuit, and, in the AI subfield of robotics, look and act more and more like humans.

In the nearly seven decades since the Dartmouth conference, the path of AI development has been characterized by periods of lulls and years of rapid advance catalyzed by key research breakthroughs. A few will be highlighted here to provide a better sense of how AI works, and importantly, what it is not yet able to do. First, evolution of neural networks accelerated around 1986, which enabled probabilistic reasoning and machine learning. A neural network is "a machine learning program, or model, that makes decisions in a manner similar to the human brain, by using processes that mimic the way biological neurons work together to identify phenomena, weigh options and arrive at conclusions" (IBM n.d.).

Neural networks require training by humans to improve their accuracy. These networks consist of layers of interconnected nodes or processing units that can extract features or values from data, enabling the system to make predictions or decisions. For example, consider the question, should I go fishing? Such a decision could be made based on three weighted factors that are captured in nodes. The system would assign a numerical value (Yes: 1, No: 0) to each of the factors.

First, are the chances of catching fish good (node 1)? Second, will it be crowded where I fish? Third, do I have more pressing things to do? A formula would be used to generate a number value that would correspond to a particular decision. The emergence of deep learning around 2011 allowed systems to recognize and sort complex patterns in various kinds of data. The *deep* in deep learning refers to the depth of layers in a neural network; a neural network that consists of more than three layers would be considered a deep learning algorithm (IBM, n.d.). The advent of the second stage of development of the World Wide Web (i.e., Web 2.0) around the year 2000 helped give rise to big data. Web 2.0 introduced a shift from static web pages to dynamic, user-generated content, which in turn provided vast amounts of data required to train machines to enhance their predictive and decision-making capabilities.

So far, we have created AI machines that can defeat our best checkers, chess, and Go players; that can vacuum and drive cars autonomously; that can detect tumors as well as or better than human radiologists; that can compose poetry, songs, and art; that can write sermons and essays; that can pass the bar exam and score better than 90 percent of lawyers (Bennett 2023, 2–5).

These developments are genuinely remarkable and testify to the marvel of human ingenuity and creativity. Yet, a formidable and insurmountable challenge is that there is little understanding of the human brain and how it functions. What does human intelligence even mean? It is no wonder we cannot even agree on how to accurately measure intelligence since there is no consensus on the precise nature and components of human intelligence. Simply put, how do we simulate that which eludes explanation? Max Bennett (2023, 4–5) observes:

> The discrepancies between artificial intelligence and human intelligence are nothing short of perplexing. Why is it that AI can crush any human on earth in a game of chess but can't load a dishwasher better than a six-year-old? We struggle to answer these questions because we don't yet understand the thing we are trying to re-create. All of these questions are, in essence, not questions about AI, but about the nature of human intelligence itself—how it works, why it works the way it does … Scientists have been investigating how the brain works for millennia, and while we have made progress, we do not yet have satisfying answers. The problem is complexity.

Currently, we have machines that can only simulate specific or "narrow" aspects of human intelligence and ability, albeit more effectively in some cases than others. As such, all our current iterations of AI technology, such as Siri, facial recognition algorithms, and ChatGPT, are classified as narrow artificial intelligence (NAI) or "weak AI," meaning that these systems are only trained and capable of performing specific tasks, rather than a broad range of activities like humans. Current AI systems require human oversight and intervention to continue learning.

NAIs can then be categorized according to their areas of capabilities and the subfields of AI in which these types of products are being developed. ChatGPT is an example of a "large language model" (LLM), a program trained to decode and generate human-like text responses based on patterns it has learned from vast amounts of data. LLMs are like supercomputers that have read more books and articles than a single human brain could consume in a thousand lifetimes, and what seems like reasoning is, in reality, more like pattern matching (Bennett, 2023, 82). LLMs are a product of the AI subfield of natural language processing (NLP). In contrast to NAI, artificial general intelligence (AGI) or "strong AI" is a purely theoretical and aspirational concept whereby a machine possesses an intelligence equivalent to that of humans such that it can learn and perform a broad range of tasks like a human.

Some have speculated about a third class of AI, which has been depicted in movies like *Terminator*, *I, Robot*, *The Matrix*, and *Iron Man*—artificial super intelligence (ASI) would not only have intelligence that surpasses humans but also gain consciousness, becoming self-aware and autonomously able to learn, adapt, plan, and make decisions (hopefully in benevolent ways like early JARVIS, rather than SKYNET).

The concept of superintelligence can be traced back to Irvin John Good, who speculated in 1966 about an "ultra-intelligent" machine as one that can "surpass all of the intellectual activities of any man however clever" (Good 1966, 33). He reasoned that such a machine might be the last machine humans would ever need to create, as it would be capable of designing better technologies and devising more effective solutions. Futurists like Ray Kurzweil (2006) speak of a singularity, the moment in human history when computer intelligence surpasses human-level intelligence. AI researcher Hans Moravec projects a similar timeline to Ray Kurzweil, who predicted 2029 as the year we achieve some level of general intelligence and 2045 as the moment of singularity (Thacker 2019). As Bennett has noted, the history of AI has reflected significant advances but also unfounded optimism. In the 1960s, AI pioneer Marvin Minsky proclaimed that "from three to eight years, we will have a machine with the general intelligence of an average human being" (Bennett 2023, 2).

However one feels about the plausibility of achieving AGI, it is not easy to deny that just in the past few years remarkable leaps have been made around natural language processing and LLM chatbots, so that at least in the narrow set of tasks it is being trained to do has become seemingly more capable and human-like. Furthermore, we should be aware that AGI is a goal that companies like OpenAI are actively pursuing: "Our mission is to ensure that artificial general intelligence—AI systems that are generally smarter than humans—benefits all of humanity" (Altman 2023).

OpenAI released ChatGPT, built on their GPT-3.5 model, in November 2022. In a conversation with Bill Gates in January 2024, OpenAI CEO Sam Altman hinted at the development of GPT-5 and its significant improvement toward becoming a more general, multimodal model, with expectations of exponential growth in the years to come (Gates 2024).

OpenAI granted access to its more advanced GPT-4 model to paid subscribers in March 2023. Other well-funded companies and startups, such as Mistral, Grok, and Gemini, are developing their competing LLMs. Given the rapid rate of development, there is genuine, even existential level concern among technology insiders and innovators about where we are headed with AI development, as exemplified in an open letter released on March 22, 2023, signed by notable figures like Yoshua Bengio, Elon Musk, and Steve Wozniak, calling on "all AI labs to immediately pause for at least 6 months the training of AI systems more powerful than GPT-4" (Future of Life Institute 2023). The letter argues:

> Contemporary AI systems are now becoming human-competitive at general tasks, and we must ask ourselves: *Should* we let machines flood our information channels with propaganda and untruth? *Should* we automate away all the jobs, including the fulfilling ones? *Should* we develop nonhuman minds that might eventually outnumber, outsmart, obsolete and replace us? *Should* we risk loss of control of our civilization? Such decisions must not be delegated to unelected tech leaders. **Powerful AI systems should be developed only once we are confident that their effects will be positive and their risks will be manageable** … AI labs and independent experts should use this pause to jointly develop and implement a set of shared safety protocols for advanced AI design and development that are rigorously audited and overseen by independent outside experts. These protocols should ensure that systems adhering to them are safe beyond a reasonable doubt. … Humanity can enjoy a flourishing future with AI. (Future Life Institute, 2023, emphasis in original)

It is encouraging to see conceptual language and value commitments related to human flourishing and the common good in this letter and in the guiding principles published by leading AI developers like GoogleAI and OpenAI. Christians can and should find consonance with general values like fairness, transparency, accountability, and bias mitigation that is commonly part of such conversations. In fact, these align with the six AI ethical principles the Roman Catholic Church called for: transparency, inclusion, responsibility, impartiality, reliability, and security and privacy

(Vatican 2020). However, we must also recognize that there are vastly different assumptions and beliefs about what this future vision of human flourishing entails, how it will unfold, and the role that technologies like AI will play in this human story. The following section will examine a Christian perspective on humanity, technology, and the telos of human history in contrast to another common account of human flourishing, rooted in a materialist worldview.

Humanity, Technology, and the Telos of Human History

There are notable examples of widespread existential crises and questioning following significant, paradigm-shifting scientific discoveries and technological innovations. Copernicus's heliocentric theory prompted questions about humanity's place in the cosmos; Darwin's theory of evolution through natural selection raised questions of human origins and our relationship to other species; developments in quantum mechanics have spurred questions about the nature of reality and causality; and advances in genetic engineering and biotechnology have confronted us with ethical and philosophical dilemmas wrapped up in questions about the nature and value of human life and human identity. Accordingly, the rapid advances in artificial intelligence have provoked reflections about what it means to be human and where humanity is headed. Bennett (2023, 364) asks:

> And so we stand on the precipice of the sixth breakthrough in the story of human intelligence at the dawn of seizing control of the process by which life came to be and of birthing superintelligent artificial beings. At this precipice, we are confronted with a very *unscientific* question, but one that is, in fact, far more important: What should humanity's goals be?

Indeed, what is the telos or end goal of human progress, and how do we achieve this goal? One worldview that frequently emerges when discussing AI development and its implications for shaping our future is technicism. Technicism centers on technology as the primary driver of human and societal advancement. Technological innovation is the means by which humanity will overcome its problems and limitations and push forward toward an evolved, technologically superior utopian future. Any deficiencies or problems associated with existing technology can and should be addressed by developing and implementing more effective technology.

Technicists often frame the human story in terms of the inevitable mechanism of Darwinian evolution. The telos of this story commonly involves the transcendence of the inherent fragility and weakness of the human body and the brain following the singularity. Kurzweil (2002, 53) prophesies: "I regard the freeing of the human mind from its severe physical limitations of scope and duration as the necessary next step in evolution. Evolution, in my view, represents the purpose of life. That is, the purpose of life—and of our lives—is to evolve."

John Dyer (2022) has astutely observed that for technicists who "don't see God as an anchoring point for reality, technological progress has become a new story that offers means of salvation and a source of future hope" (171) and that technicism "has all the elements of a good religion, offering parallels to the Christian story" (174). That is, explanatory theories like technicism contain assumptions and claims that offer a divergent anthropological, soteriological, and eschatological account, separate from one that is distinctly Christian. A biblically informed Christian story offers a vastly different account of what it means to be human, how our weakness and broken world will be remedied, and what the telos of human history looks like.

I am convinced that the Christian metanarrative offers the most compelling and comprehensive explanation for all that I see and experience in the world. It is a divinely revealed script that rightly orients us to our true identity and purpose and rightly orders our ambitions and hopes. What follows is a concise version of God's redemptive story that addresses these questions, as well as explains how technology fits into the narrative.

This story reminds me that everything God originally created was *tov* (well-formed, beautiful, good), and the first humans worked cooperatively to cultivate and build upon what God had initiated, exercising divine authority in expanding the reflections of God's glory and goodness throughout the world. Being created in the image of God could also mean that humans reflect or image the internal communion present within God in their vertical and horizontal relationships. Humans were designed for a harmonious, interdependent community. Also, humanity's vocation was and is to reflect and replicate the Creator's wise stewardship in a Garden of unfettered potential for the flourishing of all within the created order.

Humans image God by living as his divine representatives. This means that we cannot simply offload our responsibilities to love God and our neighbors to a robot or a virtual pastor. As God's image bearers, humans were bestowed with remarkable intellectual, affective, and creative capacities. This is expressed, among other things, in creating and using technology in pursuit of our divinely mandated vocation to be fruitful and multiply. As Marshall McLuhan helpfully described it, a medium or technology can be understood simply as an extension of our bodies or minds (McLuhan 1994, 7). Clothing is an extension of our skin; a hammer is an extension of our hand, a spoken word extends human thought, and so forth.

We also repeatedly see God using technology, such as Noah's Ark, to advance his purposes. McLuhan provided a helpful evaluative grid, which he called a "tetrad" (see Figure 4.1), for assessing the societal impact of technological adoption (McLuhan and Powers 1989; Lee 2022). McLuhan's tetrad prompts critical and necessary reflection for Christians seeking to be wise and responsible stewards. For example, in addition to considering how AI can enhance our divine calling, what might it erode and obsolesce as we increase our reliance on AI tools?

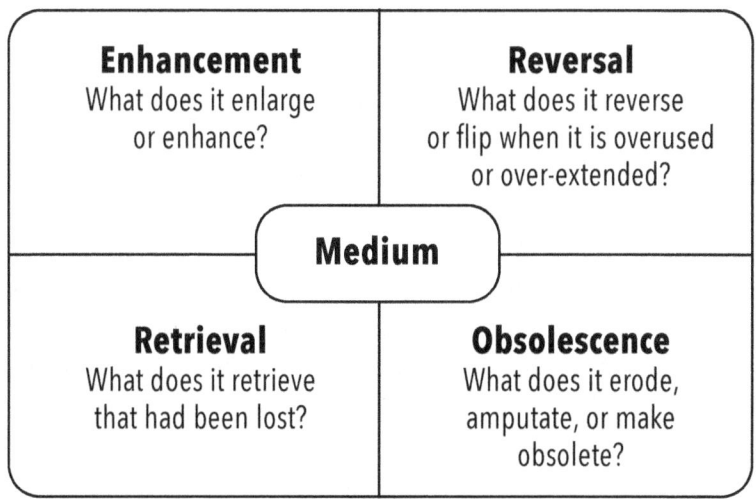

Figure 4.1: McLuhan's Tetrad

Carefully anticipating what might be at stake if AI use becomes overextended is especially prudent, given the human proclivity to place ourselves, rather than God, at the center of it all. The heart of human rebellion can take on various forms: When it comes to technology, human history bears witness to numerous examples of how humans, driven by selfishness and a desire for power, are prone to misusing technology in ways that harm both others and themselves. For example, while humans have developed medicines and other medical interventions to prolong life and fight against the mortal consequence of the Fall, we simultaneously find new, inventive, and more efficient ways to kill and exploit each other.

While technology can amplify and extend in constructive, redemptive ways, it can also amplify and extend our selfish desires, which, if left unchecked, will only enable us to harm and destroy ourselves and each other more efficiently. Therefore, we should ask what values embedded in the technology contradict God's vision for humanity and the world. What harmful or destructive tendencies might the use of this technology elicit societally and personally, given my particular weaknesses and habits of the heart?

Technological rebellion can also take the form of misplaced trust, such as in the idolatry of technicism, whereby we look to technology to deliver us from all that ails us and our world rather than trusting in and following God's unfolding redemptive work to heal all forms of brokenness through Christ and by the Spirit. God invites us to join his reclamation project of renewing all things under Christ rather than repeating the folly of the residents of Shinar and the Tower of Babel, who sought to use technological ingenuity in a futile attempt to return to Eden and secure for themselves that which God promised to supply.

We can discern patterns in the biblical story that grace and mercy follow on the heels of human failures and that what God has always desired from us is trust and mutual love. As we see in the *protevangelium* and thereafter throughout the biblical story, divine judgment is coupled with divine promise, climactically in the more significant exodus that Jesus secured through his life, death, and resurrection.

In Christ, God is reconstituting a new humanity as Jesus, the God-Man who himself is the full revelation of the image of God and is also the image of humanity's telos. We are being renewed in the image of the Son (Rom 8:29; 2 Cor 3:18), so ultimately, it is in looking at Jesus that we see what it means to be fully human as God intended. The arc of the human story will not lead to some posthuman future that is brought on by creating machines in our own image, who will then deliver us. Rather, our deliverance will come through the complete restoration of the image of God in us. Wise, God-honoring engagement with AI and other emerging technologies must be rooted in a clear, convicted Christian understanding of who we are and what role technology plays in the divine story. We must recognize and reject false, competing metanarratives that lead to disordered loves, loyalties, and longings.

Conclusion

A Pew Research report, based on a national survey conducted in July and August of 2023, surmised that while most Americans are aware of AI (90 percent say they heard at least a little about AI and about a third say they've heard a lot about it), their ability to identify and understand specific uses of the technology is "developing" (Faverio and Tyson 2023). Also pointing to increasing anxiety about "the increased use of artificial intelligence in daily life," 37 percent of US adults in 2021 indicated that they were "more concerned than excited," compared to 52 percent in 2023 (Faverio and Tyson 2023). It is not just the uninformed public masses, whose imaginations of a dystopic future ruled by superintelligent machines has been shaped by Hollywood movies.

This lack of understanding around ubiquitous technology that is increasingly consequential for our lives and the heightening societal anxiety about the place of AI in our society and its role in humanity's future reveals a potential gap in our discipleship that the church must address. In an age of rampant technological overdependency, cell phone addiction, and indiscriminate digital consumption, we within the church must offer better guidance and intentional discipleship that helps cultivate wisdom around technological engagement, including AI.

Technological overdependency tends to move us further away from life-giving, life-shaping embodied human community, and towards us becoming more like cold, detached machines incapable of expressing empathy and compassion rather than like Jesus, who showed us what it means to be fully human. The rapid development of AI has provoked existential angst and deep questions about the essence of humanity. This existential crisis presents an opportunity for Christians to share the true and hope-inducing message that to be human means we have been fashioned by and belong to a loving Creator, and that this missionary God, who has been upholding and pursuing us from the very beginning, will in his timing and chosen manner, bring to completion the full redemption of humanity in Christ. Let us be clear that even while affirming that technology—such as garments of skin used to cover Adam and Eve's shame and boats that transported Paul on his missionary journeys—has always been part of the advancement of God's mission, our hope is ultimately not in technology but in the God who alone has the power to deliver us.

The working group that collaboratively produced the Seoul Statement for the Fourth Lausanne Congress (L4) undertook a discernment process of identifying topics that are salient for the global church today and warrant clearer guidance than what previous Lausanne documents have provided. The entire seventh section of the Seoul Statement is devoted to calling for wisdom and discernment around technology and rightly asserts that the "Christian worldview informs our responses to and stewardship of these technological advancements." Regarding AI, the Seoul Statement (2024, 94) beckons Christians, "especially those who work in this industry, to engage both in the development and use of this technology that honors the Creator and human creativeness by promoting safe, equitable, and dignifying applications."

How would this approach apply to the creation and deployment of the AI robot pastor envisioned at the beginning of this paper? Given the declining number of young people entering the pastorate to replace an aging clergy in places like the United States and the dire shortage of theologically trained pastors in places like China, an AI would undoubtedly seem to be an efficient solution. But would such technology honor the Creator and the dignity of unique human creativeness? My preliminary impression is that an AI pastor seems to me to be something quite different from, say, Paul's use of parchment technology to extend and disseminate his teachings and edify believers. In the long line of priesthood, from ancient Levitical priests to the incarnated Christ, the Great High Priest, and now a ministry extended to all believers, I see a sacred calling that defies mere efficiency. Furthermore, it is a sacred human calling that is not ours to offload to nonhumans. I'm open to being convinced otherwise.

This is just the beginning of the complex questions emerging from rapidly developing technologies that we must prayerfully consider and proactively discern together as a community. For all that remains unclear,

I can say with confidence that if we are to be rightly related to emerging technologies like AI, we must wholeheartedly operate with this posture of upward rather than inward self-worship: "Some trust in chariots and some in horses, but we will trust in the name of the LORD our God" (Ps 20:7).

References

Altman, Sam. 2023. "Planning for AGI and Beyond," February 24. https://openai.com/blog/planning-for-agi-and-beyond.

Bennett, Max S. 2023. *A Brief History of Intelligence: Evolution, AI, and the Five Breakthroughs That Made Our Brains*. Mariner Books.

Bernstein, Jeremy. 1981. "Marvin Minsky's Vision of the Future." *The New Yorker*, December 6. https://www.newyorker.com/magazine/1981/12/14/a-i.

Dyer, John. 2022. *From the Garden to the City: The Place of Technology in the Story of God*. 2nd ed. Kregel.

Faverio, Michelle, and Alec Tyson. 2023. "What the Data Says about Americans' Views of Artificial Intelligence." Pew Research Center, November 21. https://www.pewresearch.org/short-reads/2023/11/21/what-the-data-says-about-americans-views-of-artificial-intelligence/.

Future of Life Institute. 2023. "Pause Giant AI Experiments: An Open Letter," March 22. https://futureoflife.org/open-letter/pause-giant-ai-experiments/.

Gates, Bill. 2024. "Sam Altman." *GatesNotes*, January 11. https://www.gatesnotes.com/Podcast?podcast=s2e0.

Good, I. J. 1966. "Speculations Concerning the First Ultraintelligence Machine." In *Ray Kurzweil vs. the Critics of Strong A.I.*, edited by Franz L. Alt and Morris Rubinoff. Vol. 6. Elsevier.

Grieshaber, Kirsten. 2023. "Can a Chatbot Preach a Good Sermon? Hundreds Attend Church Service Generated by ChatGPT to Find out." *AP News*, June 10. https://apnews.com/article/germany-church-protestants-chatgpt-ai-sermon-651f21c24cfb47e3122e987a7263d348.

IBM. 2024. "What Is Artificial Intelligence (AI)?," August 9. https://www.ibm.com/think/topics/artificial-intelligence.

IBM. N.d. "What Is a Neural Network?" https://www.ibm.com/topics/neural-networks.

Kurzweil, Ray. 2002. "The Evolution of Mind in the Twenty-First Century." In *Are We Spiritual Machines? Ray Kurzweil vs. the Critics of Strong A.I.*, edited by Jay W. Richards, et al. Discovery Institute.

Kurzweil, Ray. 2006. *The Singularity Is Near: When Humans Transcend Biology*. Penguin Books.

Lee, Michael Hakmin. 2022. "The Medium Is the Message: Reflections on Disciple-Making in the Age of Social Media." In *Communication in Mission: Global Opportunities and Challenges*, edited by Marcus Dean, et al. Evangelical Missiological Society Series, no. 30. William Carey Publishing.

McCarthy, J., M. L. Minsky, N. Rochester, and C. E. Shannon. 1955. "A Proposal for the Dartmouth Summer Research Project on Artificial Intelligence." *AI Magazine* 27 (4). https://doi.org/10.1609/aimag.v27i4.1904.

McLuhan, Marshall. 1994. *Understanding Media: The Extensions of Man*. MIT Press.

McLuhan, Marshall, and Bruce R. Powers. 1989. *The Global Village: Transformations in World Life and Media in the 21st Century*. Oxford University Press.

Thacker, Jason. 2019. "Nine Months Later: An Assessment of an Evangelical Framework for Artificial Intelligence." The Ethics & Religious Liberty Commission, December 17. https://erlc.com/resource/nine-months-later-an-assessment-of-an-evangelical-framework-for-artificial-intelligence/.

Turing, Alan M. 1950. "Computing Machinery and Intelligence." *Mind* 59 (236): 433–60.

Vatican. 2020. "Rome Call for AI Ethics," February 28. https://www.vatican.va/roman_curia/pontifical_academies/acdlife/documents/rc_pont-acd_life_doc_20202228_rome-call-for-ai-ethics_en.pdf.

Wooldridge, Michael. 2021. *A Brief History of Artificial Intelligence: What It Is, Where We Are, and Where We Are Going*. Flatiron Books.

Chapter 5

AI and the Future of Missions

Becoming an Alternative Creaturely Community in an Age of Machines

Jessica A. Udall

For the past few semesters in the intercultural studies and research classes I teach, there has been at least one—if not several—cases of students who use AI to write their research papers for them. While I do use AI checkers to confirm my intuition, I have developed an ability to sense an AI-generated paper on the first read-through. These papers are simultaneously extremely well-written yet strangely vague and lacking individuality. The machine's voice rings hollow.

These encounters with AI-generated content have brought me face to face with a phenomenon which we will all be grappling with on some level as AI becomes more ubiquitous. In the past few months, for example, in conversations with a radiologist, a Bible translator, and an English teacher, they all described to me that their workplaces had either just added an AI component to doing their jobs or were seriously considering doing so. If AI has not begun to affect a given person's daily life in some way, it likely will soon.

The church and its associated institutions, such as theological schools and mission-sending organizations, are also encountering opportunities to adopt AI within their systems and practices. People are currently working to create AI Christian music artists to sing in the metaverse (MacInnis 2022, 18) and AI Bible translators who can work faster than their human counterparts (Wycliffe Bible Translators 2022), as well as using it for more mundane applications such as help with sermon preparation and research for seminary assignments.

The developments in AI are happening so rapidly that ethicists struggle to keep up. This chapter will suggest that instead of seeking to philosophize about individual applications of AI as they are developed, it is more helpful to cultivate a set of questions that will help us to think clearly and Christianly about any type of AI we encounter in the coming months and years, interrogating it as to how it will form us individually and as a community and making decisions regarding if and how to use it based upon this inquiry. Those involved in missions must be aware of both the potential and pitfalls associated with AI in order to understand the times and make wise decisions regarding its use in various mission applications.

The Potential and Pitfalls of AI in the Mission of God

Research Assistant or Ghost Writer?

Because they have been trained on vast datasets of information from across the internet, AI tools can serve as excellent research assistants for pastors, professors, and students alike, saving time in aggregating relevant resources for review. This is a net positive, but the pitfall comes when those employing the AI tools take things one step further: when pastors get AI to write their sermon outlines or entire sermons for them, when professors outsource the creation of lesson plans, or students ask AI to write their papers for them. What is lost in each of these scenarios? I would argue that when we give AI the responsibility to craft raw data into the final product, we may gain a usable product, but we lose something of the expression of our own humanity along the way, whether in learning, teaching, or preaching.

In an article praising the use of AI to support and even facilitate pastoral ministry, Yi-Li Lin (2023) says, "Preaching—be it preparing a sermon or delivering the words to a congregation—is a process that currently involves a speaker, the influence of numerous people living and dead, and the Holy Spirit. I believe that within these actions, there is room for the work of AI too."

While generally positive about the use of AI in creating sermons, Lin (2023) does concede: "Obviously, however, a 100 percent AI-generated sermon would miss the context of the speaker and the congregation." Abby Perry makes a similar point with regard to the place of AI in higher education in a generally positive article, which still states categorically: "AI can never replicate a teacher's ability to consider context when evaluating a student's needs, abilities, or contributions" (Perry 2023, 78).

Indeed, context is something that AI is not able to easily or accurately integrate. When various students of mine have turned in AI-generated papers, the "tell" that made me recognize it as not their own work before even using an AI checker was the lack of context. While extremely well-written and organized, synthesizing impressive amounts of information, the papers lacked the voice of the individual student and vaguely missed the mark of the particular assignment, especially with regard to application in a particular setting, tending instead towards sweeping generalities.

Unfortunately, this is a continuation and entrenchment of what is a modern, society-wide, Enlightenment-influenced problem: we seek after more and more information, not realizing that this information is not beneficial for us and can even become unhealthy for us—through information overload—if we do not possess the soft heart (Heb 3:15) and skill for applying this information wisely and well in our actual contexts: our daily lives lived in particular communities.

Let us return to Lin's article about the potential of AI to help time-strapped pastors gain back time for relational pastoral ministry (an admirable goal) and for whom "there is never enough time for sermon preparation" (Lin 2023). Lin's enthusiasm raised this question in my mind: "Could it be possible that the extra research pastors believed they needed—and turned to AI for—was not needed at all?" By asking this question, I in no way mean to discourage the deep study of the word of God. Yet I would like to suggest that what is needed in the digital age is not primarily the aggregation and articulation of information (because any one of the parishioners in the church could have aggregated that same information themselves within a few minutes, based on this author's own description), but the embodied fellowship of simply encountering God's word together and considering how to live as his followers in their particular context. What matters most in Christian leadership in the modern age is less about the information that they have been able to acquire (on their own or by proxy) and more about their wisdom and practices.

Discussions like these raise fundamental questions: What is a pastor? What is a professor? I would argue that they are more than simply talking heads sharing AI-generated information. If they were only this, they could be replaced by robots. But as a society, we somehow know that they are more, thus we are "suddenly grappling with the matter of human distinctiveness" (Lucky 2023, 49). While functionally, AI bots can replicate many of the things that humans can do, they are not made in the image of God, which is "an ontological status that can be granted only by the Lord, bestowed by the same breath of life that animates dry bones. It's mysterious, not mechanical" (50).

Likewise, learning is about more than the transfer of information—more than a thumb drive or airdrop taking documents from one device and copying them to another—it is a co-mingling of humanity in which mysterious alchemy is at work. When people come together in their full humanity, all of them—leaders and laypeople, professors and students—come away changed. This is what discipleship is about, and it requires active human interaction to reach its full potential.

In an academic setting, Perry (2024, 74) observes: "With every advantage that AI offers, it demands something in return. Many educators fear that classroom learning will be left paying the price as students gain access to a tool without the knowledge of how to use it well or wisely." In practice, I have noticed that when I gently confront students who have submitted AI-generated papers, they invariably are under significant stress and feel compelled to generate the AI paper because they did not feel they had the time to write a paper themselves. In each case, I seek to emphasize to them that if they had communicated honestly and personally with me and told me about their situation, I would have granted them an extension so that they could do their own work and get the full benefit of the learning process without short-circuiting it for the sake of expediency.

Pastors do not have this option, of course—they cannot ask their congregation for an extension until Thursday, when they are supposed to preach on Sunday. While I am not a pastor myself, I have learned much from friends who are. Particularly on the subject of the tension between time for sermon preparation and time for relational pastoral ministry, I have learned from the example of Pastor Chris Sicks of One Voice Fellowship in Falls Church, Virginia, which is a diverse, multi-lingual church—many of whose members are new to the US and need a significant amount of pastoral support. In an interview for an article I was writing at the time, Sicks shared with me that he has learned to "just stop and say, 'This may not be a great sermon, but it's a good sermon, and it communicates the Gospel. Now, I'm going to go have coffee with a brother from the church rather than spending another two hours on the sermon." This commitment to adequate but not over-preparation is healthy and human and a way of leading by example.

Missional Implications. It is hard to overstate the effects that AI is having and will have on our society, and it is essential to consider their implications. Indeed, "the AI technologies being created and imagined today raise ethical questions about data curation, algorithmic agency, social inequities, and the future of every dimension of life" (Paulus 2022, 6). As Christians, we must think about AI from a faith perspective, inquiring about its effects on our souls, not merely viewing it in terms of a "technical perspective," but instead recognizing that the connection of AI and the spiritual life of virtue as a topic is "intrinsically interdisciplinary and requires drawing upon technical, theological, social, and philosophical resources" to adequately and helpfully engage it. While the field of technology raises good AI-related questions, it lacks the resources to answer them. When the Christian Church seeks to engage these questions, conversely, "they also have the spiritual vocabulary to address them" (Lucky 2023, 47).

As the body of Christ in the digital age, one of our roles is to remember what it means to be human in a world where there is so much confusion on this subject. To be human is to be inherently limited yet connected to a limitless God. In Scripture, we see the dire consequences of forgetting this fact and attempting to be like God in his incommunicable attributes (Gen 3:11). Indeed, "when humans, who are in the image of God, exercise their technological powers independently or in defiance of their Creator, their dominion mandate is transmuted into a curse" (Williams 2021, 106). Indeed, when we strive for God-like power, we become strangers to each other and even, in some sense, to ourselves. Thus, "while Christians are called to be part of all intellectual and creative pursuits on earth, we should not be seeking to transcend our humanity through AI" (Huizinga 2022, 130).

The way of wisdom is instead to focus on becoming like God in his communicable attributes by cultivating virtue: love, patience, forbearance, faithfulness, and the like. The goal of a Christian pastor, professor, or student is, therefore, not to transcend the limits of their own abilities but rather to be honestly present within them, faithfully doing what they are capable of without seeking to cover their limitations by robotic means. This does not absolutely preclude the use of AI in sermon preparation, lesson preparation, or research for assignments. Still, it does bring up a continual question—which should be truthfully engaged with by each user in each instance—as to whether AI helps or hurts us along the way in our pursuit of virtue (cf. Schuurman 2023, 155).

Questions. Questions to determine whether and how to use AI as a research assistant while preventing it from becoming a ghostwriter include:

- Are we utilizing AI tools to assist us in research, driven by the simple desire to aggregate raw data that we will then use to craft our sermon, lesson plan, or research paper faithfully, leveraging our own limited but God-given abilities?
- Or are we using AI to cover for the fact that we are stretched too thin and are living beyond our human limits?

Balm for Loneliness or Agent of Relational Atrophy?

Many AI companies have created AI companions that claim to help people struggling with social anxiety, loneliness, and other mental health struggles. These companions range in presentation from supportive friends to ever-responsive romantic partners to empathetic therapists. Usage of these companions understandably sky-rocketed during the pandemic, when in-person interactions were at an all-time low for most people. Yet their popularity has remained even when COVID-era restrictions have been lifted.

Neuro-divergent users have reported practicing their upcoming in-person social interactions to gain confidence. Those for whom conventional therapy is financially out of reach have benefitted from using an AI therapist—the principles of cognitive behavioral therapy, for example, are relatively simple to train a bot to convey effectively. Yet, for many users, the results are not so positive.

Regardless of who they present as, the common denominator between the majority of these companions is that they are trained by their user to respond in ways that are pleasing to the user, thus creating a number of problems if over-relied on (and due to the addictive and friction-free nature of technology, over-reliance is an ever-present possibility). If accommodation is only flowing one way—that is, the trained-to-be-supportive bot is adapting to the user, this creates the ultimate one-person echo chamber. At best, this atrophies the user's capacity for dealing with real human relationships, which involve a give-and-take with people who are not capable of complete supportiveness at all times and who, biblically speaking, should sometimes lovingly confront others (Matt 18:15–17). At worst, such overreliance enables abusive behavior by humans towards their AI companions (Bardhan 2022).

It may be tempting to dismiss this last problem as unimportant—what does it matter how a person treats a machine who does not have feelings? The harm, I would argue, is not to the machine but to the user since "AI systems [can] nudge humans toward repeated practices and habits [which] will inevitably shape and form users toward virtue—or vice" (Schuurman 2023, 158). Humans are shaped and formed through their interactions with AI in ways that will translate to interactions with humans. Derek Schuurman observes that "A common pitfall is to anthropomorphize our machines and, in so doing, to elevate machines and reduce the distinctiveness of human beings" (158). Indeed, when we start treating machines more like humans, we start treating humans more like machines, and this leads nowhere good.

In a world with self-checkouts, automated ordering screens at restaurants, self-check-in ticketing kiosks at airports, and touchless grocery pick-up, society is already moving in a direction that prefers technological interaction to human interaction. Having an exchange with a screen is orderly, efficient, and low effort. Comparatively, interactions with humans are messy, time-consuming, and require social effort. It is nearly impossible to avoid more interactions with screens than we had ten or even five years ago, but we cannot pretend that the increased time spent interreacting with screens instead of humans is not shaping us.

Likewise, even for those who are simply seeking to study the Bible for their own edification, AI tools form us in helpful or harmful ways, depending on how they are used. Kaitlyn Schiess (2023, 23–25) observes: "We are turning to AI tools for our Bible questions out of a good desire to understand God's Word, but our use of such tools often trains us to expect easy and immediately accessible answers to questions that might require longer messier, and more collaborative work. Our desire for objectivity is often a desire to be freed from the constraints of community." Indeed, our daily practices form us, and we must ask in what direction they are forming us.

Missional Implications. Post-pandemic, it is undeniable that, as a society, our social muscles have atrophied. Years of Zoom meetings, online church, and remote work and school have caused many in my social circles to admit that, though they are not proud of this fact, they now feel exhausted by in-person relationships and gravitate more towards virtual experiences. This is understandable, but it should not be accepted by Christians as the new norm. Real-world, in-person relationships are what tether us to essential aspects of our humanity, and the Christian church should be a haven of concretely (not digitally) connected humanity as we move into an increasingly AI-driven world. In this way, "we may be the salt and light to others who find themselves increasingly isolated, despite having thousands of followers in digital communities" (Baker 2022, 128).

One credible argument is that, whether we like it or not, people are on social media, so we should go to them there. However, we must not assume that that is where they or we should primarily stay. Outreach into virtual reality should aim to invite people into real-world communities. Thus, AI/digital church efforts should be viewed with caution, with a focus better allocated to evangelistic efforts in these domains with an eventual discipleship goal of drawing converts into in-person church communities.

It has been widely recognized that though modern society tends to lead to a sedentary existence, this can be recognized and resisted through intentional movement throughout the day. Similarly, although modern society tends to make low-quality, high-calorie foods the most readily available, these can be avoided by intentionally seeking out healthier alternatives. No one denies that this kind of intentionality takes effort, but it is possible, and most people acknowledge this path as the only way to live a long, healthy, happy life.

I argue that this same intentionality and effort must be engaged in with regard to modern society's move toward AI ubiquity. The friction and frisson of human-to-human relationships are necessary for the cultivation of "one another" commands, which are so often found in Scripture: loving one another, bearing with one another, and serving one another is not possible except when there is "another" in proximity. When we lose this aspect of daily life, we lose part of the essence of being a human in God's created order.

Questions. Questions to determine whether and how to use AI as a balm for loneliness while preventing it from becoming an agent of relational atrophy include:

- Am I using AI tools to help prepare and support me in cultivating real-world relationships?
- Or am I using AI tools as a replacement for real-world relationships?

The Church: Rememberers of Creatureliness in an Age of Machines

In an age of AI, the Christian church has the potential to be a haven of reality in which we communally remember what it means to be human, thus becoming a truly alternative community that shines like a city on a hill and keeps us connected to our creatureliness and thus our rightly ordered relationships with other creatures and with our Creator God. To be this kind of alternative community, however, requires that we ourselves rightly understand ourselves as limited creatures created by a limitless God for connection with him and others in community, not as machines plugged into other machines in a mechanized universe.

While there is a strong desire in our society right now to dive head-first into AI technology and transcend our current limits, there is also a weariness of screens, a disillusionment with not knowing whether anything seen online is true, and an uneasy sense that things seem less and less real. There is a hunger for authenticity, embodiment, simplicity, and community. This is what the church can offer if we recognize and respond to the Real: primarily God, the ultimate Reality, and then the real world and real community of people that he has placed us in (which provide friction as a reality check!). We are called to faithfully exercise dominion according to our God-given abilities while resisting the ever-present urge to transcend our creatureliness and become God-like in ways we were never meant to do. Leaving omnipresence, omniscience, and omnipotence to him, we can be a missional community inviting others to join our life-giving liturgies of presence, knowing God and knowing others, and spiritual empowerment while living an embodied, creaturely existence. This is the "life to the full" (John 10:10) that Jesus gives and which no technological augmentation can ultimately supersede.

As Christians, we may use technology for the glory of God, but we must not become enamored by it or by the vision of ourselves transcending our humanity with it. Instead, we must be aware that what we use shapes us. We must recognize that we are not just atomized heads (with a tendency to become atomic in 140-character bursts!) spouting information. We are living in embodied communities that mystically make up the church, which is itself a body. Since we become like what we behold, the question before us in a mechanized age is this: will we become more like bots ourselves or more like the body of Christ himself?

Much intentionality is needed if today's church is to embody an alternative creaturely community that is attractive to those who are eventually looking to eschew a screen-based reality. For this to be possible, Christians must not be shaped by the mores of this age but must stand apart from them enough to be distinct and noticeable among the homogeneity of digital norms. Doing so does not necessitate completely rejecting all technology, but it does require a healthy skepticism of innovations that whisper promises of transcendence. From the original garden until now, trying to be more than human—whether individually or collectively—has always ended in futility, while connecting with the Creator of humans vertically and then with other humans horizontally has led to flourishing.

Practically speaking, maintaining a critical distance from transcendence-oriented technology and rooting ourselves in a creaturely community may take many forms, including:

- Maintaining a human connection with God through regular unplugged prayer and worship.
- Maintaining a human connection with the creation through noticing and giving thanks for its beauty and taking care of it with a stewardship mindset, as well as recognizing and acknowledging our human dependence on it for light and sustenance.
- Maintaining a human connection to other humans socially with the humble acknowledgment that we were made for person-to-person physical connection, and thus seeking to have interactions of varying levels of depth in person whenever possible instead of defaulting to the mediation of screens.
- Maintaining a human connection to others in learning communities—teachers to students and students to teachers—seeking to communicate in our own authentic voices instead of employing AI to obscure it and make us look better, and only using AI (if at all) as a tool that assists us and resisting the

temptation to let it take the lead and thus halt and stultify our own human attempts to teach and learn.

- Maintaining a human connection to other humans in a local expression of the body of Christ, assuming that one is physically capable of attending an in-person church, recognizing its particularity as part of its essence and refusing to replace it with an exclusively online version despite its apparent convenience and possible superior production value.

- Maintaining a human connection with other humans as a pastor with the congregation, refusing to outsource the essential personal labor of love that is their own humble study of the word of God and subsequent sermon preparation. Thus, pastors will show up as their full human selves to equip and build up the body of Christ with what they have been able to glean, perhaps with the assistance of AI with regard to initial information gathering, but while maintaining their own soul's integrity as a fellow-human communicator of the gospel. This is in contrast to allowing that privilege and joy to be usurped by what is literally a soul-less entity.

While the reader will likely have discerned the author's rather anti-AI stance while reading this chapter, even those who regard AI with optimism or in whose fields where it is objectively helpful can benefit from using these philosophical questions and also formulating their own so as to use these new and rapidly advancing tools well and wisely. This moment is an inflection point—in the years to come, it will become increasingly difficult to recall a world without AI. Humans, in general, and for the purposes of this chapter, Christians, will do well to take time now to contemplate who we are and who we are becoming. While we stride into an unknown and rapidly changing future, we maintain equilibrium and anchor ourselves by remembering our creaturely identity that is rooted in the very beginning. This identity is carried with us always as a reminder of our essential humanity in relationship with the only omnipresent, omniscient, omnipotent Creator, who alone offers a healthy means of flourishing transcendence through the indwelling of his fruitful and empowering Holy Spirit.

References

Baker, Phillip M. 2022. "Reinforcement in the Information Revolution." In *AI, Faith, and the Future: An Interdisciplinary Approach*, edited by Michael J. Paulus, Jr., and Michael D. Langford. Pickwick.

Bardhan, Ashley. 2022. "Men Are Creating AI Girlfriends and Then Verbally Abusing Them." *Futurism*, January 18. https://futurism.com/chatbot-abuse.

Huizinga, Gretchen. 2022. "Righteous AI: The Christian Voice in the Ethical AI Conversation." PhD diss, University of Washington.

Lin, Yi-Li. 2023. "I Used ChatGPT for Six Months to Help My Pastoral Ministry. Here's What Worked." *Christianity Today*, September 1. https://www.christianitytoday.com/ct/2023/august-web-only/chatgpt-ai-ministry-pastoral-taiwan.html.

Lucky, Kate. 2023. "AI Will Shape Your Soul: But How is Up to Us." *Christianity Today*, October: 40–50.

MacInnis, Adam. 2022. "Let the Algorithms Cry Out." *Christianity Today*, March: 17–19.

Paulus, Jr., Michael J. 2022. "Introduction." In *AI, Faith, and the Future: An Interdisciplinary Approach*, edited by Michael J. Paulus, Jr., and Michael D. Langford. Pickwick.

Perry, Abby. 2024. "AI Meets Academia: Balancing Innovation and Tradition in Higher Education." *CT Advertising* 68 (1): 73–92.

Schiess, Kaitlyn. 2023. "Scripture Through the Eyes of AI." *Christianity Today*, December: 23–25.

Schuurman, Derek C. 2023 "Virtue and Artificial Intelligence." *Perspectives on Science and Christian Faith* 75 (3): 155–61.

Williams, Stephen. 2021. "What Is It to Be a Person?" In *The Robot Will See You Now: Artificial Intelligence and the Christian Faith*, edited by John Wyatt and Stephen N. Williams. SPCK Publishing.

Wycliffe Bible Translators. 2022. "Translation Technology: Accelerating the Spread of God's Word," July 21. https://www.wycliffe.org/blog/posts/translation-technology-accelerating-the-spread-of-gods-word.

Chapter 6

Gaming as a New Frontier in Missiology

Andrew Feng, Nick Wu, and Kyle Lee

Introduction

For Christians, Matthew's Great Commission is fundamental: namely, the goal of spreading the gospel and making disciples of all nations. Traditionally, this involved physical journeys to geographically distinct cultures. With an estimated 3.3 billion active participants worldwide, the expanding realm of online gaming represents an emerging and compelling frontier with significant potential for mission efforts (Clement 2024). However, in the current modern landscape of Christianity, a newer, broader understanding of "nations" must be affirmed to engage with gamers more effectively as a whole. The extensive level of engagement within the gaming community suggests that it is not merely a niche market but rather a microcosm of the global online population itself.

This chapter explores the viability of the gaming world as a mission field. It will examine the characteristics of the gaming community that facilitate connection and relationship building. Additionally, the chapter will analyze how the themes explored within video games can serve as a platform for discussions of faith and Christian principles. Ultimately, the goal of this study is to demonstrate that the world of online gaming presents a captivating, unexplored arena for Christian outreach.

Gaming Around the World

The global gaming population is far from monolithic. Figure 6.1 shows that, notably, 2.36 billion gamers reside in the Asia-Pacific and Middle East/Africa regions, aligning with the strategically significant "10/40 window"—a demographic encompassing roughly 65 percent of global internet users (Zandt 2023 and Meltwater 2024).

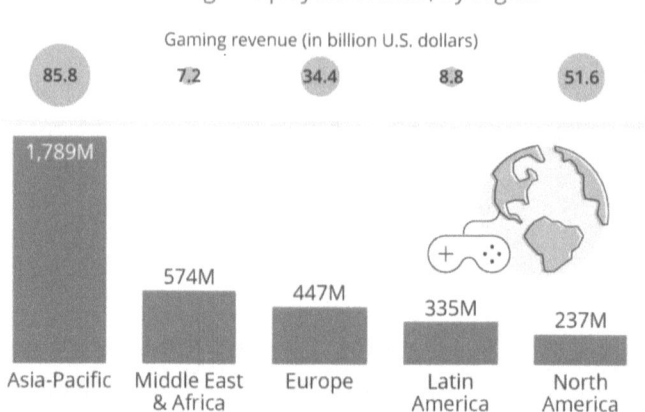

Figure 6.1: Video Game Players Around the World
Source: Zandt (2023)

With 68 percent of gamers gravitating towards smartphones as their primary platform, the gaming community transcends physical limitations and socio-economic barriers. The pervasiveness of gaming is further underscored by the fact that eight out of ten internet users engage with video games in some way (Clement 2023; Zandt 2023).

Consider, for example, *EVE Online*, a Sci-Fi spaceship battler Massive Multiplayer Online Role-Playing Game (MMORPG), known for its complex economic mechanics and strategic depth. Its player base, while concentrated among males aged 25–45 in IT, engineering, and finance professions, exemplifies the deep investment some gamers make in virtual worlds. With a daily player count of nearly one hundred thousand and player financial losses exceeding $700,000 during a single in-game war, *EVE Online* showcases the dedication and strategic thinking of its player base (MMO Populations 2024).

League of Legends (*LoL*) is a free-to-play MOBA (Multiplayer Online Battle Arena) where players collaborate as a team of five to destroy an opposing team's base in a fast-paced, reactionary game environment. *LoL* has over 140 million users—most averaging between 16–30 years old—and features a significantly more diverse community in terms of gender, background, and ethnicity than *EVE Online*. The total viewership for the

League's annual esports finals exceeded 100 million unique viewers, with a peak single-match viewership of 6.4 million (*Sports Business Journal* 2023). This represented a 25 percent increase in engagement compared to the previous year. For comparison, the NBA playoffs viewership peaked at 5.4 million that same year (NBA 2023). With the recent release of a TV show, spin-off video games, media, and merchandise, League has established itself as a cultural shaper.

This diverse range of games, with their varied player demographics, highlights the immense potential of the gaming world as a mission field. From the strategic thinkers of *EVE Online* to the team-oriented players of League, gaming communities offer connections with a broad audience that transcends traditional geographical and cultural boundaries—many of whom live and play games in the 10/40 window.

Games inherently foster social interaction and teamwork, creating fertile ground for building relationships and communities within the virtual world. Many online games necessitate communication and collaboration to achieve success. In games like *EVE Online*, the complex player-driven economies require the formation of guilds and alliances. Members strategize together, share resources, and forge bonds through shared experiences—even virtual losses of $700,000 can become a story that strengthens the community. Similarly, MOBA games like League require rapid communication, team chemistry, and coordination.

A Case Study: *League of Legends* as an Evangelistic Tool

A real-world example from our research: Cason wasn't the most fervent gamer on campus, but he knew it was the key to spending time with Shawn, his easy-going friend with an infectious laugh. Shawn wasn't religious, but *League of Legends* was his passion, so Cason, with slightly rusty skills, started queuing up for matches alongside Shawn.

Initially, their conversations centered on in-game strategies and friendly banter. However, as they climbed the League ladder, late-night gaming sessions became a space for more meaningful conversations. Cason, initially hesitant, began sharing stories about his faith and the campus Christian group he was involved with. Shawn, ever the skeptic, would listen with good humor, occasionally throwing in a playful jab.

The League community itself became a bridge. Cason invited Shawn to join in with some of his friends from the Christian group, who also enjoyed gaming. The initial awkwardness melted away as they discovered a shared passion for virtual battles. The group's camaraderie and genuine warmth started to chip away at Shawn's skepticism.

Over their four years in college, their League sessions morphed into invitations to weekly Bible studies. Shawn, though initially hesitant, found himself drawn to the group's open discussions and authentic care. He still had questions and doubts, but the judgment-free environment fostered by Cason and his friends created a space for him to explore.

By graduation, Shawn wasn't just a League buddy; he was a close friend and a regular at the Bible study group. A newfound appreciation for the Christian faith replaced his previous skepticism over the course of late-night gaming sessions with the community that embraced him, controller in hand. Cason's willingness to meet Shawn on his turf, the camaraderie of the gaming community, and the authenticity of the Christian group built a bridge of faith that extended far beyond the virtual battlefield.

Narratives Within Video Games

Many video games, by their very nature, grapple with complex themes that resonate deeply with the human experience. These themes, often mirroring real-world moral questions, present a unique opportunity for Christians to engage with gamers on a deep level, initiating conversations about faith and values.

Consider the core narratives that drive countless video games: the struggle between good and evil, the weight of sacrifice, and the possibility of redemption. These are not merely plot devices; they are fundamental questions that have occupied humanity for millennia. As gamers confront these themes within the virtual world, a natural curiosity may arise. Gamers ask themselves, "Why are we drawn to stories of good versus evil? What motivates characters to make immense sacrifices? Is redemption truly possible?"

These questions can serve as springboards for Christians to connect with gamers and share their faith perspective. Imagine a post-game discussion where a player ponders the moral ambiguity of a character's actions. A Christian might offer their interpretation, drawing parallels to biblical narratives or teachings on forgiveness and redemption. This type of organic dialogue allows faith to be presented not as a set of rules but as a framework for understanding the complexities of the human condition, the very themes explored within the game itself.

While games like *League of Legends* and *EVE Online* present clear narratives, not all games fall neatly into this category. Popular titles like *Call of Duty: Warzone* and *Fortnite* focus heavily on competition, reflexes, and combat, with the narrative playing a relatively minor role in the overall experience compared to the gameplay itself.

While some video games lack overt narratives exploring morality, their appeal extends far beyond mere gameplay. Take *Fortnite*, a global phenomenon where millions engage in a cartoon battle royale. The core objective—securing victory royale—may not explicitly mirror Christian themes. However, a 2018 LendEDU poll, cited by *Variety*, reveals that a significant portion of players (63 percent) view *Fortnite* as primarily a social space for cultivating and developing friendships (Eriksen 2021).

Furthermore, games like *Fortnite* offer players a surprising degree of creative freedom with its ever-changing, build-as-you-go mechanics. Players can design elaborate structures, participate in player-created challenges, and even express themselves through in-game avatars and emotes. The sheer amount of time and money people invest in games like *Fortnite* is astounding. While some may view countless hours spent in virtual worlds as frivolous, Christians can recognize this dedication as a form of passion and commitment. The aforementioned LendEDU poll (Ericksen 2021) highlights that a staggering 83 percent of *Fortnite* players have purchased cosmetic items for their avatars despite these items offering no competitive advantage. This dedication highlights the significance of self-expression and the pleasure players derive from virtual spaces.

Understanding Gaming Culture: A Message to the Players

While the potential of gaming as a mission field is clear, at first glance, its culture and community are not. Gaming culture isn't a monoculture. Each gaming platform (PC, Xbox, PlayStation, and so on) has its own subculture, and even individual games sport different player characteristics, nuances, and language. To effectively engage with gamers, Christians must strive to understand these complexities.

The concept of gamer personas, as outlined in a report by *Newzoo*, can be a helpful paradigm for understanding gamers (*Newzoo* 2023). The idea categorizes gamers into distinct groups based on their motivations, preferred genres, and gaming habits. For instance, *EVE Online* attracts the "Strategizer" persona, according to the *Newzoo* framework. These players are drawn to complex game mechanics, long-term strategy, detailed planning and forecasting, and the intellectual challenge of navigating an in-game free market economy. Their online interactions are likely to be more strategic and analytical, with a focus on in-game goals and objectives.

League, on the other hand, would be more appealing to the "Socializer" and "Achiever" personas. Socializers enjoy the community and relational aspects of online gaming, seeking to build friendships and experience the camaraderie that gaming fosters. Achievers, meanwhile, are driven by competition and the pursuit of mastery within the game. Engagement with these players would likely benefit from a more casual and community-oriented approach, emphasizing teamwork and the shared experience of the game.

By understanding these core motivations and tailoring an approach accordingly, Christians can connect with gamers on a deep level. Those who engaged deeply with the strategy of *EVE Online* may find casual, lower-level conversations around *EVE Online* lacking in substance due to a lack of investment and skill in their beloved game. Socializers within *League of Legends* might be more receptive to conversations about faith that build on shared experiences fostered by the game. They may also be more open to casual engagement with new players.

Beginning Strategies of Engagement

Playing the Games

The most effective strategy for reaching gaming communities is to actively participate in the games. This doesn't require becoming a professional gamer, but rather demonstrating a genuine interest in the hobby that gamers hold dear. Joining guilds in *EVE Online* or participating in ranked matches of *League of Legends* allows Christians to connect with players on a shared level, fostering trust and rapport. Authentic engagement goes beyond simply being present; it involves strategizing with teammates, celebrating victories, and commiserating over losses—all while exemplifying good sportsmanship and Christ-like character.

Imagine a Christian with a fervent desire to share their faith with passionate basketball players. This well-intentioned individual shows up at a local court with the best of intentions, but he has a critical flaw—no experience with the game. He can't shoot, dribble, or even understand the basic rules. Instead of attempting to learn the game or its language, he stands on the sidelines, occasionally shouting Bible verses or theological concepts in strange parlance, calling a jump shot an "attempt" or a made basket a "scored goal."

This scenario perfectly illustrates the pitfalls of inauthentic engagement within the gaming community. Just as a clueless spectator wouldn't resonate with basketball players, Christians who lack genuine interest and knowledge in gaming will struggle to connect with gamers.

The basketball players share a passion for the game, a language of strategy, and a respect for skilled competitors. The outsider, lacking these things, cannot connect on a fundamental level. Similarly, gamers are passionate about the mechanics, narratives, and communities within their chosen games. Even worse, the basketball players might view the outsider's presence as a nuisance, a disruption to their enjoyment of the game. Similarly, gamers may perceive a Christian who only shows up to preach in-game as inauthentic or disingenuous. Worst of all, by failing to engage in the game, the outsider misses opportunities to build relationships and trust with the players.

Creating Content

Another avenue for authentic engagement involves content creation. Gamers are a highly engaged online community, and many consume content related to the games they enjoy. Christians can leverage platforms like YouTube or Twitch to stream gameplay, offer tutorials, or even create faith-based content that intersects with the gaming world. Imagine a series exploring the moral complexities of player choice within RPGs or a channel that analyzes the themes of redemption and sacrifice found in video game narratives. This approach allows Christians to speak the language of gamers and offer conversations about faith within a familiar space.

Finding Common Ground: Online Platforms and Communities

The vast online world offers numerous platforms where faith-based discussions can intersect with gaming. Discord servers dedicated to specific games or Christian gaming communities can provide fertile ground for connection. Participating in discussions about the latest game update can naturally lead to more in-depth conversations about the themes and values explored within the game itself.

Ultimately, the goal is not to force religious discussions into every interaction but to cultivate genuine relationships with gamers and allow opportunities for faith to emerge naturally. By being present, participating authentically, and offering a Christ-like presence within the online gaming community, Christians can create a space where gamers feel comfortable exploring questions of faith alongside their passion for gaming.

The Problem: A Digital Divide—
Why Traditional Models Struggle

The potential for Christian outreach within the gaming world is undeniable. But translating this potential into reality presents a unique challenge. Traditional models of ministry often struggle to gain traction within this environment, for at least three reasons:

1. **The Ephemeral Nature of Gaming**: Unlike established cultures with relatively stable traditions, the internet's culture is constantly evolving. Content posted on Twitter (now X) can be considered old news just a day later. Fifty years ago, a news headline would have lasted weeks; today, they last minutes, at best. Similarly, new games emerge, existing games receive patch updates that significantly alter gameplay strategies, and trends shift rapidly. Video game "seasons" often change every six months, twice as fast as traditional sports leagues. By the time a ministry meticulously crafts a strategy for one game, the next big release may already overshadow it.

2. **Missionaries vs. Mega-Corporations**: Traditional models of missions often involve diligent missionaries spending years immersing themselves in a particular culture. With a rapidly changing gaming landscape, those unfamiliar may struggle to find the time and money to understand the gaming world. Massive budgets of gaming

companies like Riot Games (creators of *League of Legends*) or popular streamers are culturally savvy and have been for years. Even still, these companies and entities often still get this process wrong. With the general lack of institutional knowledge, how can Christians compete?

3. **Beyond Preaching**: There is a need for authenticity. Gaming culture is not a passive audience waiting to be preached to. Gamers crave authenticity and genuine connection. Ministries or churches that approach the online gaming community solely with the intent of religious conversion are likely to be met with skepticism and resistance.

A Case Study: Hilton vs. Airbnb

The challenge of engaging with gamers through traditional ministry models presents a situation analogous to the struggles faced by established hospitality giants, such as Hilton, in today's digital landscape. According to a recent study, while core aspects of faith, such as discipleship and theological exploration, remain important, college students are actively engaged with a broader digital ecosystem that encompasses platforms like Instagram, TikTok, YouTube, and streaming services. This parallels the experience of a Marketing Manager at Hilton (a company with a well-established brand and significant revenue). The Marketing Manager observed that the company struggled to connect with a younger demographic (under thirty) who gravitate towards the unique experiences and influencer-driven marketing of competitors like Airbnb (*Statista* 2024).

Companies like Hilton are missing the experiential shift of consumers. Hilton's focus on hotel amenities—the "For the Stay" experience—doesn't resonate with younger generations as much as Airbnb's emphasis on "Living Like a Local." Traditional hotels only recently began to offer high-speed Wi-Fi, a valuable commodity to younger generations, while Airbnb has provided these services from the get-go.

Hilton is also losing the influencer battle. Hilton's belated foray into influencer marketing pales in comparison to Airbnb's strategy of partnering with travel enthusiasts who genuinely align with their brand. However, replicating Airbnb's approach within the gaming world presents a unique challenge. While prominent Christian figures like David Platt exist, they often belong to a different generation and may not resonate with younger gamers. Similarly, partnerships with other established churches or figures, such as Hillsong or Mark Driscoll, have been tarnished by controversy, potentially alienating the very audience these efforts aim to reach.

Replicating influencer-level production will be challenging. Effectively penetrating these digital markets requires significant expertise, financial resources, manpower, talent, and unwavering commitment. The recent "He Gets Us" campaign, despite its well-publicized multi-million-dollar budget and professional production value, exemplifies the complexities involved (CNN 2023). While these 30-second commercials garnered attention, they are not the long-form content typically found on YouTube and podcasts, nor are they crafted in the same style and language as the Instagram and TikTok culture landscape.

The question is whether any denomination, let alone a local church is prepared to manage public relations and release weekly a substantial volume of high-quality video and audio content (15 to 100 hours, which requires between 45 and 900 hours of manpower in total) for the foreseeable future, operating with a multi-million-dollar budget for this endeavor alone. YouTubers and other content creators dedicate their full-time efforts to crafting engaging, relatable content that understands the nuances of each platform, the trends, and the je ne sais quoi that keep viewers hooked.

On the other hand, churches often lack the same level of dedicated resources or the deep understanding of these platforms to create content that captures the attention of millennial, Gen Z, and Gen Alpha audiences. While the gospel will always be valuable and true, translating it into the language and style appealing to the younger generations is another matter entirely.

A Proposed Solution: Innovation and Collaboration

The rapid evolution and inherent complexities of the gaming world present a unique challenge to established religious structures. Traditional models of ministry are designed for slower-paced environments and often struggle to gain traction within a digital ecosystem. Solutions require a paradigm shift within religious institutions to move away from a one-size-fits-all approach and toward understanding gaming culture. Here are four suggestions for a proposed solution:

1. **Meeting Gamers Where They Are**: Churches can emulate Jesus's approach with the woman at the well by partnering with

established Christian gamers and influencers who already possess credibility and trust within the gaming community (John 4). These individuals, who are well-versed in gaming culture, can serve as a bridge between established religious structures and the target audience. Their lived experiences and relatable perspectives allow them to connect with gamers on a deeper level, fostering a more receptive environment for faith-based discussions.

2. **Empowering Young Voices**: Just as Jesus empowered his disciples, churches can nurture young people's passions for gaming and the gospel. With opportunities to develop their gaming skills and hone their content creation abilities, young churchgoers can become powerful voices within the gaming community. Furthermore, encouraging them to explore ways to integrate their faith journey into the games they play provides an authentic and organic platform for faith exploration within the digital landscape. Churches can take this concept a step further and move beyond simply offering a few gaming consoles in the youth room. Consider establishing dedicated computer and gaming cafes within the church itself. These cafes could provide a welcoming space for young people to connect, play games, and engage in faith-based discussions in a natural and organic setting.

3. **Building Bridges with Industry Professionals**: Industry professionals in the gaming world may be under the same roof as a church. Churches would do well to forge partnerships with game developers, esports organizations, or even Christian content creators already working in the gaming environment and in their pews. By establishing these connections, religious institutions gain access to a wealth of knowledge about the gaming community and its dynamics.

4. **Learning from the Past, Adapting for the Future**: The core principles of missions remain unchanged. Even in the digital age, building trust, fostering a learning culture and language, and genuinely connecting with people remain crucial components. The church has been very good at these tasks over the years and will undoubtedly continue to do so. However, to reach the 3.3 billion online gamers, it will require dedicated learning and understanding. Relying on youth and industry professionals is not enough; the church must seek to grow in understanding while remaining cognizant of the obstacles at hand.

In essence, engaging with gamers in the digital age necessitates a move beyond outdated methodologies. By fostering genuine connections, empowering young voices, collaborating with industry professionals, and adapting traditional mission principles, churches can create a space where faith can find fertile ground within the dynamic world of video games.

Conclusion: Equipping the Church for Gaming Missions in the Digital Age

The world of online gaming presents a vast and dynamic mission field, teeming with billions of potential connections. While traditional outreach models may struggle to resonate within this ever-evolving landscape, the potential for fostering faith conversations and building authentic relationships with gamers remains immense.

Indigitous US stands ready to equip the church for this exciting challenge. Our ministry is founded on the principle of understanding cultural contexts and utilizing innovative tools for outreach. Recognizing the limitations of traditional outreach models within the online gaming environment, Indigitous US implemented a multifaceted approach to gain a deeper understanding of the gaming community and its unique needs. This approach centers on two key pillars: fostering fresh perspectives from within the gaming world and establishing collaborative partnerships with industry professionals.

A team of interns—passionate gamers themselves—were recruited to provide insight. Their lived experiences within the gaming culture proved invaluable. These interns weren't just casual players; they were deeply embedded in specific gaming communities. Some specialized in the fast-paced, technical world of fighting games, like *Street Fighter* and *Super Smash Bros.*, while others specialized in first-person shooters, such as *Overwatch*. Their understanding of the nuances of these communities, from preferred communication styles to the underlying motivations of players, provided a crucial lens through which to view outreach efforts.

Indigitous US is undertaking similar efforts, such as the "Hack in a Box Workshop," which utilizes design thinking principles to drive innovative solutions to traditional problems. This workshop can be used to gain an understanding of gamer demographics and motivations. By unpacking personas like the "Strategizer" and "Socializer," churches can tailor their approach to resonate with specific gaming communities or other areas of ministry they wish to reach.

The road to success in this digital mission field requires more than just understanding the landscape. It necessitates building trust and fostering genuine connections with gamers by:

1. Partnering with Christian gamers and influencers who already possess credibility and trust within the gaming community.
2. Empowering young people with a passion for gaming and faith to create content and build communities that resonate with their peers.
3. Creating dedicated spaces within churches, such as gaming cafes, that provide a welcoming environment for gamers to connect, play games, and explore their faith in an organic setting.

The challenges are undeniable. The rapid pace of change in the gaming industry demands adaptable approaches. However, by partnering with young adults and savvy gamers and dedicating time, resources, and space to them, churches can enhance their understanding and ability to reach the gaming community worldwide.

References

Clement, Jessica. 2023. "Video gaming worldwide - Statistics & Facts." *Statista*, June 3. https://www.statista.com/topics/1680/gaming/.

Clement, Jessica. 2024. "Leading devices used to play games worldwide Q4 2023." *Statista*, February 18. https://www.statista.com/statistics/533047/leading-devices-play-games/.

CNN. 2023. "See the 'big money marketing' of Jesus that's set to air during the Super Bowl." *CNN*, January 27. https://edition.cnn.com/videos/us/2023/01/27/jesus-campaign-he-gets-us-superbowl-kansas-right-wing-lead-foreman-vpx.cnn.

Eriksen, Kaare. 2021. "As Epic Diversifies, 'Fortnite' Is Still the Focus." *Variety*, June 16. https://variety.com/vip/as-epic-diversifies-fortnite-is-still-the-focus-1234997746/.

Meltwater. 2024. "2024 Global Digital Report." https://www.meltwater.com/en/global-digital-trends.

MMO Populations. 2024. "Eve Online Player Count." https://mmo-population.com/r/eve.

NBA. 2023. "2023 NBA playoffs are most-watched in 5 years." *National Basketball Association*, June 13. https://www.nba.com/news/2023-nba-playoffs-are-most-watched-in-five-years.

Newzoo. 2023. "New free report: Meet the gamers of 2023 and see how they engage with video games." *Newzoo*, June 20. https://newzoo.com/resources/blog/how-consumers-engage-with-video-games-in-2023.

Sports Business Journal. 2023. "2023 League of Legends Worlds streaming creates record-breaking media value." *Sports Business Journal*, December 7. https://www.sportsbusinessjournal.com/Articles/2023/12/07/esports-shikenso-media-value.

Statista. 2024. "Revenue of Hilton Worldwide Holdings from 2009 to 2023." https://www.statista.com/statistics/297760/revenue-of-hilton-worldwide-holdings-inc/.

Zandt, Florian. 2023. "Which World Region Has the Most Gamers?" *Statista*, August 8. https://www.statista.com/chart/30559/number-of-video-game-players-by-region/.

Chapter 7

The Final Frontier of Mission
Space Tourism, Lunar Colonies, and the Future of Interplanetary Mission

Stephen Stallard

Introduction: Space as the Final Frontier of Mission

After the Apollo lunar missions, humans expected to touch the stars once again, yet decades passed with little forward progress in the exploration of outer space. The American Space Shuttle program faced tragedy and was eventually retired. The scientific research conducted on the International Space Station (ISS) and via the Hubble and James Webb telescopes has been the most successful element of the space agenda of the last few decades. With mixed results in space, humans turned their focus back to the "pale blue dot" that we call home (NASA 2019). The frontier was closed until the billionaires re-opened it. Elon Musk, Jeff Bezos, and, to a lesser extent, Paul Allen and Richard Branson constitute a group of wealthy tech moguls that have been dubbed "The Space Barons" (Davenport 2018). With their lofty ambitions and hefty fortunes, these tech titans have propelled humanity into another global space race. Unlike the first space race, the new space race is not limited to global superpowers, which pitted the United States against the Soviet Union. Instead, Space Age 2.0 involves numerous companies and countries vying for positions in low-Earth orbit and beyond.

Elon Musk did not merely establish PayPal, sell electric vehicles, and take over Twitter (renamed X); he also launched a Tesla into space (space.com 2018). As the eccentric leader of SpaceX, Musk has, perhaps more than any other individual, helped refocus our attention on the heavens. Musk's goal is to help humanity become an interplanetary species capable of surviving what he believes is an inevitable extinction-level event on Earth (Davenport 2018, 37–38). If an asteroid were to strike the Earth one day, we would need a Plan B.

For Musk, Plan B is a city on Mars (SpaceX.com n.d.). At the SpaceX online store, you can purchase a T-shirt that says, "Occupy Mars." More provocatively, SpaceX has even sold one that says, "Nuke Mars," since Musk has theorized that deploying nuclear weapons in the Martian atmosphere might trigger processes that could help to terraform the planet. Musk has leveraged his wealth and connections to put rockets, cargo, and people into space. His brash talk and erratic personality have masked his creative genius, enabling him to fight for the reopening of the space frontier.

Jeff Bezos, by contrast, is a low-key billionaire spaceship enthusiast. His Blue Origin company has pioneered a new industry: space tourism. Using Blue Origin vehicles, wealthy tourists have blasted into low-earth orbit for a brief experience of weightlessness and a stunning view of the earth from space, unintentionally providing people with an experience of transcendence (Stallard 2022). Bezos has a different goal than Musk, but his objective is no less ambitious. Concerned about climate change and pollution, Bezos wants to outsource all heavy industry to outer space. He reasons that if we can successfully extract minerals and energy from the solar system, the Earth can be preserved as a pristine environment for life and play. In this scenario, industrial colonies would dot the solar system from the asteroid belt, to space stations, to the Moon (Rubenstein 2022, 18–23).

These interplanetary dreams have thus far not been universally embraced. Some writers are concerned about the continued weaponization of space and the potential for a space-related nuclear holocaust on earth (Bowen 2023; Deudney 2020). Other more progressive thinkers are concerned about the ethics of space exploration and are wary of projecting an imperialistic sense of manifest destiny into the galaxy (Schwartz, Billings, and Nesvold 2023).

Rubenstein (2022, xi) has even asked, "How might we approach outer space without bringing our most destructive tendencies along with us?" Her question is valid. However, her presuppositions as a pseudo-pantheistic-Jewish religious thinker blind her to a fundamental reality: humanity is inescapably predisposed to sin because of our ancient fall. The only solution is redemption. So, if we are sending sinners into space, then, as I will argue throughout this essay, we should send missionaries to proclaim the gospel on this new frontier.

Please note that this essay is squarely focused on presenting the gospel to *humans* in outer space. A variety of theologians have written about some of the theological and missiological issues involved in a potential future encounter with extraterrestrials (Peters, Hewlett, and Moritz 2018; Lewis 1967, 2013; Weidamann 2016). I am skeptical (for both theological and scientific reasons) that we will ever encounter intelligent alien life. Hence, the focus of this essay is on the gospel's missionary encounter with human cultures in outer space. If we do encounter extraterrestrials in my lifetime, I will have to revisit this question.

It is not merely private enterprise that is re-blazing a trail to the stars; multiple countries harbor serious space ambitions. To position itself to participate in a space economy that it estimates will be worth 1 trillion dollars by 2040, the European Union plans to partner with NASA to land an astronaut on the moon by the end of the decade (ESA n.d.). Japan is devoting 6 billion dollars to its space program and aims to land a craft on the surface of the moon (Roeloffs 2023). Indonesia has a long record of interest in space and has recently partnered with SpaceX to launch a satellite into orbit (Dhayita 2024). Israel unsuccessfully attempted to land its Beresheet spacecraft on the Moon (NASA n.d.), potentially depositing micro-animals on the lunar surface (Halon 2019). India recently landed an unmanned mission on the south pole of the moon, cementing its place as "the fifth great space power" (Duchaine 2023). China and Russia have plans to follow and hope to establish a joint base in the same vicinity by 2036 (Hutchinson 2024). Since NASA also plans to establish a manned outpost there, the lunar south pole could become relatively crowded, at least by lunar standards (Fox 2022). It could conceivably become a multicultural, multi-faith outpost.

With companies and countries competing and partnering to establish dominance in outer space, it is not inconceivable to imagine an interplanetary existence fifty years into the future. While Musk's Martian City seems farfetched, other possibilities seem within grasp: orbital hotels, lunar mining colonies, and solar space stations (Foust 2022). If any of these possibilities materialize, a future generation of missiologists will need to craft strategies for deploying missionaries to outer space. The goal of this essay is to provide the next generation of missiologists with models that they can utilize as they seek to evangelize the final frontier. The intent is to spark a conversation about the future of interplanetary missions before we are left behind by fast-moving events.

As Lou Cornum notes, "The frontier never closes. Not in California, not in the 19th century. If it isn't the West, it's the moon, then cyberspace, and then Mars. The frontiers do not close but rather lap over each like waves where people and capital crash and flow" (Cornum 2023, 70). If Elon Musk and Jeff Bezos get their way, outer space will become the new missional frontier. To be ready to bear witness on that missional frontier, evangelical missiologists, and missionaries will need to consider both the history and future of religion in outer space.

History of Religion in Space

Religious practice has been a consistent feature of the brief history of spaceflight. Since humanity is fundamentally religious, we should expect that religion would be a part of the history of space travel. The following sections will provide brief overviews of religious rituals in outer space. Attention will be devoted to Christian, Jewish, and Muslim practices during spaceflight.

Christianity in Outer Space

The first race to the moon was a geopolitical endeavor. The United States and the Soviet Union were competing to ensure dominance on the world stage. For many, the contrasting ideologies of capitalism and socialism were underwritten by Christian or atheist dogmas. The United States saw itself as a beacon of democracy, and many Americans saw themselves as bearers of the good news in a world threatened by atheistic Communism. Against that backdrop, the first American astronauts engaged in striking displays of Christian religious practice, both overtly and covertly.

Prior to humanity's lunar landing, a series of manned missions tested various technologies and prepared astronauts for the challenges of space travel. One of those missions was Apollo 8, which took place from December 21 to December 27, 1968. Oliver (2013, 128) notes, "The highlight of the Apollo 8 mission, for audiences back on Earth, was the crew's prime-time broadcast from lunar orbit on Christmas Eve. … toward the end of the broadcast, they took turns reading the opening passages from Genesis, concluding with the tenth verse." After wishing their viewers a "Merry Christmas," the three astronauts signed off, leaving the world below in a luminous moment of transcendence. This broadcast, viewed live by a billion people, had a profound impact on one who would later become "The Pope's Astronomer" (McKeown 2023).

A more secluded expression of the Christian faith transpired on the surface of the moon when one of the first astronauts to set foot there celebrated communion privately in his spaceship. Prior to the Apollo 11 mission, the mainline Protestant Buzz Aldrin consulted with his pastor on the theological significance of the historic spaceflight. His pastor gifted him a chalice which Aldrin then used on the moon to commemorate the death of Christ (Oliver 2013, 11–12, 35, 41).

The lunar visitors did more than privately practice their faith; they also left behind religious mementos. A tiny disc bearing goodwill messages from seventy-three world leaders was deposited on the moon. One of those world leaders was Pope Paul VI, whose message was the text of Psalm 8 (NASA 1969). Another permanent reminder of humanity's presence on the moon is the official United States commemorative plaque left behind by the astronauts. President Nixon's speechwriter William Safire remembered that the inclusion of the term "AD" on the plaque was a subtle way of referring to God (Muir-Harmony 2020, 2). Communist cosmonauts could claim that they had not found God in outer space, but astronauts claiming to be Christians would leave behind a record of enduring faith.

After the early days of the Space Age, traces of the Christian faith could still be found in the stars. A Baptist deacon took to space a piece of the plane that Jim Elliot flew in on his way to missionary martyrdom (Roach 2009). Bagpipes were used to play "Amazing Grace" on board the International Space Station (Inocencio 2022). Christianity has proven itself to be resilient, even in the cold confines of outer space.

Judaism in Outer Space

When should you observe Shabbat when you are in orbit, and experience sixteen sunrises in twenty-four hours? Rabbis have grappled with this question on behalf of Jewish astronauts (Konikov 2008). Observant Jews in outer space face several challenges, including procuring freeze-dried kosher food and praying toward Jerusalem (Shurpin n.d.). Perhaps the most notable Jewish astronaut thus far has been Dr. Jeffrey Hoffman, an astronomer who embarked upon five space shuttle missions and two spacewalks.

Hoffman famously took Judaica to outer space. He was the first to spin a dreidel in zero gravity, the first to take a menorah into orbit, and the first to read from a kosher Torah in outer space (Center for Jewish History n.d.). Jewish astronauts have built upon his legacy as they have continued to observe their faith off-earth (Dinner 2023). For Hoffman, his faith was a private matter, one rarely discussed within the confines of NASA. However, he did choose to practice the rituals of his faith while in orbit. From the space shuttle, Hoffman even had the chance to explain the significance of Hannukah on a live television broadcast.

Islam in Outer Space

In 1985, the Saudi Prince Sultan bin Salman rocketed into space aboard the Space Shuttle Discovery (Gornall 2020). As the first Muslim in outer space, the prince was a pioneer for Muslim astronauts. He recited the entire Qur'an while in orbit and fasted during Ramadan (Wilford 1985).

Bin Salman did find it necessary to modify some of the traditional Muslim rituals, such as praying five times a day and facing Mecca during prayer. At speeds of over seventeen thousand miles per hour, it wasn't easy to pinpoint the location of the city that holds such significance to Muslims. Salman remarked, "In space, by the time you find Mecca, it's gone" (Wilford 1985).

Muslims face many challenges when they attempt to practice their faith in orbit. Islamic scholars in Malaysia even issued a fatwah designed to guide Muslim astronauts in the interplanetary observance of their faith (Rhude 2018 and Kalhoro 2023). It included details about how to pray when one cannot kneel in zero gravity. Oktar believes that Muslims must settle in space, ideally before "anti-religious forces" (Oktar 2023, 2). However, he notes that there would be challenges: "When Sputnik went into space, it threatened the God of the Christians. Today, space exploration mainly threatens the God of Muslims" (Oktar 2023, 9). He cites a potential problem: Muslim astronauts living on a space station in orbit around Venus would witness the sun rising from the West, which, in Qur'anic interpretation, would signal the end of days (Oktar 2023, 11). Despite such hermeneutical and methodological obstacles, Oktar believes that Muslims must press forward into the cosmos.

Summary

The rituals of Christianity, Judaism, and Islam have been extensively practiced in outer space. Other examples of spaceflight spirituality could also be cited. For instance, several astronauts have experienced epiphanies in orbit, ones that seem to align with eastern religious practices (Weibel 2020, Kanas 2020). Even the non-professional astronaut William Shatner experienced the Overview Effect, which perhaps neatly aligns with his animistic worldview (Dunn and Taber 2021). Plausibly, this has led to the birth of an alternative religious movement (Bjørnvig 2013). Soviet cosmonauts, by contrast, were steeped in atheism, and the first allegedly declared that he could not find God in outer space. C. S. Lewis responded to this alleged claim with his essay "The Seeing Eye" (Lewis, 1967). Based on this brief history of humanity's sojourn in space, it is apparent that religious practice has often been a key feature in the personal lives of space travelers. What remains to be seen is if there is a future for religion in outer space.

Future of Religion in Space

Many writers have chronicled NASA's historical (if tenuous) embrace of Christianity (Mersch 2013). Yet, as society has secularized, so have expectations regarding the American space program. Oberhaus argues, "Space was once dominated by protestant Christians, but we may finally be on the cusp of turning space into a truly universal form of spiritual exploration" (Oberhaus 2019). Predicting the shape of the world to come is fraught with difficulty, but it is likely that interplanetary societies will be characterized by secularism and multi-faith multiculturalism.

Secularism

The Protestant veneer of American civil religion has been stripped away, and in its place is a newly empowered secularism. It is this secular ideology that could shape the future of interplanetary life. What would be the features of a secular outpost, whether on the moon, on an asteroid, or on an orbital resort? We can predict the future shape of these secular societies by noting two features of the historical progression of secular societies on earth. First, science will probably be prized above all else. It might function as a pseudo-religion that promises to actualize our utopian dreams. Scientists will be the priests and priestesses of this new outer space philosophy.

Second, continuing in the trajectory of the Enlightenment, religion will be privatized. The devout Jewish Astronaut Jeffrey Hoffman has already noted that he and his colleagues at NASA did not discuss religion. They stayed focused on their job and quarantined religion to the realm of private belief.

Lesslie Newbigin prophetically challenged Western culture's embrace of the separation of "public facts" from "private beliefs." He argued, "A serious commitment to evangelism, to the telling of the story which the church is sent to tell, means a radical questioning of the reigning assumptions of public life. It is to affirm the gospel not only as an invitation to a private and personal decision but as public truth which ought to be acknowledged as true for the whole of the life of society" (Newbigin 1991). Newbigin would undoubtedly reject the smothering embrace of scientism and would have the church recover its voice as the counter-society that speaks for God at the intersection of the gospel's missionary encounter with culture.

On the interplanetary missional frontier, this role will be vital but difficult. In this future society, religion will no doubt be tolerated so long as it is observed in private. Any religion that makes grand claims about the cosmos and about humanity (as most of the world religions do) will find it difficult to break through the secular wall that the scientific establishment dominates. Devout Christians, Jews, Muslims, and others will be welcomed participants in spaceflight, but they will be expected to privatize their faith.

Multi-Faith Multiculturalism

The second likely feature of outer space outposts (whether research labs, mining colonies, or resorts) is multi-faith multiculturalism. Mersch (2013) maintains, "It goes without saying that America was a very different country 40 years ago, and will no doubt be a very different country when human beings finally venture further out into the solar system. Explorers of every stripe will be allowed to practice their faith on their voyages—Christians, Jews, Muslims, Hindus, Buddhists, and others." Since Indonesia, Israel, and India all have a space agenda, it is reasonable to predict that a future orbital resort or mining colony could be staffed by Muslims, Jews, and Hindus. The multicultural ethos of the outer space horizon will lend itself to a multi-faith environment.

If a diverse set of countries and companies achieve their goals for the next decade, the lunar South Pole could become the most distant multi-faith outpost of our lifetimes. With Russian, Chinese, and American astronauts living there, the missional frontier will have moved from this planet to its moon. It takes little imagination to conceive of the multicultural character of this new frontier. Communist taikonauts, Russian (Orthodox?) cosmonauts, and American astronauts from diverse religious backgrounds will partner and compete at the Moon's South Pole. Their proximity as lunar neighbors will no doubt prompt a rich cultural interchange. We can hope that Christian space workers (regardless of their country of origin) would bear witness to Christ in this multi-faith context. The question remains: how could Christians bear witness to the risen Lord in outer space? What models of mission could be fruitful on this evolving missional frontier?

Potential Models for Space Mission

Space engineers are taught an axiom: "Space is hard" (Davenport 2018). Space missiologists need their own axiom: space mission is even harder. In outer space, there are limited resources to sustain human life. Whether in a research lab in earth orbit or on a lunar mining colony, there will be a finite amount of food and oxygen (Frank 2023). Everyone in space (at least in the initial years) will need to demonstrate their worth to the mission. They will need to prove they are worthy of tapping into the scarce resources available. Given the extreme conditions and high costs involved in outer space life, outer space missions will be challenging.

The history of Christian missions, however, is in part the story of pioneering missionaries who reached the frontiers in creative ways. In the first millennium of Christianity, everyday Christians migrated and took the gospel to places as far as Mongolia and Persia (Hanciles 2021). Later, teams of monks built monasteries and brought the gospel to the violent frontiers of Medieval Europe (Smither 2016). Moravians traveled to the West Indies and successfully partnered with local Christians to catalyze "an indigenous black movement that was birthed in the slave quarters" (Sensbach 2005). Baptists and Methodists innovated in mission by creating the model of the "Circuit Riding Preacher" who traveled the frontier to bear witness to Christ. Jones (2021) notes, "These circuit-riders were self-sufficient, often living off the land, and they died young because of it." The United Methodist Church records that Francis Asbury declared, "We must reach every section of America, especially the raw frontiers. We must not be afraid of men, devils, wild animals, or disease. Our motto must always be Forward!" (United Methodist Church 2018). That pioneering mentality was also dear to Portlander Jim Elliot, who was martyred along with some of his missionary colleagues as they sought to bring the gospel to a missional frontier in Ecuador. The history of Christian mission demonstrates that the frontier ought not be shirked, simply because it is hard. If outer space is the final frontier of mission, we will need to explore creative models that will enable Christians to bear witness in outer space. In this essay, two models will be briefly proposed: bi-vocational mission and chaplaincy.

Bi-Vocational Mission

Bi-vocational approaches to the mission are as old as the New Testament (1 Cor 4:12). In this approach, Christian workers make their living by engaging in a trade and bearing witness to Christ. Intriguingly, this model has already been used in outer space. American Astronaut Shannon Lucid was born in China and spent time living in a concentration camp (Stella 2019). The child of missionaries to China, she adopted the pioneer spirit of her parents. Lucid became a pilot and flew her father to revival meetings in Oklahoma (Oklahoma Medical Research Foundation n.d.).

Eventually, she spent 188 days aboard the Russian space station Mir—the first American woman to do so (Broad 1996). Prior to her liftoff, her home church recorded a special space-themed church service. The recording, which included a sermon directed towards the cosmonauts, was sent into space so that it could be given to Russian space travelers (Weibel 2016 and Jones 1996). This is the only known instance of potential evangelism in outer space. Intriguingly, Lucid's Bible was not the first aboard the Mir. She noticed a Russian Gideon's Bible was already there (Davison 1998).

Although little is known about Lucid's private conversations with the cosmonauts, her sojourn on the Mir provides us with a tantalizing foretaste of the possibilities for the future of bi-vocational missions in outer space. Given the high cost and rigorous demands of space flight, Christians should be prepared to serve bi-vocationally in outer space. Like Lucid, they could demonstrate, through their training, skills, and experience that they belong on the mission. Christians in outer space can serve as pilots, scientists, security, and support staff. When they deploy, they can bear witness to the Lordship of Christ as they embed themselves within the fabric of a long-term outer space community. In this way, perhaps Antarctica is a glimpse of the future for bi-vocational missions on the Moon. There, research scientists conduct religious services at one of the six chapels on the ice (Patowary 2022; Springer 2014). Perhaps lunar explorers will one day follow in the footsteps of their polar predecessors.

Chaplaincy

Chaplaincy provides a second potential model for space missions. Alan Baker notes that chaplaincy thrives in the framework of "cooperative pluralism." In this approach, chaplains do not proselytize but are "present in the lives of others through personal character, integrity, compassion, values, and example. It leads to invitations for the chaplain to discuss faith" (Baker 2021, 97). Evangelical chaplains are available to bear witness to Christ upon request. They conduct themselves in such a way that they demonstrate their trustworthy character, thereby facilitating potential gospel conversations. This is a less direct approach to the Christian mission but one that might be viable in outer space.

Some might wonder if chaplains would ever be allowed to consume the scarce resources available to humanity in outer space. The answer might be "yes." Food scientists have already argued that the morale of space explorers is an important consideration in designing outer space food systems (Douglas, Zwart, and Smith 2020). Those who send workers into space must not simply adopt a utilitarian perspective. They should endeavor to launch holistically healthy people into space. Although this would include nutritional and psychological health, evangelicals should make the case that this ought to also include spiritual health. Indeed, Kim believes that we should consider the spirituality of space explorers as one important component of the success of their mission. He argues, "An astronaut's attitudes of positivity, confidence, assurance, and trust, which are the socio-cultural elements of religious psychiatry, should not be underestimated as a mental tonic for communal sustainability during long-term space exploration" (Kim 2023, 14).

Corporate and military institutions have recognized this reality and invested in chaplains to ensure the health and success of their workforce. While their motives are not entirely altruistic, organizations as diverse as hospice facilities and the United States Navy have created opportunities for evangelical Christians to provide spiritual care to hurting people. Even the newly minted Space Force has earth-bound chaplains. One leading Space Force Chaplain even wondered: "If a base camp is established on the moon one day, maybe we will have the opportunity to setup and operate a chapel on the moon. … Wherever the … Guardians of the Space Force go, they will always need a chaplain to provide for their free exercise of religion and spiritual care" (Campbell 2021). Although chaplaincy does provide certain constraints, it ought to be considered alongside bi-vocationalism as a possible model for Christian missions in outer space.

Conclusion: To Boldly Go with the Gospel

In response to the explosion that doomed the Space Shuttle *Challenger*, Ronald Reagan declared "We're still pioneers" (Reagan 1986). Countries like Israel and India and entrepreneurs like Elon Musk and Jeff Bezos continue to demonstrate that the space frontier has been reopened. As a species, we are still pioneers, and we are experiencing a renaissance of space travel. Tourists have spent a few minutes in orbit and scientists and explorers are preparing for longer sojourns on both the Moon and Mars. Although this emerging frontier presents challenges to Christian missions, evangelicals should eagerly seek opportunities to follow their neighbors into space to bear witness to Christ there.

The environment of outer space may be uniquely positioned to spark feelings of transcendence. Ted Peters poignantly notes that when you look at the stars from earth, "Infinity enters your soul. The human psyche is stirred by our experience with the sky above and with the greater sky behind it, cosmic space. Like an angel, cosmic space comes to us bearing a message from the God who transcends it" (Peters, Hewlett, and Moritz 2018, 3–4). If this is what humans experience on Earth, what might they feel in outer space when gazing at God's creation?

Although he never ventured into space, Augustine can give us a clue. Searching for God, he looked to the stars, and was told, "'Nor are we the God you seek,' … And I said to all these things … 'Tell me about my God … With a loud voice they cried out: 'he made us'" (Augustine 1953). When we look at the stars, whether from earth, from orbit, or from the moon, they speak to us (Ps 19:1–4). Future missionaries will likely stand on the moon, tap into that sense of transcendence, and proclaim to their fellow travelers that God created the cosmos. Future missionaries should seize that chance, and present-day missiologists should begin planning for this missional opportunity.

Outer space appears to be the final frontier of missions. Evangelicals should ready themselves for the challenge of bearing witness to the risen Lord on this new frontier. It will require innovation and sacrifice. Yet that is what Christians have done and will do. We follow the flow of people, to boldly go with the gospel to a remote tribe, a distant corner of the internet, or even to outer space.

References

Augustine. 1953. *Confessions*. Catholic University of America.

Baker, Alan T. 2021. *Foundations of Chaplaincy: A Practical Guide*. Eerdmans.

Bjørnvig, Thore. 2013. "Outer Space Religion and the Overview Effect: A Critical Inquiry into a Classic of the Pro-Space Movement." *Astropolitics* 11 (1–2): 4–24. DOI: 10.1080/14777622.2013.801718.

Bowen, Bleddyn. 2023. *Original Sin: Power, Technology and War in Outer Space*. Oxford University Press.

Broad, William J. 1996. "Record-Setting Astronaut Remained Very Down-to-Earth." *New York Times*. Newspapers.com.

Campbell, Julie. 2021. "Space Force Chaplain Fills Historic Role in New Military Branch." *Church of God Ministries*, March 16. https://www.jesusisthesubject.org/space-force-chaplain-fills-historic-role-in-new-military-branch/.

Center for Jewish History. 2018. "Jews in Space: Meet Astronaut Jeffrey Hoffman," May 7. https://www.cjh.org/jewsinspace/.

Cornum, Lou. 2023. "'Event Horizon' and 'The Space NDN's Star Map.'" In *Religion and Outer Space*, edited by Eric Michael Mazur and Sarah McFarland Taylor. Routledge.

Davenport, Christian. 2018. *The Space Barons: Elon Musk, Jeff Bezos, and the Quest to Colonize the Cosmos*. PublicAffairs.

Davison, Mark. 1998. "NASA Shuttle-Mir Oral History Project. Edited Oral History Transcript," June 17. https://historycollection.jsc.nasa.gov/JSCHistoryPortal/history/oral_histories/Shuttle-Mir/LucidSW/LucidSW_6-17-98.htm.

Deudney, Daniel. 2020. *Dark Skies: Space Expansionism, Planetary Geopolitics, and The Ends of Humanity*. Oxford University Press.

Dhayita, Kun, H. M. 2024. "Astropolitical Developments in Indonesia: Are They the Same as Developed Countries?" *Modern Diplomacy*, January 2. https://moderndiplomacy.eu/2024/01/02/astropolitical-developments-in-indonesia-are-they-the-same-as-developed-countries/.

Dinner, Josh. 2013. "NASA Astronaut Spins the Dreidel for Hannukah aboard International Space Station." *Space.com*. https://www.space.com/astronaut-jasmin-moghbeli-iss-dreidel-hanukkah-video.

Douglas, Grace L., Sara R. Zwart, and Scott M. Smith. 2020. "Space Food for Thought: Challenges and Considerations for Food and Nutrition on Exploration Missions." *The Journal of Nutrition* 150 (9): 2242–44. https://doi.org/10.1093/jn/nxaa188.

Duchaine, Daniel. 2023. "Enter India, the Fifth Great Space Power." *The Space Review*, December 4. https://www.thespacereview.com/article/4702/1.

Dunn, Marcia, and Rick Taber. 2021. "William Shatner, TV's Captain Kirk, Blasts into Space." *AP News*, October 13. https://apnews.com/article/shatner-blue-origin-launch-09705724072c0ecad2674c8511f0fcab.

European Space Agency. n.d. *ESA Vision*. https://vision.esa.int/.

Frank, Heather. 2023. "Next-Level Astronaut Food." *World Magazine*, June 1. https://wng.org/roundups/next-level-astronaut-food-1685649855.

Foust, Jeff. 2022. "Commercial Space Stations: Labs or Hotels?" *The Space Review*, October 10. https://www.thespacereview.com/article/4462/1.

Fox, Alex. 2022. "Four Things We've Learned about NASA's Planned Base Camp on the Moon." *Smithsonian Magazine*, August 29. https://www.smithsonianmag.com/science-nature/four-things-weve-learned-about-nasas-planned-base-camp-on-the-moon-180980589/.

Gornall, Jonathan. 2020. "35 Years Ago, Saudi Prince Sultan bin Salman became the first Arab, Muslim and Royal in Space." *Arab News*, June 17. https://www.arabnews.com/node/1691201/amp.

Halon, Etyan. 2019. "Did Beresheet's Crash Spill Thousands of 'Water Bears' onto the Moon?" *Jerusalem Post*, August 7. https://www.jpost.com/israel-news/did-beresheets-crash-spill-thousands-of-water-bears-onto-the-moon-597849.

Hanciles, Jehu J. 2021. *Migration and the Making of Global Christianity*. Eerdmans.

Hutchinson, Allie. 2022. "China and Russia are on Track to set up a Moon Base by 2036 – Here's the Plan." *Inverse*, May 20. https://www.inverse.com/innovation/horizons-china-russia-moon-base.

Inocencio, Ramy. 2022. "The Story of 'Amazing Grace.'" *CBS News*, December 25. https://www.cbsnews.com/news/the-story-of-amazing-grace/.

Jones, Jim. 1996. "Minister Sending Sermon to Space Station." *The Seguin Gazette-Enterprise*. Newspapers.com.

Jones, Peyton. 2021. *Church Plantology: The Art and Science of Planting Churches*. Zondervan.

Kalhoro, Amna. 2023. "The Final Frontier for the Faithful: Islamic Rulings on Space." *E-International Relations*, May 17. https://www.e-ir.info/2023/05/17/the-final-frontier-for-the-faithful-islamic-rulings-on-space/.

Kanas, Nick. 2020. "Spirituality, Humanism, and the Overview Effect during Manned Space Missions." *Acta Astronautica* 166: 525–28. https://doi.org/10.1016/j.actaastro.2018.08.004.

Kim, David W. 2023. "Psycho-Religious Experiences in Deep Space History: Astronaut's Latent Countermeasures for Human Risk Management," *Aerospace* 10 (626): 1–18. https://doi.org/10.3390/ aerospace10070626.

Konikov, Zvi. 2008. "Shabbat in Space." *Chabad.org*, January 31. https://www.chabad.org/library/article_cdo/aid/632169/jewish/Shabbat-in-Space.htm.

Lewis, C. S. 1967. *The Seeing Eye and Other Selected Essays from Christian Reflections*. Ballantine Books.

Lewis, C. S. 2013. *The Space Trilogy*. HarperCollins.

McKeown, Jonah. 2023. "Jesuit Astronomer Remembers the First Christmas in Space." *National Catholic Register*, December 25. https://www.ncregister.com/cna/jesuit-astronomer-remembers-the-first-christmas-in-space.

Mersch, Carol. 2013. "Religion, Space Exploration, and Secular Society." *Astropolitics* 11 (1–2): 65–78. DOI: 10.1080/14777622.2013.801933.

Muir-Harmony, Teasel. 2020. *Operation Moonglow: A Political History of Project Apollo*. Basic.

NASA. 1969. "Apollo 11 Goodwill Messages," July 13. https://www.nasa.gov/wp-content/uploads/2024/05/apollo-11-goodwill-messages.pdf.

NASA. 2019. "Voyager 1's Pale Blue Dot," February 14. https://science.nasa.gov/resource/voyager-1s-pale-blue-dot/#hds-sidebar-nav-3.

NASA. n.d. "Beresheet." https://science.nasa.gov/mission/beresheet/.

Newbigin, Lesslie. 1991. *Truth to Tell: The Gospel as Public Truth*. Eerdmans.

Oberhaus, Daniel. 2019. "Spaceflight and Spirituality: A Complicated Relationship." *Wired*, July 16. https://www.wired.com/story/apollo-11-spaceflight-spirituality-complicated-relationship/.

Oklahoma Medical Research Foundation. n.d. "Out of this World." https://omrf.org/findings/out-of-this-world/.

Oktar, Süleyman. 2023. "Islam and Space Exploration." *Astropolitics* 21 (2–3): 112–26. DOI: 10.1080/14777622.2023.2274116.

Oliver, Kendrick. 2013. *To Touch the Face of God: The Sacred, the Profane, and the American Space Program, 1957–1975*. John Hopkins.

Patowary, Kaushik. 2022. "The Churches of Antarctica." *Amusing Planet*, May 30. https://www.amusingplanet.com/2022/05/the-churches-of-antarctica.html.

Peters, Ted, with Martinez Hewlett, Joshua M. Mortiz, and Robert John Russell. 2018. *Astrotheology: Science and Theology Meet Extraterrestrial Life*. Cascade.

Reagan, Ronald. 1986. "Address to the Nation on the Explosion of the Space Shuttle Challenger." Reagan Presidential Library, January 28. https://www.reaganlibrary.gov/archives/speech/address-nation-explosion-space-shuttle-challenger.

Rhude, Kristofer. 2018. "Muslims in Outer Space: Islam Case Study – Technology." Harvard Divinity School, Religion and Public Life. https://rpl.hds.harvard.edu/religion-context/case-studies/technology/muslims-outer-space.

Roach, Erin. 2009. "Home Again, Astronaut Encourages Missions." *Biblical Recorder*, October 23. https://www.brnow.org/news/Home-again-astronaut-encourages-missions/.

Roeloffs, Mary Whitfill. 2023. "Modern Space Race: Japan Pledges $6.6 Billion for Developing Space Sector as U.S. and China Plan Historic Missions." *Forbes*, November 21. https://www.forbes.com/sites/maryroeloffs/2023/11/21/modern-space-race-japan-pledges-66-billion-for-developing-space-sector-as-us-and-china-plan-historic-missions/.

Rubenstein, Mary-Jane. 2022. *Astrotopia: The Dangerous Religion of the Corporate Space Race*. University of Chicago Press.

Saudi Gazette. 2020. "'Seven Days in Space' Tells Prince Sultan Story of Fasting, Praying in Space." *Saudi Gazette*, April 30. https://saudigazette.com.sa/article/592495.

Schwartz, James, Linda Billings, and Erika Nesvold, eds. 2020. *Reclaiming Space: Progressive and Multicultural Visions of Space Exploration*. Oxford University Press.

Sensbach, Jon F. 2005. *Rebecca's Revival: Creating Black Christianity in the Atlantic World*. Harvard University Press.

Shurpin, Yehuda. n.d. "How to Observe Judaism in Outer Space." *Chabad.org*. https://www.chabad.org/library/article_cdo/aid/4168250/jewish/How-to-Observe-Judaism-in-Outer-Space.htm.

Smither, Edward L. 2016. *Missionary Monks: An Introduction to the History and Theology of Missionary Monasticism*. Cascade.

Space.Com. 2018. "Watch SpaceX's Falcon Heavy launch a Tesla Roadster on 5th anniversary of debut flight." https://www.youtube.com/watch?v=sTNd8PnQMoU.

Springer, Carly M. 2014. "What It's Like to Attend Church in Antarctica." *LDSLiving*, September 9. https://www.ldsliving.com/what-its-like-to-attend-church-in-antarctica/s/76763.

Stallard, Stephen. 2022. "Space Tourism and the Search for God," *Transform*, August 4. https://transform.westernseminary.edu/resources/space-tourism-search-for-god.

Stella, Fred. 2019. "Spirituality and Space Travel," *WGVU News*, July 8. https://www.wgvunews.org/common-threads/2019-07-08/spirituality-and-space-travel.

United Methodist Church. 2018. "The Hard Road of a Methodist Circuit Rider." https://www.youtube.com/watch?v=5zRXChPJOFE.

Weibel, Deanna. 2016. "Pennies From Heaven: Objects in the Use of Space as Sacred Space." In *Touching the Face of the Cosmos: On the Intersection of Space Travel and Religion*, edited by Paul Levinson and Michael Waltemathe. Connected.

Weibel, Deanna. 2020. "The Overview Effect and the Ultraview Effect: How Extreme Experiences in/of Outer Space Influence Religious Beliefs in Astronauts." *Religions* 11 (8): 418. https://www.mdpi.com/2077-1444/11/8/418/htm.

Weidamann, Christian. 2016. "Did Jesus Die for Klingons Too? Christian Faith and Extraterrestrial Salvation." In *Touching the Face of the Cosmos: On the Intersection of Space Travel and Religion*, edited by Paul Levinson and Michael Waltemathe. Connected.

Wilford, John Noble. 1985. "Man in the News; Saudi Prince on Space Voyage: Sultan Salman Al-Saud." *New York Times*, June 19. https://www.nytimes.com/1985/06/19/us/man-in-the-news-saudi-prince-on-space-voyage-sultan-salman-al-saud.html.

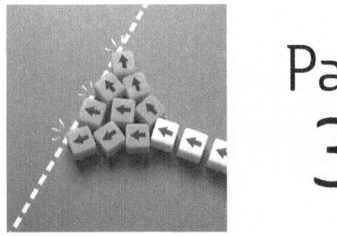

Part
3

Equipping for the Future

Chapter 8

Do You Believe in Magic?
Equipping Frontier Missionaries to Engage with Animistic Muslim Practices

David Taylor (Pseudonym)

Introduction

Frontier missions is facing an unprecedented time of both crisis and opportunity. It is a time of crisis for a number of concerning reasons. First, research shows that there are over 2 billion unbelievers in the world who are part of a frontier people group. According to the evangelical missiological database Joshua Project, "A Frontier People Group (FPG) is an Unreached People Group (UPG) with virtually no followers of Jesus and no known movements to Jesus, still needing pioneer cross-cultural workers." These groups have "0.1 percent or fewer Christian Adherents and no confirmed, sustained movement" (Joshua Project n.d.).

In terms of geographical location, 72 percent of frontier people groups reside in South Asia, 9.9 percent are in Central Asia, 5.5 percent in the Middle East and North Africa, and 5.1 percent in West and Central Africa. A staggering 54.5 percent of all frontier people groups are Muslim, which means there are slightly over one billion frontier Muslims who are in desperate need of missionaries. However, for every thirty missionaries that go to a reached area of the world, there is only one missionary that goes to an unreached or frontier people group (Lewis 2018, 159, 161–62).

Despite the massive number of unreached peoples in the world, Western missionaries today have an extraordinary opportunity to reach those with the least access to the gospel. Largely due to modern technology, travel, and business opportunities which open the door to closed areas, the unreached can be reached within one's lifetime. However, Western missionaries must be prepared to encounter the worldview of animism or folk religion if they are to successfully fulfill the Great Commission in frontier lands. The world of popular or folk Islam poses an especially unique challenge to the Westerner.

In this chapter, the terms *folk Islam* and *Muslim animism* are used interchangeably. Namely, a "mixture of traditional religious beliefs and practices with orthodox Islam" (Hadaway 2021, 5). Today's foremost authority on popular Islam, Bill Musk defines popular or folk Islam as a combination of "indigenous beliefs and practices" with "formal Islamic creed and practice" (Musk 2004, 182). The term *popular Islam* is also synonymous with folk or animistic Islam. *Ordinary Muslims* are Muslims who practice popular or folk Islam (Musk 2004).

When Westerners hear words such as *magic*, *witches*, and *genies*, images of Harry Potter and Halloween often come to mind. Yet Western missionaries working in frontier Islamic lands must be equipped to engage with the spiritual realities and worldviews of the common Muslim. The majority of Muslims worldwide practice a form of folk Islam with animistic beliefs and practices. Shaitans, jinns, the evil eye, witchcraft, and a wide variety of magical and superstitious practices pervade the lives of most Muslims. However, many Western missionaries are unprepared to engage with the magic-influenced worldview that is common throughout the Islamic world.

The worldview of many Christians from the West has been influenced by outside factors such as the Enlightenment, secularism, and cultural evolution. In addition, internal factors inside the church such as cessationism and dispensationalism often impact the way Christians view the relationship between spiritual and material realities. Any form of Christianity that perceives reality to be split between the material and spiritual worlds will often answer the problems of this world through science and reason, while answering the ultimate and eternal questions with the gospel (Hiebert and Shaw 2000, 16–19).

These factors have contributed to Christians viewing animistic Muslim practices as not representative of "true" Islam and the study of them as irrelevant to the task of spreading the gospel (Hiebert and Shaw 2000, 18–19). However, the testimonies of former Muslims and national practitioners in frontier lands demonstrate that conversion from Islam often happens as a result of the gospel's power to confront magical and animistic practices. Therefore, Western missionaries need a wholesome and biblical understanding of the spirit world in order to address Islamic magical practices with the gospel. Western missionaries face several obstacles to understanding and engaging with Muslim animistic practices. These barriers include: a secularized biblical hermeneutic, dispensational theology, cessationism, and a deficient understanding of the gospel's power over the spirit realm. Missionaries to frontier Muslim lands must double-check their theological and hermeneutical presuppositions and listen to the voices of Majority World Christians if they are to successfully minister the gospel to folk Muslims.

Magic in Islam

It is vitally important that Western missionaries study the topic of magic in Islam because the supernatural and magical realm affects nearly every Muslim's life. Most Muslims deeply fear spells, witch doctors, jinns, shaitans, and other forms of magical practices. Muslims are greatly concerned about how to protect themselves from black magic and how to use magical practices for their advantage. Most Westerners are unaware of the way Muslims think about and interact with the supernatural world which can greatly hinder their ministries.

According to the *Oxford Classical Dictionary*, magic is "a manipulative strategy to influence the course of nature by supernatural ('occult') means" (Versnel 2016, 1). Muslims traditionally have divided magic or *sihr* into two categories: white magic and black magic. White magic can refer to a charm or incantation which manipulates someone into thinking they are perceiving reality correctly when he is not. *Sihr* can also refer to a "falsification of the reality of things and of actions," comparable to "falsehood," "trickery," and "astrology."

As black magic, *sihr* can be "applied to any action effected through recourse to a demon and with his assistance" (Fahd 1997, 567). Typically, white magic is thought to provide restoration and protection, while black magic is thought to cause harm or destruction (Collinson 1977, 8, 10). Magical beliefs and practices have influenced virtually all corners of the Muslim world. One seasoned missionary and scholar has estimated that around 70 percent of Muslims participate in folk practices (Parshall 2015, 2).

Why are magical practices so prevalent in Islamic lands despite the fact that we have entered the modern era? Wouldn't the rapid technological advancement and globalization of our world dispel such beliefs? Popular or folk Islamic practices are still prevalent due to the human desire to be close to the divine. Muslims seek to manipulate reality through questionable methods due to their lack of intimacy and trust in their deity's character. In Islam, Allah is remote and distant; therefore, Muslims turn to magic and unorthodox practices in order to access the divine and manipulate reality (Grant 1987, iii).

Most Western Christian missionaries have had little training or experience with popular Islamic practices. However, they must study these magical practices if they are to engage with the vast majority of Muslims worldwide. The Islamic magical world is a vast topic that could fill a whole book, but for this section, I will focus on three of the most common topics in Islamic animism: the Qur'an, the evil eye, and spiritual beings. I will also examine how Muslims believe they can protect themselves from these evil forces.

Magical Use of the Qur'an

Many standard Christian introductions of the Qur'an focus on its theological and historical content. Undoubtedly, these are important topics for any missionary to understand. Yet a majority of Muslims worldwide admire the Qur'an not so much for its historical or theological value, but rather view the words of their holy book as magical. One scholar summarized the Muslim attitude towards the Qur'an in this way, "Among the masses there is probably more faith in the magical uses of the book than there is understanding of its contents" (Donaldson 1937, 254). This insight demonstrates how Muslims typically view the Qur'an as an amulet which helps them to manipulate or control their lives rather than a book to be interpreted according to sound exegesis and historical methods.

Muslims believe that the Qur'an helps them attain good fortune and health. For example, Surah 65 is used to cure a toothache if verses are "written on paper and hung over the ear on the side of the aching tooth and [then] it will cure the pain" (Donaldson 1937, 258). This Surah also provides protection, "If one writes the 58th verse of Ya Sin, which is called the heart of the sura and therefore the heart of the Koran, in the form of a square at sunset, and keeps it on his person, no snake, scorpion or other injurious animal will molest him." Additionally, Muslims seek to improve their memory and physical strength by writing Surah 65:10 on a piece of paper, tying it with a blue cord, and burying it in a grave (260).

The Qur'an can also be used in many malicious ways to manipulate and harm others. One example is Surah 2:7 which is known for its ability to reveal secrets when it has been written on a green mud bowl, washed in rain water, and then sprinkled on a sleeping person. Supposedly, the suspect will then reveal any evil secrets or deeds. Another example is Surah 3:122–24, if it is written on a water pot or horse skin and then placed in someone's house, their home will be destroyed. The Qur'an is also thought to be able to kill enemies using voodoo practices, "A man makes a mask of his enemy's face … writes verses 30–33 of Surah 5 on the face of the image and the enemy's name on the back of it. He sticks a dagger into the head where the name is written, at the same time saying, 'O angels of God, do this to this person,' and the enemy will be struck dead" (Donaldson 1937, 261).

Another popular practice throughout the Muslim world is to run water over written qur'anic verses and then drink it for healing or as a cure from magic (Assimalhakeem 2020; Islam Q&A 2008). A similar tradition is seen in the Hadith which states, "Whenever the Prophet went to bed every night, he used to cup his hands together and blow over it after reciting Surat Al-Ikhlas, Surat Al-Falaq and Surat An-Nas, and then rub his hands over whatever parts of his body he was able to rub, starting with his head, face and front of his body. He used to do that three times" (Sunnah.com, n.d.). Even the words of the Qur'an are believed to have magical powers according to Islamic thought, thus Muslims attempt to literally "consume" its words. Examples abound of the Qur'an being used for magical and superstitious purposes, but the main point is that Muslims use the Qur'an more as an amulet to manipulate reality rather than a scripture to be understood.

The "Evil Eye"

A highly prevalent topic in the Muslim world unlike in the West is the "evil eye." It is best explained by those who have experienced it firsthand. Veteran missionary to Muslims, Bill Musk, describes it well, "The fundamental concept of the evil eye is that precious persons or things are constantly vulnerable to hurt or destruction caused by other people's envy" (Musk 2004, 23). In her PhD dissertation on the evil eye, Jeonghee Yun provides a similar definition, "The Evil Eye refers to the belief that certain individuals possess an eye whose powerful gaze can harm or destroy any object or possession and cause illness … The belief system holds that all persons and things are vulnerable to the Evil Eye, especially children, the beautiful, the successful, and what is most valuable and essential to survival" (Jeonghee Yun 2023, 29–30). Due to this belief, Muslims live in a state of paranoia caused by the evil eye and its effects.

The evil eye can also be termed the envious eye. Jeonghee Yun elaborates on the connection between envy and one's gaze when she writes,

> In Islam, the Evil Eye (*ayn* or *hasad* in Arabic) is linked to envy. It is believed the envious Evil Eye, aroused by looking at other people's fortunes and God-bestowed blessings and favors, can cause serious harm and illness to animals and people. It is feared and blamed for any misfortune, especially those involving young children and nursing mothers. Strangers and persons with physical deformity are suspected of possessing the Evil Eye. Sickness is often explained by a curse or the Evil Eye. Especially in the case of mental illness or disability, the Evil Eye and envy are often used as the main explanation since many Muslims believe that having a disabled child is due to envy. (Jeonghee Yun 2023, 47–48)

It is apparent that in Muslim culture the ethical and magical realms should not be separated, as in the case of the evil eye.

Since the concept of the evil eye is foreign to most Western missionaries, a few examples will help illustrate this prominent belief. A respected Arab news site reports the story of a Syrian housewife who is afraid of the evil eye because of her nice home and marriage. She claims that her friend cast the evil eye on her home which caused a room to be set on fire. The same site also tells of a Saudi housewife who repeats the phrase *Mashallah* (meaning "God wills it" or "as God has wished it") when she receives a compliment in order to drive away bad fortune from the evil eye (Al-Jassem 2010).

In her interviews with Jordanian women, Jeonghee Yun explored the reported cause and effect of the evil eye. One participant stated that her mother developed cancer and died because her neighbor was jealous that she worked outside the house. The evil eye can reportedly hurt loved ones, as another participant told the story of how a mother looked at her beautiful daughter at a wedding and blinded her. After the mother died the daughter's eyesight came back (Jeonghee Yun 2023, 123, 127). Musk reports of a Yemeni woman who was unable to breastfeed her child because of another woman's evil eye (Musk 2004, 22).

The origins of the evil eye can be found in Muslim sources, mainly the Hadith but also some passing references in the Qur'an. For example, Surah 113 states, "Say: I seek refuge in the Lord of the Daybreak, from the evil of that which He created; from the evil of the darkness when it is intense, and from the evil of malignant witchcraft, and from the evil of the envier when he envieth." In fact, Surah 113 (Al-Falaq) and Surah 114 (Al-Nas) are called *al-Mu'awwidhatayn* (the Protectors) and are recited by Muslims for protection against various types of evil (Jeonghee Yun 2023, 105–106).

The Hadith contains several references to the evil eye. For example: "The influence of an evil eye is a fact; if anything would precede the destiny it would be the influence of an evil eye, and when you are asked to take bath (as a cure) from the influence of an evil eye, you should take bath" (Sunnah.com, n.d., "Sahih Muslim 2188—The Book of Greetings"). Aisha reportedly stated, "The Prophet ordered me or somebody else to do Ruqya (if there was danger) from an evil eye" (Sunnah.com, n.d., "Sahih Al-Bukhari 5738—Medicine").

The evil eye is seen as extremely powerful and qur'anic magic (known as *ruqyah*) must be performed to cure someone of its effects per the advice of the Hadith, "Asma' said: 'O Messenger of Allah! The children of Ja'far have been afflicted by the evil eye, shall I recite Ruqyah for them?' He said: 'Yes, for if anything were to overtake the Divine decree it would be the evil eye'" (Sunnah.com n.d., "Sunan Ibn Majah 3510—Chapters on Medicine"). Both the Qur'an and Hadith testify to the fear and power of the evil eye in Muslim culture.

Jinn

On the surface, Muslims appear to believe in the same spiritual beings as Christians, but in reality their conception of angels, demons, and other spiritual beings is totally different from the biblical worldview. The Islamic worldview is heavily influenced by these spiritual beings. Missiologist Paul Hiebert has rightly pointed out that Westerners often have "excluded the middle" by dismissing the reality of entities such as spirits, demons, angels, and their interaction with the affairs of humankind. In the Global South, these beings are involved in this world and not in an abstract realm (Hiebert 1982, 40–41, 43). Oftentimes the most influential type of spiritual beings in animistic Islam are the jinn. Western missionaries must understand these creatures if they are to engage with magical Islamic practices.

The jinn (or genies in English) are perplexing creatures and difficult to define. The Qur'an states that they were made of fire (15:27). The jinn can be either good or bad and participate in human-like activities such as propagation, eating, and drinking (Grant 1987, 270–72). Zwemer helpfully summarizes their identity by stating, "The Jinn are considered to be like men, capable of future salvation and damnation; they can accept or reject God's message. … Mohammed was sent to convert the Jinn to Islam" (Zwemer 1920, 125–26). Although jinn are not necessarily evil, they are generally thought of as being malicious. Many Muslims are afraid of these strange beings (Musk 2004, 33).

The Qur'an and Hadith contain multiple references to the jinn. Surah 72, known as Al-Jinn, is about how some jinn accepted Muhammad's message of Islam. Yet not all jinn are peaceful, as the Hadith reports, "The Prophet said, 'A strong demon from the Jinns came to me yesterday suddenly, so as to spoil my prayer, but Allah enabled me to overpower him, and so I caught him and intended to tie him to one of the pillars of the Mosque so that all of you might see him, but I remembered the invocation of my brother Solomon … so I let him go cursed'" (Sunnah.com n.d., "Sahih Al-Bukhari 3423—Prophets" 2024).

Another Hadith relates the story of a young man who killed a snake with a spear but died simultaneously with the snake. Apparently, this snake was actually a good jinn who converted to Islam. In response Muhammad gave these instructions, "There are jinn in Madina who have become Muslim. When you see one of them, call out to it for three days. If it appears after that, then kill it, for it is a shaytan" (Sunnah.com n.d., "General Subjects").

Muslims believe Iblis leads the evil jinns (known as shaitans) in opposing Allah and his prophets (Grant 1987, 279). They also harm people through possession and by distracting humans from worshiping Allah (Qur'an 6:112). Jinn can possess not only humans but also inanimate objects like trees and animals. They are often blamed for unusual events and calamities (Laughlin 2015, 5, 8). Therefore, Muslims resort to a variety of folk practices in order to protect themselves and find deliverance from jinn.

There are numerous stories of jinn terrorizing Muslims. For example, seasoned missionary Bill Musk reports of a female jinn named A'isha Qandisha. She seduces men to sleep with her and if she is successful, the man becomes her slave for the rest of his life. He can save himself only if he recognizes her and plunges a knife into the earth (Musk 2004, 34).

Missiologist Earl Grant also relates several stories about jinn, "Muslims in Palestine will not call a doctor on Wednesday; Wednesday and Saturday nights are considered dangerous because the demons go at these times to the wells with their waterskins to draw water." In Algeria and Sudan, jinn can steal children and replace them with their own deformed jinn children (Grant 1987, 276–77).

In order to rescue people from jinn possession and oppression, Muslims use a variety of techniques. Ruqyah is one of the most popular magical techniques in the Muslim world. In Muslim thought, "'Ruqyah' is the practice of treating illnesses through Qur'anic āyāt and invocations as prescribed by the Messenger of Allah. … It provides a cure for evil eye, magic and physical ailments … The Qur'an is the complete healing for all mental, spiritual and physical diseases; all the diseases of this world and the Hereafter" (Ummah Welfare Trust, n.d., 2). Despite often being used as a means of cursing others, the Qur'an claims to have healing powers that can be used during ruqyah to expel evil spirits and undo magical curses and spells. Surah 17:82 describes its healing power as follows, "And We reveal of the Qur'an that which is a healing and a mercy for believers though it increase the evil-doers in naught save ruin."

A popular manual for performing ruqyah lists several steps to protect and rid oneself of evil. The main steps are making du'a (intention), reciting qur'anic verses, and consistently performing ruqyah. Believers should also wash themselves (wudu), send salutations (salawat) upon Muhammad, and recite ayats into their hands and rub it over themselves. If someone is performing ruqyah for another, he/she can put their hand on the patient, recite ayats and blow (Ummah Welfare Trust, n.d., 3–5).

Ruqyah can also protect one from the evil eye. The manual suggests, "One should pray Ruqyah on water, especially the last 3 Sūrahs of the Qur'an and bathe with it daily for 10–20 days until the symptoms [of the evil eye] disappear … The last 3 Sūrahs of the Qur'an are the strongest protection against envy, evil eye, magic and jinn" (Ummah Welfare Trust, n.d., 7). Connected with ruqyah is repeating the phrase "Mashallah" in order to protect oneself from the evil eye, "This protective formula is carefully employed in all situations of congratulation or admiration" (Musk 2004, 25).

Muslims also read Ayat al-Kursi and the adhan (the call to prayer) for protection from jinn and black magic. A person afflicted by black magic can also recite the ruqyah prayers over olive oil and rub it over the body. Other food sources such as black seed, cow's milk, dates, and zamzam water can help cure illness and the effects of magic. Reciting ayats such as the last two verses of Surah al-Baqarah provides protection from jinn and evil, as does mentioning Allah's name when entering a home or eating (Ummah Welfare Trust, n.d., 7–9, 11).

This brief introduction to magical practices and beliefs in Islam should help the Western missionary to understand that Muslims do not "exclude the middle" but live in deep fear of the spirit world. Muslims find protection from evil forces and black magic through reciting the Qur'an, saying prayers, and following superstitious practices. Western missionaries may find it extremely difficult to effectively address these practices from a biblical perspective—I will explain why in the next section.

Obstacles for Western Missionaries

Missionaries who have been influenced by secular worldviews may face several obstacles when engaging with Muslim animism. Therefore, they must re-examine three prevalent presuppositions when thinking about Islam and magic: a secular and Enlightenment influenced biblical hermeneutic, dispensationalism, and cessationism. I will examine each of these in light of the worldwide church and how these obstacles can hinder effective engagement with Muslim animists.

Biblical Hermeneutic

In general, Western believers have been influenced by the deistic worldview of the Enlightenment which in turn may cause them to read the Bible as functional deists. Westerners often assume that if something cannot be perceived by the five senses, then it is not real. Furthermore, they may think that the spiritual realm or what cannot be assessed empirically does not impact the physical realm and vice versa. However, in the Bible, "God controls physical phenomena and all so-called natural laws. Angels do his bidding. Demons actively and energetically oppose his kingdom. Miracles, physical healing, and gifts of the Holy Spirit are essential elements that constitute *reality* (Storms 2021, 16–17, emphasis in original)." This functional deistic worldview is not shared by Christians or Muslims living in the Majority World. Muslims' theology is faulty because it is based on the Islamic scriptures rather than the Bible, but they do have a keen awareness of the supernatural world which many Westerners do not understand.

Although there is a wealth of biblical resources available today in the Western world, the presuppositions and biases of Western believers often prevent them from reading the biblical text as the original authors saw it. As a result, they may be ignorant or confused about how the Bible can address the situations and needs of folk Islam. The Western church has been influenced by modernism and the scientific method in such a way that it often approaches the Bible with a bias against the strange, supernatural texts that seem to contradict how Westerners interpret reality (Heiser 2015, 12–15).

I am in no way suggesting that the Islamic understanding of the supernatural realm is theologically accurate. However, I am suggesting that the supposed magical experiences of Muslims, which keep them bound in fear and terror, need to be addressed biblically. The Western missionary who simply dismisses the bizarre supernatural events in both the Bible and the Muslim world can be a major roadblock to helping Muslims understand and experience the life-changing power of the gospel.

One of the most helpful ways for a Western student of the Bible to overcome biases is to admit presuppositions and read the thoughts of others living in different contexts. Scholar Craig Keener insightfully remarks, "Welcoming a multicultural range of perspectives to the table checks biases far better than welcoming only a single perspective … dialogue can help all of us to hear … the biblical text and how it speaks to our various situations" (Keener 2016, 85).

Keener goes on to name two specific areas where the thinking of Western churches and seminaries needs to be challenged by the Majority World church, namely the spirit realm and miracles. The reality of spirits, spirit possession, and witchcraft is accepted by Majority World Christians because they experience these entities every day. In addition, these believers seek to replicate the miracles found in the Bible and experience the supernatural realm that the Bible speaks of daily. Simply put, non-Western Christians have no reason to object to the reality of miracles and assume that God can perform them today (Keener 2016, 88–92, 94–95).

As of 2020, Christians (including numerous branches and types) were recorded geographically as follows: Africa—667 million; Latin America—612 million; Europe—565 million; Asia—379 million; North America—268 million; and Oceania—28 million (Zurlo 2019). These numbers demonstrate that the majority of Christians worldwide live in the Global South and therefore do not have the same Enlightenment and secular-influenced worldview as most Westerners have. Contrary to the view that Majority World Christians usually subscribe to "liberation theology" or have unorthodox beliefs, many believers in the Global South have a high view of biblical authority and would be viewed as conservative in Western circles. At the same time, these believers tend to "have a special interest in supernatural elements of scripture, such as miracles, visions, and healings," and for them "ideas of supernatural warfare and healing need not the slightest explanation, and certainly no apology. They are at the heart of lived Christianity" (Jenkins 2006, 4, 7–8, 11).

Along with the Enlightenment-influenced hermeneutic, a dispensationalist hermeneutic is one of the more popular hermeneutical-theological presuppositions many evangelical Christians hold to in the West. Dispensationalists read the Bible as containing "dispensations" or certain manners in which God related to humanity at different time periods. They also see a strict distinction between the Old and New Testament, believe the church is not the new Israel, and typically do not read the Bible as one, unifying story in the same manner as covenant theologians. Historically (in part due to early Brethren influence), dispensationalists have been fond of interpreting the Bible apart from commentaries and historical creeds. Dispensationalists have often viewed the Bible as its own commentary or concordance and not relied on theological works of those outside of their own camp (Pietsch 2015, 96–114).

The dispensational hermeneutic can impact Western missionaries in a few ways. First, it can unnecessarily divide the Bible into parts (dispensations) where God only dealt in a certain matter for a specific time period. For example, dispensationalists often view the book of Acts as a special dispensation where God worked signs and wonders through the apostles and then stopped performing miracles "regularly" after the apostles died. God's actions through his people in the past which were extraordinary and miraculous are not viewed as replicable but only historical. In other words, believers should not expect God to work in miraculous ways today similar to how he did in the Bible because these scriptural events are examples to learn from but not imitate due to the fact that they took place during particular dispensations.

Second, a dispensationalist hermeneutic may discourage believers from hearing other Christian voices because dispensationalism often claims to be the hermeneutical key which renders all other theological systems irrelevant. Westerners need to hear what their brothers and sisters from the Global South have to say because Western Christendom does not have a monopoly on biblical interpretation.

I am not suggesting that Majority World Christians necessarily have an advantage on biblical interpretation because they are not Western. The Western church has made tremendous contributions to the universal church which all believers should be thankful for. However, I am pointing out that if Western Christians want to engage missionally with the Global South, then they need to understand the way Majority World Christians think about the supernatural realm. Westerners can learn much from their brothers and sisters in the Global South on how to think biblically about the "middle zone" of spirits, angels, demons, and supernatural encounters. Besides re-assessing their hermeneutical presuppositions, one of the other ways in which Western missionaries can learn from Majority World believers is by re-examining the theological doctrine of cessationism through a biblical lens.

Cessationism

For most Christians worldwide, the idea that the signs or miraculous gifts of the Holy Spirit have ceased is irrelevant if not bizarre. The debate over cessationism and continuationism is not a pertinent topic of discussion for most Christians worldwide. In fact, cessationism can be an impediment to the growth of Majority World churches, especially in many Islamic countries where medical care is poor and popular religion relies on magic.

Cessationism can hamper missionary effectiveness in multiple ways. First, cessationist missionaries may have difficulty ministering to folk Muslims who are being oppressed by demonic forces and need prayer for healing or deliverance. If the missionary views ministry to folk Muslims through a cessationist and Enlightenment-influenced lens they may have difficulty ministering to animistic Muslims who are heavily influenced by the supernatural. In addition, most Majority World churches in the Muslim world are not cessationist but strongly believe in the sign gifts, which may prevent the Western missionary from serving alongside Majority World Christians.

Cessationists are not all in agreement with what gifts are still operational. Some believers may fall into the "open but cautious" camp, while others may label Pentecostals/Charismatics as unbiblical. Scholar Tom Schreiner outlines his cessationist position which many cessationists would likely agree with, "Over the years I've become convinced that some of the so-called charismatic gifts are no longer given and that they aren't a regular feature of life in the church. I am thinking particularly of the gifts of apostleship, prophecy, tongues, healing, and miracles (and perhaps discernment of spirits)" (Schreiner 2014).

Another definition of cessationism as well as continuationism is given by theologian Sam Storms who states:

> A cessationist is someone who believes that certain spiritual gifts, typically those of a more overtly supernatural nature, ceased to be given by God to the church sometime late in the first century AD (or more gradually through the course of the next few centuries). Cessationists do not deny that God can on occasion still perform miracles, such as physical healing. But they do not believe the spiritual gift of miracles or the gift of healing is given to believers today. Whereas "healing" still exists in the life of the church, "healers" do not. God's people may still experience miracles, but God no longer empowers "miracle workers." A continuationist, by contrast, is a person who believes that all the gifts of the Spirit continue to be given by God and are therefore operative in the church today and should be prayed for and sought after. (Storms 2021)

I am not proposing that there is a cause-and-effect type of relationship between continuationism and the effectiveness of a missionary to Muslims. The effectiveness of a missionary primarily comes down to his or her character and reliance on God's grace. However, I am asserting that cessationism can be a contributing factor to missionaries not effectively engaging with Muslim animistic worldviews. The reason is simple: if one believes that healings, miracles, and other "sign" gifts are not normative, how will they engage with national believers who rely on God to work in miraculous ways? If God does not "normally" work through the miraculous, then how will cessationist missionaries respond to Muslims living in the Global South who need deliverance from demons, sickness, and evil spirits? In addition, how will Western missionaries support and integrate into indigenous churches which are often composed of converts who have experienced healing, deliverance, exorcism, and who now minister using these "signs and wonders" in evangelism?

By not subscribing to a continuationist position, Western missionaries put themselves in a position of skepticism towards both Majority World Christians and Muslims who claim to experience evil magical powers. Skepticism towards the miraculous instead of embracing God's power can prove detrimental to the growth of the church. Keener notes an insightful story of some Western missionaries who left behind gospel booklets in Africa. Upon returning they found "a flourishing church with NT-like miracles happening daily because there had been no missionaries to teach that such things were not to be taken literally" (Keener 2016, 95). As this story demonstrates, Western missionaries can hinder church growth by teaching cessationism.

One of the foundational assumptions of cessationism is that God does not normally perform miracles today like he did in the Bible, especially in the book of Acts. Yet Christians around the world report miracles that resemble those that took place in the book of Acts with no hint that these are somehow "not normative" for God to perform (Keener 2011). Cessationists must come to terms with the fact that there is a supernatural world in which evil spirits are actively seeking to kill and destroy humankind, but that the risen Christ is still at work today just as he was in the pages of the Bible to heal those oppressed by the enemy.

The biblical authors and characters believed that witchcraft, evil spirits, and demonic possession were serious issues that needed to be dealt with by the power of God. The continuous pattern throughout Scripture clearly shows that God's people engaged with the spiritual world through healings, signs and wonders, exorcisms, and the like. For instance, in the Old Testament the miraculous gifts were typically reserved for the prophets, but in the New Testament the work of the Spirit is expanded as he makes his gifts available to all new covenant believers.

Furthermore, Paul plainly states in 1 Corinthians 12:31 and 14:1 that believers should pursue gifts such as prophecy, healings, miracles, helps, teaching, etc. These passages and others provide explicit grounds where Christians should seek the Holy Spirit's gifting in the so-called "sign" or "miraculous" charisms. From a biblical perspective there is strong precedent to expect God to work today in supernatural ways to reach the lost, just like he did in the pages of Scripture. Of course, God's miraculous works today do not mean that salvation history is being repeated, or that the scriptural canon is open.

However, Majority World Christians today often experience similar supernatural and miraculous phenomena as the biblical characters did. Craig Keener in his scholarly assessment of miracles in the universal church provides eyewitness testimony from the continents of Asia, Africa, Latin America, and the Western world of miraculous healings, similar to those the early church experienced (Keener 2011). Cessationist believers who live like functional deists should reassess their own assumptions about the interaction between the natural and supernatural worlds. They can look at the Bible with an awareness that many Christians are not cessationist and experience God glorifying his name in frontier lands through the miraculous.

My goal here is not to discourage cessationists from being missionaries. Rather, my goal is to alert Western missionaries of biases and presuppositions that often affect the way they think biblically about the supernatural realm. Brothers and sisters in the Majority World usually (but not always) have a more biblical view of the way the physical and spiritual worlds interact than Western cessationists. This is partly because their cultures have not been desensitized to the supernatural world through the influences of secularism, deism, the Enlightenment, and the scientific method.

As this brief study has shown, Westerners need to be aware that the Bible supports the view that God still works in miraculous ways like he did in the pages of Scripture. If Westerners are to engage with the dark forces of Islam, then they need to have an accurate understanding of God's world and how he has equipped the church to overcome the forces of evil.

Application

Thus far I have examined some of the most prevalent Islamic magical practices as well as a few major reasons why Western missionaries may have difficulty effectively addressing them. Now I will briefly look at how frontier missionaries can biblically engage the powers of darkness in their ministry. As Paul reminds us in Ephesians 6:10–20, Christians must use God's power and resources in order to wrestle the spiritual forces of evil. Ministry to Muslims can only be effective with God's written word and the Holy Spirit who reveals the living Word.

Although I have referenced several instances of Muslims claiming to experience evil spiritual forces, not every report of an encounter with the dark arts and evil beings is factual. Tragedies, illness, and erratic behavior can have a mainly psychological, biological, or emotional cause. It is possible that out of fear or superstition unbelievers falsely attribute a malady to magical forces. Missionaries should seek out a gifted mentor (preferably a national) to understand how to minister to those claiming to be affected by magic. In addition, missionaries must pray for the gift of discernment to determine if an affliction was caused by satanic influence. Instead of being skeptical of the Holy Spirit's miraculous works, Christians should be open to how God wants to glorify his name in a given situation as well as discerning if any sign or supernatural encounter accords with Scripture.

Westerners can often dismiss the reports of those who claim to have had genuine encounters with the dark spiritual world because they appear to be fanciful or bizarre. Although unbelievers from the Global South are not regenerate and are under the bondage of sin, they are not stupid. It would be presumptuous to assume that all Muslims living in fear of dark magic are perceiving reality incorrectly. Missionaries should approach those claiming to suffer from spiritual forces with a sense of humility and reliance on God to show them the root cause of any issue.

All evil, whether it be sickness from black magic, disease from a virus, sin addiction, or demon possession, is a result of the fall. Therefore, the answer to any form of trauma and evil is always the gospel of Jesus Christ. Islam by its very nature is anti-Christ because it teaches a false Jesus (Isa) who is not the divine Savior of the world. What every Muslim needs is a biblical revelation of the true person and work of Jesus Christ. It is only through a new identity in Christ that someone can find peace with God, others, and oneself.

Regardless of whether or not a Muslim experiences a miraculous sign, the ultimate miracle is the new birth. The greatest display of power was when the Son of God defeated Satan through his death and resurrection and procured forgiveness of sins for his people. If this message is not believed by Muslims, then miraculous signs become pointless. All healing from the powers of black magic must point to Christ who defeated sin, death, and Satan. Physical healings and displays of miraculous power culminate in the regeneration of a person's spirit from death to life.

Although repentance and faith in Jesus is the main goal of ministering to animistic Muslims, deliverance from satanic and magical forces are often effective means of leading Muslims to Christ. Since God typically uses people to accomplish his work of sharing his love and power, missionaries must understand their God-given authority over the spiritual forces. Luke 10:1–12, 17–20 provides a biblical foundation for the spiritual authority of Christians. In this passage "average, non-apostolic followers of Jesus are given the same authority as the apostles over Satan and his forces … It would appear that the commissioning, authorizing, and empowering of the seventy-two (some texts read 'seventy') is a prelude to the ministry of the larger universal body of Christ" (Storms 2017, 151–52). Western missionaries need to take advantage of the power delegated to them by the risen Christ if they are to minister effectively in frontier Islamic lands.

The ministry of healing is another useful method of displaying the gospel's power to Muslims. There are countless testimonies of Muslims coming to faith through healing (Blanc and Yacob 2021). This form of ministry is needed in Muslim lands because the Qur'an is typically used to treat sickness and spiritual oppression. From a Christian perspective, Muslims are using a satanically inspired book to find healing and deliverance, even though Satan came to steal, kill, and destroy. Missionaries can follow the examples of Scripture by laying hands on the sick and praying for healing in Jesus's name. Furthermore, many Muslims live in lands with little or poor medical care. God may choose to heal people regularly through supernatural means as a witness to the gospel in lands with poor medical resources.

Frontier missionaries have the opportunity to take the gospel to Muslim countries which were once completely closed to any outside Christian influence. As a result, they now face the unexpected challenge of magical and animistic Islamic practices which Satan uses to keep Muslims in fear and bondage. Animistic religion and magical worldviews are often unknown to the Western believer and can be a major hurdle to ministering to Muslims. However, through listening to global Christian voices, questioning the philosophical and theological foundations of secularism, cessationism, and dispensationalism, and declaring the gospel in word and power, Western missionaries to frontier Muslim lands can effectively engage with magical Islamic practices.

Resources

Al-Jassem, Diana. 2010. "The Evil Eye an Obsession for Most Middle Eastern Families." *Arab News*, December 31. https://www.arabnews.com/node/364262.

Assimalhakeem. 2020. "Is It Permissible to Write Any Part of the Quran, Wash It and Drink the Water for Cure Assimalhakeem." Video. YouTube. https://www.youtube.com/watch?v=e8EbQ_zGYS8.

Blanc, Jean L., and Youssef Yacob. 2021. *Algerian Church Revival*. LOGOS Ediciones.

Collinson, Bernard. 1977. *Occultism in North Africa*. The North Africa Mission.

Donaldson, Bess Allen. 1937. "The Koran as Magic." *The Muslim World* 27 (3): 254–66. doi:10.1111/j.1478–1913.1937.tb00355.x.

Fahd, T. 1997. "Sihr." In *Encyclopedia of Islam*, edited by P. Bearman, Th. Bianquis, C. E. Bosworth, E. van Donzel, and W. P. Heinrichs. 2nd ed. Brill.

Grant, Earl. 1987. "Folk Religion in Islam: Its Historical Emergence and Missiological Significance." PhD diss., Fuller Theological Seminary.

Hadaway, Robin. 2021. *The Muslim Majority: Folk Islam and the Seventy Percent*. B&H Publishing Group.

Heiser, Michael. 2015. *The Unseen Realm: Recovering the Supernatural Worldview of the Bible*. Lexham Press.

Hiebert, Paul G. 1982. "The Flaw of the Excluded Middle." *Missiology: An International Review* 10 (1): 35–47. doi:10.1177/009182968201000103.

Hiebert, Paul G., and R. Daniel Shaw. 2000. *Understanding Folk Religion: A Christian Response to Popular Beliefs and Practices*. Baker Books.

Islam Q&A. 2008. "Writing Qur'aanic Verses on a Vessel so That It Can Be Washed and the Water Drunk by One Who Is Sick." *Islam Question & Answer*, April 19. https://islamqa.info/en/answers/111809/writing-quraanic-verses-on-a-vessel-so-that-it-can-be-washed-and-the-water-drunk-by-one-who-is-sick.

Jenkins, Philip. 2006. *The New Faces of Christianity: Believing the Bible in the Global South*. Oxford University Press.

Jeonghee Yun, Safia. 2023. "The Evil Eye Through the Eyes of Young Jordanian Muslim Women." PhD diss., Columbia International University.

Joshua Project. N.d. "Definitions Unreached/Least Reached (UPGs)." https://joshuaproject.net/help/definitions#unreached.

Joshua Project. N.d. "Frontier Unreached Peoples." https://joshuaproject.net/frontier.

Keener, Craig S. 2011. *Miracles: 2 Volumes: The Credibility of the New Testament Accounts*. Baker Books.

Keener, Craig S. 2016. *Spirit Hermeneutics: Reading Scripture in Light of Pentecost*. Eerdmans.

Laughlin, Vivian. 2015. "A Brief Overview of al Jinn within Islamic Cosmology and Religiosity." *Journal of Adventist Mission Studies* 11 (1): 67–78. doi:10.32597/jams/vol11/iss1/9/.

Lewis, R. W. 2018. "Clarifying the Remaining Frontier Mission Task." *International Journal of Frontier Missiology* 35 (4): 154–68.

Musk, Bill. 2004. *The Unseen Face of Islam: Sharing the Gospel with Ordinary Muslims at Street Level*. Monarch Books.

Parshall, Philip L. 2015. *Bridges to Islam: A Christian Perspective on Folk Islam*. InterVarsity Press.

Pickthall, Mohammed Marmaduke. 1953. *The Meaning of the Glorious Quran: Text and Explanatory Translation*. Mentor.

Pietsch, B. M. 2015. *Dispensational Modernism*. Oxford University Press.

Schreiner, Thomas. 2014. "Why I Am a Cessationist." *The Gospel Coalition*, January 22. https://www.thegospelcoalition.org/article/cessationist/.

Storms, Sam. 2017. *Practicing the Power: Welcoming the Gifts of the Holy Spirit in Your Life*. Zondervan.

Storms, Sam. 2021. *Understanding Spiritual Warfare: A Comprehensive Guide*. Zondervan.

Sunnah.com. N.d. "General Subjects." *Sayings and Teachings of Prophet Muhammad*. https://sunnah.com/urn/418530.

Sunnah.com. N.d. "Sahih Al-Bukhari 3423—Prophets." *Sayings and Teachings of Prophet Muhammad*. https://sunnah.com/bukhari:3423.

Sunnah.com. N.d. "Sahih Al-Bukhari 5017—Virtues of the Qur'an." *Sayings and Teachings of Prophet Muhammad*. https://sunnah.com/bukhari:5017.

Sunnah.com. N.d. "Sahih Al-Bukhari 5738—Medicine 5738." *Sayings and Teachings of Prophet Muhammad*. https://sunnah.com/bukhari:5738.

Sunnah.com. N.d. "Sahih Muslim 2188—The Book of Greetings." *Sayings and Teachings of Prophet Muhammad*. https://sunnah.com/muslim:2188.

Sunnah.com. N.d. "Sunan Ibn Majah 3510—Chapters on Medicine." *Sayings and Teachings of Prophet Muhammad*. https://sunnah.com/ibnmajah:3510.

Ummah Welfare Trust. N.d. "Ruqyah A Remedy for Illnesses, Evil Eye, Magic and Jinn from the Qur'an and Sunnah." https://uwt.org/wp-content/uploads/2019/03/Ruqyah-Booklet.pdf.

Versnel, H. S. 2016. "Magic." *Oxford Classical Dictionary*. https://oxfordre.com/classics/display/10.1093/acrefore/9780199381135.001.0001/acrefore-9780199381135-e-3865.

ZA Blog. 2021. "Understanding Cessationism from a Continuationist Perspective." *Zondervan Academic*, December 10. https://zondervanacademic.com/blog/understanding-cessationism-from-a-continuationist-perspective.

Zurlo, Gina. 2019. "Who Owns Global Christianity?" *Gordon Conwell*, December 11. https://www.gordonconwell.edu/blog/who-owns-global-christianity/.

Zwemer, Samuel Marinus. 1920. *The Influence of Animism on Islam; an Account of Popular Superstitions*. The Macmillan Co.

Chapter 9

Mobilizing Generation Z for the Great Commission

A Model Based on Proven Strategies in Business and Fast-Growing Next Gen Ministry

Billy McMahan[1]

Introduction

In today's rapidly evolving cultural landscape, Generation Z (born between 1997 and 2011) represents a pivotal generation within and beyond the church. Defined by their digital fluency, pervasive anxiety, and deep longing for authenticity and social impact, Gen Z poses unique challenges and opportunities for ministries seeking to engage them meaningfully. As previous models of outreach and discipleship lose their effectiveness, the church must rise to the occasion with innovative, intentional strategies tailored to this emerging generation.

This research seeks to answer the question: How can the church effectively disciple Generation Z to become Great Commission-focused followers of Jesus? To achieve this goal, the study will first explore the defining characteristics of Gen Z to understand their worldview and desires. Second, it will examine adaptations in the business world that resonate with Gen Z workers to uncover transferable principles. Third, the study will draw upon key traits of some of the fastest growing next-generation ministries to identify proven approaches. Fourth, the study will briefly examine a biblical example involving the calling of the next generation. Finally, it will propose a comprehensive, reproducible model for discipling the next generation, equipping churches and everyday believers to raise future leaders who will advance the kingdom of God.

---

1 Portions of this chapter are taken from my earlier work: McMahan (2024).

Six Defining Characteristics of Gen Z

As we dream of walking the long, dusty road of discipleship with this emerging generation, we must first understand some of their unique, defining characteristics. Understanding these defining characteristics assists the church as we seek to reach, disciple, and send young leaders for mission. These characteristics influence how members of Gen Z approach relationships, purpose, and the gospel. By understanding these six defining traits, ministries will be better equipped to lead Gen Z toward kingdom-minded work, develop them in ways that strengthen their relationship with Christ, and mobilize them as dynamic contributors to the Great Commission.

Generation Z is commonly defined as those born between 1997 and 2011. This means that by the end of 2024, Generation Z will be between the ages of thirteen and twenty-seven. The youngest Gen Zers are in seventh grade, while the oldest have entered the global workforce over the last several years. With that age group in mind, consider these six defining traits of this emerging generation.

1. Developing Through Rapid Change

In 2018, the *New York Times* invited readers under twenty-two to suggest a name for the generation following the millennials. Among the responses, the term "Delta Generation" stood out. Kelsy Hillesheim, one of the participants, explained, "Delta is used to denote change and uncertainty in mathematics and the sciences, and my generation was shaped by change and uncertainty" (Bromwich 2018). She described how events like a recession, job loss, terror attacks, war, and contentious elections had shaped her generation's experiences.

Since Kelsy's interview, her observations have only become more ingrained. To her list, we can now add a global pandemic, widespread natural disasters, ongoing conflicts, increased racial tensions, and an escalating sense of instability. Regardless of what name we use to describe Generation Z, it is undeniable that their lives have been defined by instability and change. While global and political events have contributed significantly to this, we must also consider the instability within their homes due to high divorce rates.

Gen Z expects change. This reality comes with positives and negatives. First, it makes them slow to trust. There is a feeling that very few things are trustworthy. Constant change also uniquely equips them for Great Commission work. Moving to a new country, learning a language, and adapting to cultural norms and a new environment require adaptability. This emerging generation is uniquely equipped to move in and out of change more smoothly than previous generations. They have been adapting to change their entire lives, removing at least one barrier inherently found in cross-cultural mission work.

2. Digital Addiction

Gen Z is the first generation to grow up entirely in the internet age. Most cannot remember life before smartphones, earning them the nickname "iGen" to reflect their complete immersion in the iPhone era. Smartphones and social media have become defining features of their daily lives, shaping how they interact with the world and with one another.

According to Gallup's *Familial and Adolescent Health Survey*, teenagers aged thirteen to seventeen spend an average of 4.8 hours daily on social media platforms such as YouTube, TikTok, and Instagram (Rothwell 2024). This amounts to 33.6 hours per week, 134.4 hours per month, and 1612.8 annually. This means that, in just 5.5 years, the average teenager would have spent an entire year on social media. These numbers exclude additional screen time for schoolwork, television, video games, or other digital activities, underscoring the dominant role of social media in their lives.

The internet has become more for this generation—it is their space for shopping, socializing, and seeking answers to life's questions. Previous generations would go to a trusted mentor or friend, millennials would go to Google to look up answers to big questions, but Gen Z goes to TikTok and Instagram. According to a recent study, 64 percent of Gen Z users have used TikTok as a search engine to find answers to questions (Adobe Express 2024). It is a refuge where they escape, find entertainment, and fill every slow, awkward, or uncomfortable moment. For this generation, online spaces are a part of life and a primary environment shaping their identity and worldview.

3. Desire to Be Known and in Community

Generation Z could aptly be called the "Lonely Generation," as they are experiencing a profound mental health crisis. While technology and social media have fostered unprecedented global connectedness, they have also contributed to rising rates of loneliness, depression, anxiety, and other mental health issues. Many young people feel isolated and disconnected despite being more "connected" than any previous generation. A 2019 Cigna study revealed that 73 percent of respondents aged eighteen to twenty-two reported "sometimes or always feeling alone" (Coombs 2023). By 2021, post-pandemic data showed this number had climbed to 79 percent, highlighting the intensifying impact of loneliness on Gen Z (Buechler n.d.).

These statistics align with real-life experiences in ministry. Conversations with Gen Z often reveal a deep sense of isolation, with loneliness being the most common response to questions about their well-being. This generation craves meaningful community and genuine connection. As Wytsma and Swoboda note in *Redeeming How We Talk*, "It is not that the amount of information or words has declined, but rather that deep, transformative, and redemptive communication has fallen victim to the new realities of modern culture" (Wytsma 2018). The rise of social media has replaced deep connections with surface-level interactions, often robbing young people of the ability to engage in meaningful relationships.

This loss of connection is damaging mental health and every aspect of life. For Gen Z, isolation is compounded by societal pressures such as cancel culture and a diminished capacity for healthy conflict resolution. While social media provides a temporary escape, it often deepens feelings of disconnection. The loneliness and mental health struggles shaping this generation also illuminate their need for genuine, transformative relationships and authentic community. Addressing these needs is essential for Gen Z's well-being and spiritual growth.

4. Desire to Change the World

Generation Z is acutely aware that the world is broken. They see its effects daily—on social media, in the news, and their own experiences with loneliness and depression. This generation does not need to be convinced that change is necessary; they witness it constantly. Gen Z lives in a world of rapid change, and they expect it. Roberta Katz, a former senior research scholar at Stanford, notes that this generation has "an expectation of constant change" (De Witte 2024). Having grown up in an environment of perpetual transformation, they refuse to tolerate what is broken. As a result,

Generation Z is deeply committed to creating change. They believe in their ability to influence the future and want to be positive changemakers. Their desire to make a difference stems from seeing the world evolve and their strong sense of responsibility to help shape that change.

Gen Z is particularly passionate about fighting for justice. They are not willing to stand by when they perceive injustice, especially toward marginalized groups. Gen Z will fight hard for causes that matter to them, and their commitment to fighting for what they believe in shows their deep desire to bring about meaningful change in the world.

Many emerging adults throughout history have expressed a desire to change the world. This desire is heightened in this generation due to their unsettled upbringing and the influencer age in which they find themselves. While the longing for world change, meaningful impact, and big dreams seems to mark the twenty-somethings of every generation, this longing is increased among Gen Zers. Listening carefully to ad campaigns, music, and the popular influencers of culture makes it clear. The church can capitalize on this hunger and send them out as changemakers for kingdom growth.

5. Desire for Mentorship

The next generation is eager for mentorship, seeking guidance, feedback, and on-the-job training to help them grow and achieve their aspirations. Gen Z has big dreams and values the support of older, more experienced individuals to help them navigate their goals. According to the Adobe Future Workforce Study, 83 percent of Gen Z workers believe having a workplace mentor is crucial for career development. However, only 52 percent feel they currently have one, highlighting a significant gap in the mentorship they seek (Adobe Communications Team 2023).

This need for guidance and development is mirrored in Barna's *Resilient Pastor Series*, which paints a concerning picture of the church's role in developing and discipling next-generation leaders. The study found that 75 percent of respondents believe it is becoming harder to find mature young Christians who want to become pastors. Additionally, 71 percent are concerned about the quality of future young leaders, and 79 percent agree that churches are failing to train the next generation of Christian leaders (Barna 2023). These findings suggest a disconnect between Gen Z's hunger for mentorship and the church's efforts to provide it.

The church must rise to the challenge of meeting this generation's need for guidance and discipleship. Jesus's final command to "Go and make disciples of all nations" calls believers to invest intentionally in the next generation. Returning to Jesus's discipleship model, the church can equip Gen Z to become the leaders and changemakers they aspire to be while grounding it in Biblical, God-given realities. This generation is hungry for mentorship, and the church has the opportunity—and responsibility—to step into that role. If the church fails to step into this role, someone else will.

6. The Corrective Generation

There is hope for the next generation, even as the church grapples with how to engage them effectively. In 2023, the world witnessed a unique move of God among Generation Z, beginning in Wilmore, Kentucky, at Asbury University. What started as a small group of leaders praying faithfully for revival blossomed into an outpouring of the Holy Spirit that drew comparisons to historic revivals like the Jesus Revolution of the 1960s. This revival was marked by something new: the role of Gen Z in leveraging social media to spread the word, drawing people from across the nation and the world to encounter God profoundly.

What stood out about this revival was the humility of Gen Z. Asbury's Pastor in Residence, Zach Meerkreebs, observed, "Gen Z is going lower," describing their posture of repentance, humility, and genuine hunger for God. Similar movements followed at Auburn University, the University of Alabama, and even in Europe, showcasing the deep spiritual yearning of this generation. Kevin Brown, President of Asbury University, described Gen Z as "a corrective to the casual Christianity that has marked our religious landscape," emphasizing their hunger for a more genuine, simple, and authentic encounter with God (Brown 2024). This desire to push against the status quo reveals a generation eager for transformative change.

The church has an incredible opportunity to lean into this hunger and guide Gen Z towards a biblically centered vision to change the world. This generation's dissatisfaction with how things have been presents an opening for the church to affirm their desires to fix what is broken and lead them to a life of submission to Jesus. While the rise of the "nones"—those claiming no religious affiliation—may be a reality, there is also great potential for radical faith among those who choose to follow Christ wholeheartedly.

As the "Corrective Generation," Gen Z invites the church to partner with them in shaping a new and dynamic future for the kingdom of God.

Adaptations in Business for Gen Z

As Generation Z enters the workforce, they bring unique values, expectations, and skills that will reshape the workplace. Businesses are feeling the changing culture of Gen Z entering the global workforce. They are racing to adopt innovative and meaningful ways of attracting, retaining, and developing Gen Z employees. These strategies emphasize alignment with Gen Z's priorities, including purpose, flexibility, growth, and collaboration.

1. Emphasis on Purpose and Impact

One strategy used in the business world to attract Gen Z employees is emphasizing "purpose" and "impact." Cindy Waxer (2022) writes, "83.1% care to work for a company or an organization that is intentional about making a positive impact in the world." Companies that can pull employees into a vision of more significant impact, purpose, and world change are more attractive to young workers.

Patagonia is finding success with this. The owner of Patagonia recently gave up 98 percent of the company by placing it into a trust. This move generates increased revenue that is being used to protect the environment. In a letter shared on the Patagonia website, Yvon Chouinard explains his heart and vision behind some of these decisions. In this letter, he writes, "Instead of 'going public,' you could say we are 'going purpose.' Instead of extracting value from nature and transforming it into wealth for our investors, we will use Patagonia's wealth to protect the source of all wealth" (Chouinard 2022).

Companies are making a concerted effort to rally their employees around a big vision of world change. They know that giving increased purpose behind the work will increase output, especially among their younger workers. It moves the motive beyond profit alone to a grander purpose.

2. Creating Environments for Personal and Professional Growth

Companies have realized the need to increase the application pool. While not a business, the US Armed Forces have been experiencing a recruiting crisis. They have not only seen a decline in overall interest levels in enlisting into the Armed Forces, but they have also seen a decrease in the number of potential recruits who would even qualify to enlist (USA Facts 2023). As a way of addressing this recruiting crisis, the US Army has invested in the development of "Early Engagement Strategies." These programs are designed to plug potential recruits into mentor relationships where students can be challenged and developed to meet the physical and mental requirements. The early results are strong, and Gen Z is responding (Winkie 2022).

Companies are also investing in a strategy called "reverse mentoring." Notable companies like Cisco, Target, and General Electric have succeeded in the new plan. With this strategy, they are leveraging the expertise and knowledge of their younger workers to train older ones. They have found areas where Gen Z is more equipped than the previous generations, specifically in technology areas. A former General Electric leader has said, "We tipped the organization upside down. We now have the youngest and brightest teaching the oldest" (Wingard 2018). Another article says, "Reverse mentorship changes the direction of the flow of information" (Kelly 2024).

Companies are realizing the next generation's hunger for mentorship and development. They also see that giving Gen Z opportunities to lead meaningfully generates increased buy-in and helps grow and develop their teams. Companies that can learn to develop young talent from within will experience increased success and retention.

3. Prioritizing Authenticity and Transparency

We are all familiar with Nike's iconic ads, which showcase world-class athletes like Michael Jordan, who are depicted as almost superhuman. From soaring dunks to a partnership immortalized in films, Nike has long emphasized image and excellence, crafting its athletes into figures reminiscent of superheroes. These ads sent a clear message: greatness was within reach—you could aspire to be like them.

In 2019, Nike shifted its approach in a way that resonated deeply with Gen Z. Partnering with *Darling Magazine*, they launched a marathon campaign that followed a woman's journey preparing for the Chicago Marathon. One ad told the story of a young woman battling self-doubt and physical challenges during her training. Scenes of her pushing through early morning runs were overlaid with a raw, inner monologue: "I have quit before. Why not quit again? It is too cold outside. I am not an athlete. My knees hurt. I do not have time." The ad concluded with her triumphant smile, wearing a Chicago Marathon finisher's medal engraved with the words, "It is only a crazy dream until you do it" (Presley 2019).

This campaign resonated with Gen Z because it embodied trust, transparency, and vulnerability—values central to their worldview. By showcasing the mental and physical struggles of training, Nike created an authentic narrative, inviting a deeper connection with the brand. The campaign did not just acknowledge the pain of pursuing big goals; it celebrated the resilience required to dream and achieve the impossible, inspiring a new generation to take on their challenges.

Key Traits from Fast Growing Next Gen Ministries

Engaging Generation Z in ministry requires a strategic and intentional approach. A recent study (McMahan 2024) on four rapidly growing next-generation ministries in church and parachurch settings uncovered five key areas of focus. These principles are not abstract ideas but practical and essential steps for equipping the next generation to live out the gospel in transformative ways.

1. **Create Space to Lead in Meaningful Ways:** Empowering Gen Z to lead taps into their desire to make a meaningful impact. This generation does not want to sit on the sidelines; they want to take ownership and contribute. When ministries trust young people with leadership opportunities—such as preaching, organizing events, or leading service projects—they grow in confidence and discover how their gifts can advance the mission of Christ.

2. **Big Vision:** Gen Z longs to see their lives as part of something bigger. This generation wants to change the world, and ministries that invite them into a kingdom mission—whether through justice initiatives, global outreach, or local service—tap into their God-given desire to make a difference. They need to see action that backs up the belief behind the action. Talk without action quickly loses credibility with the next generation.

3. **Prioritize Authenticity:** Gen Z is looking out for anything fake, and they respect leaders who are honest about their struggles and faith journeys. When leaders transparently share their honest trials with

depression and doubt, they model what it means to follow Christ in real life. Young adults will follow your lead but need you to model it and prove that it is a safe space to be themselves.

4. **Foster Meaningful Community:** The average Gen Zer has a deep-rooted longing for belonging. One of their primary felt needs is an answer to their loneliness. Ministries that create environments where young people can connect in small groups or close-knit gatherings give them a place to be known and loved. These settings provide support and encourage spiritual growth through shared experiences.

5. **Digital Engagement:** Having a digital strategy is non-negotiable. Gen Z lives in a digital-first world, and the church must show up there. Ministries that use platforms like Instagram or TikTok to share gospel-centered content are meeting this generation in their space, providing bite-sized, impactful messages that resonate. Even more important than sharing content, it must be a starting point for drawing young people into genuine relationships. Ministries that thrive in this space leverage online platforms for two-way communication, not just as a means of advertisement.

By embracing these five areas, ministries can effectively engage Generation Z and empower them to live out the gospel in ways that shape the future of the church. These focus areas speak to Generation Z's unique needs and passions and can help church leaders be more effective as they seek to reach, disciple, and send the next generation.

A Biblical Example of Calling the Next Generation into Discipleship and Mission

While there are many examples of discipleship in the Bible, the calling of Elisha by Elijah gives us a powerful picture of what it looks like to raise up the next generation. It also provides a powerful example of what God could do if we can restore discipleship into the everyday practices of believers around the world. 1 Kings 19:19–20 says,

> So Elijah went from there and found Elisha son of Shaphat. He was plowing with twelve yoke of oxen, and he himself was driving the twelfth pair. Elijah went up to him and threw his cloak around him. Elisha then left his oxen and ran after Elijah. "Let me kiss my father and mother goodbye," he said, "and then I will come with you."

The weight that Elisha felt on his shoulders from Elijah's cloak came packed with meaning. This moment is filled with cultural context that we must understand as we think about next-generation discipleship. To understand what is happening, we must understand the meaning of the cloak being placed on Elisha's shoulders. There are at least three aspects to this understanding:

1. **An invitation to surrender:** Elijah was inviting Elisha into surrender. For Elisha to follow Elijah, he must say goodbye to all he knew. He would need to say goodbye to his friends and family, stepping away from the comfort and security of home. The role that Elisha was being invited into was not an easy assignment. In chapter nineteen (the very same chapter), we see Elijah running for his life, hiding in a cave, lamenting to God that he is the only prophet left, questioning his impact and desire to continue. Elijah is inviting Elisha to surrender everything so that he can become God's messenger and God's chosen vessel. Elisha decides the mission is worth the cost. He proceeds to burn the plows and slaughter the oxen as a statement of never turning back. Elisha decided that following God was worth his surrender and that God would be faithful despite the hardship that would undoubtedly come.

2. **A call to be all that God had created him to be:** Elijah, seeking out Elisha to invite him into discipleship and mentorship, spoke volumes to Elisha. The weight of the cloak on Elisha's shoulders spoke value, purpose, and vision. Elisha would have understood that which he was being invited towards. This moment is Elijah saying to Elisha, "I see more in what you could become than what you can see in yourself." Elisha was excited and wanted to say goodbye before starting the discipleship journey.

3. **A commitment to long, slow discipleship:** In this discipleship relationship, we see a long-lasting journey and the relationship between Elijah and Elisha. Most scholars agree that Elisha spent six years learning from Elijah. Elisha watched, asked questions, and observed, and then, after six years of learning, he was sent out to carry on Elijah's legacy and make God known.

Each of these aspects is very important to understand as we start the conversation of discipling the next generation. First, we cannot force a discipleship relationship. Discipleship must be something that both sides are open to. In the case of Elijah and Elisha, God reveals to Elijah whom he should call out. We can do the same by listening to God and walking in obedience.

Second, one of the greatest gifts you can give to the next generation is the statement, "I see more in what you could become than what you can see in yourself." We must learn to make the affirmation of young leaders a regular part of our discipleship. We can cast a vision for the next generation, helping them see and accept their God-given kingdom assignment. While the next generation profoundly desires to see change, they often struggle to see and understand how they fit. They need leaders to show them how to leverage their gifting, abilities, and passions toward kingdom fruit as an offering to Jesus.

Finally, we must commit to long-term, genuine relationships and authentic love for those we disciple. They will make mistakes, and there will be times when you question the fruitfulness of time invested. Crafting next-generation leaders and disciple-makers takes time. Elijah spent six years investing in Elisha's life and kingdom potential.

We see discipleship practiced throughout Scripture. The reality is that when we disciple the next generation, there is a multiplying effect. If every one of us can learn to be disciple-makers, the number of people we can impact grows exponentially. We see this reality played out beautifully in the lives of Elijah and Elisha. At the end of Elijah's ministry, he witnessed eight of God's miracles. During his life, he had seen God do amazing things in and through his ministry. However, being commanded by God, Elijah poured his life into Elisha. In Scripture, we see that Elisha was witness to sixteen miracles. Elisha got to see God do twice as many miracles as his predecessor. So, it can be with us! This reality should help everyone understand the importance of discipleship.

Each one of us has been called to make disciples. As we make disciples, walk the long road of development, love people far from God, and give them a global vision of kingdom service, I believe we will see more people reached. We will witness unreached people groups worldwide experiencing the life and the promise offered by Jesus alone.

DREAMER Discipleship: A Model for Discipling the Next Gen Towards Life on Mission

Finally, I want to offer a method of discipleship aimed squarely at Gen Z, or as I call them, the *dreamer generation*. This method is designed for church leaders, lay leaders, and any follower of Jesus with a heart to participate in the development of future Great Commission leaders. It is discipleship rooted in trust and relationship that we have seen modeled through Scripture, calling back to that of Elijah and Elisha, Jesus and his disciples, Paul and Timothy, and others. This approach is designed to disciple, empower, cultivate missional passion, and then send them to impact the world. I am calling this method of discipling the next generation, *DREAMER Discipleship*.

If we, the church, can begin to implement and replicate this method into the fabric of church culture, church life, and the everyday practice of believers, we could see the next generation change the world and ultimately be the ones to fulfill the Great Commission. The process of DREAMER Discipleship contains the following seven components, as seen in Figure 9.1: Discover, Recognize, Envision, Affirm, Mentor, Empower, and Rejoice.

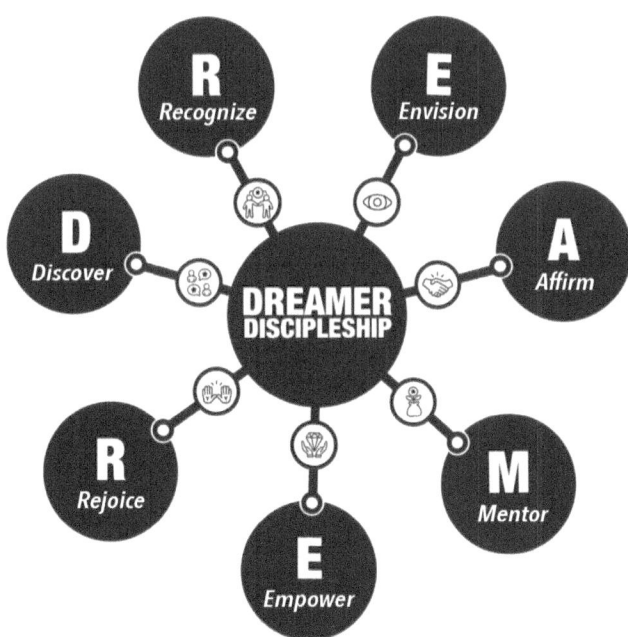

Figure 9.1: DREAMER Discipleship

Leveraging DREAMER Discipleship will take time. It will take time to establish trust with those you disciple. As you begin to build the relationship, share your stories. Share your triumphs and your challenging moments. Share your fears and failures. Share the times you saw God come through and the ones where you wrestled and questioned his goodness. Often, as we disciple others, we feel we need to have the answers. This can lead us to present only the highlight reel of our walks with Jesus, ultimately giving a rose-colored picture of journeying with Jesus. We must learn to share the realities of a journey with Jesus that experiences the hills and valleys of life. This will allow the ones we disciple to withstand the storms of life that will shake their faith. It will make them more likely to cling to hope despite the trials they are sure to face. Let's examine the components of DREAMER Discipleship one by one.

1. **Discover:** *Prioritize time to get to know and listen.*
   Meet them over coffee or take them to lunch. Use these natural settings where they feel comfortable. Ask lots of questions. Ask open-ended questions—questions that cannot be answered with one word. Start with things that interest them and build from there. As you begin to do this, you will learn what makes their eyes light up, the places where they are struggling, and the things they dream about. Get to know them. As you build trust, share your story. Find pieces of your story that relate to where they are, even sharing portions of your story that once brought you shame. This openness tells them that it is a safe place, and they no longer need to hide. Your vulnerability will invite them to follow you into openness. Find ways to challenge lies and re-establishing the conversation in hope. Sometimes, the best thing you can do is to just be with them in the struggle. Many disciple-makers are tempted to try and fix the problems rather than simply being present. Sometimes, your simple presence speaks the loudest.

2. **Recognize:** *Begin to identify what God is stirring within them.*
   Begin to prayerfully imagine the roles that they could play in the kingdom based on the giftings and dreams that God has given them. When you listen long enough, you can sense what God may be stirring inside them. As I have walked with young people, this

often shapes their dreams and desires for the future. Sometimes, it will seem like an impossible dream. Other times, you may need to help them find environments to experiment and walk with them as they process where God is leading. Clarity can begin to take shape through exposure, experience, and opportunity. As they try and experience new things, process with them. Throughout this process of discernment, they must hear the message: "God loves you; he designed and will lead and place you. He knows you better than you know yourself, and your desire is secure in him because only he can satisfy."

3. **Envision:** *Imagine unique roles they can play in advancing the kingdom.* As you begin to see the places in their lives where God is moving, start casting a vision for their potential. Help them imagine and see different kingdom roles they could play. Do not limit your imagination to ministry positions alone. Help them understand that God can use kingdom-focused leaders in business, education, medicine, science, technology, and any other assignment where he may place them. Prayer must be central. As we disciple, we point them towards God and his plans for them. Whenever possible, do this in community with other believers and the church. God will give wisdom. As the disciple-makers, we have the privilege to walk with them as they discern.

4. **Affirm:** *Help them identify and trust their God-given gifts.* As a leader and as someone who has invested time building trust and getting to know them, you need to understand your influence within that young leader's life. This is the point in the process where you, like Elijah, communicate to them, "I see more in what you could become than what you can see in yourself." You affirm their God-given design and potential. Find the places where God has gifted them and affirm them in those areas. You then have the unique opportunity to help them begin to believe that God has a role for them, and if they can abide in him, they will be used to bring him glory. Help them build confidence in God's design.

5. **Mentor**: *Lead toward personal, professional, and spiritual growth.*
   The narrative surrounding the next generation is often very negative. The narrative tends to be "They are addicted to their phones." "They have no resiliency" and "The next generation is lazy and or apathetic." What they do not hear very often is, "I am with you. Let us do this together." The next generation undoubtedly needs growth. They need to grow personally, spiritually, and professionally.

   a. Personal Growth: Emerging leaders must learn to have hard conversations. As we disciple individuals, we must coach them to have healthy relationships, deal with conflict and disagreement, and walk in humility. They need to learn how to persevere through hard things.

   b. Spiritual Growth: They must be shown how to create healthy spiritual rhythms and disciplines. Emerging young leaders need to know the value of church, the value of Scripture, and prayer.

   c. Professional Growth: They need help achieving vocational dreams. They need to begin making steps toward professional development. As the leader, you commit to walking and growing with them. Leverage your connections and relationships to connect them with others in their field of interest. During this phase, we help them begin taking steps toward God's invitation to participate in his mission.

6. **Empower**: *Give them a platform to lead and space to fail.*
   As a leader, you influence areas they do not. You will need to help them get opportunities to grow in their skill and leadership. They will need an opportunity even to begin to grow in that area. If you are a pastor, support them by sharing the platform and giving them opportunities to teach and communicate. Allow them to lead meetings. Use your influence and power to allow young leaders to grow, experiment, and fail. Do this intentionally. Let them join some of your meetings if you are a business leader. Share your influence and your platform to give them opportunities to grow. Coach and lead them by discussing areas of success and things to improve on. Help them prepare and help them reflect.

7. **Rejoice:** *Celebrate growth and impact they make.*
   There will come a time when you need to release them to chase God's given assignment. We often get to pour our lives into young people for a season before we release them to go and become all that God has. Continue your care and support into the next season. One of the greatest joys for the disciple-maker comes from watching the kingdom impact made by those you have poured your life into. Seeing how God moves in and through their service is a blessing. Rejoice when you see progress. As a leader, you succeed when they succeed. Celebrate them one-on-one and publicly. We rejoice and give all the glory to God.

The next generation is hungry for mentorship, discipleship, and coaching. They long to be seen and have big dreams of making a difference. God is stirring God-sized dreams within them, but they need help growing into the healthy leaders the world is looking for. DREAMER Discipleship offers a process of relational discipleship. It is one anchored in love, trust, and relationship. Sometimes you will be a coach; sometimes you will be a cheerleader. There will be other times when you need to be a truth-teller. You will need to learn to speak the truth in love. The impact of raising a next-generation leader can be long lasting. We dream of all that they can accomplish, but ultimately, the dream is to see them abide. We dream of seeing them find their home in Jesus and then allowing themselves to leverage their gifts and position to impact the world and bring glory to the Father.

Conclusion

Generation Z presents a unique opportunity and challenge for the church. Their characteristics—marked by a longing for authenticity, community, and purpose—demand innovative and relational approaches to discipleship. DREAMER Discipleship offers a biblically grounded and culturally relevant framework for equipping the next generation to live their lives on mission for the kingdom of God. We raise them up and watch all that God does through their lives.

The church stands at a crossroads. The need for intentional, transformative discipleship is urgent, and the reward is great. As we relearn and reprioritize discipleship among the next generation, we follow Jesus into the discipleship of young leaders. We can expect to see kingdom impact that will echo through future generations around the world. Let us dream boldly of a church where the next generation leads with conviction, serves with humility, and pursues the gospel passionately. Together, we can embrace this sacred calling to disciple Gen Z and witness their profound role in shaping the future of the church.

References

Adobe Communications Team. 2023. "Adobe Future Workforce" Study: What U.S. Employers Need to Know about Gen Z in the Workplace. *Adobe Blog*, September 27. blog.adobe.com/en/publish/2023/09/27/adobe-future-workforce-study-what-us-employers-need-know-about-gen-z-workplace.

Adobe Express. 2024. "Using TikTok as a Search Engine." *Adobe Express*, January 4. www.adobe.com/express/learn/blog/using-tiktok-as-a-search-engine.

Barna Group. 2023. "The Pastoral Succession Crisis Is Only Getting More Complicated." *Barna Group*, August 23. www.barna.com/research/pastoral-succession/.

Bromwich, Jonah Engel. 2018. "We Asked Generation Z to Pick a Name. It Wasn't Generation Z." *New York Times*, January 31. www.nytimes.com/2018/01/31/style/generation-z-name.html.

Brown, Kevin. 2024. "What the Asbury Revival Taught Me about Gen Z." *Christianity Today*, February 19. www.christianitytoday.com/ct/2024/march/asbury-revival-taught-me-about-gen-z-casual-christianity.html.

Buechler, Jessica. N.d. "The Loneliness Epidemic Persists: A Post-Pandemic Look at the State of Loneliness among U.S. Adults." *The Cigna Group News and Insights*. newsroom.cigna.com/loneliness-epidemic-persists-post-Pandemic-look.

Chouinard, Yvon. 2022. "Earth Is Now Our Only Shareholder." *Patagonia*, September 14. www.patagonia.com/ownership/.

Coombs, Bertha. 2020. "Loneliness Is on the Rise and Younger Workers and Social Media Users Feel It Most, Cigna Survey Finds." *CNBC*, January 23. www.cnbc.com/2020/01/23/loneliness-is-rising-younger-workers-and-social-media-users-feel-it-most.html.

De Witte, Melissa. 2024. "8 Ways Gen Z Will Change the Workforce." *Stanford Report*, February 14. news.stanford.edu/stories/2024/02/8-things-expect-gen-z-coworker.

Kelly, Jack. 2024. "How Gen-Z Workers and Baby Boomers Both Benefit from 'Reverse Mentoring.'" *Forbes*, February 9. www.forbes.com/sites/jackkelly/2024/02/09/how-gen-z-workers-and-baby-boomers-can-both-benefit-from-reverse-mentoring/.

McMahan, Billy. 2024. "Innovations in Engaging the Next Generation Towards Innovations in Engaging the Next Generation Towards Discipleship and Mission." *Great Commission Research Journal* 16 (2). https://place.asburyseminary.edu/gcrj/vol16/iss2/2/.

Presley, Nathan. 2019. "Darling x Nike Women Marathon Project Part I." YouTube, January 30. www.youtube.com/watch?v=7NwDzyN3p3s.

Rothwell, Jonathan. 2024. "Teens Spend Average of 4.8 Hours on Social Media per Day." *Gallup*, October 16. news.gallup.com/poll/512576/teens-spend-average-hours-social-media-per-day.aspx.

USA Facts. 2023. "Military Recruitment Is Down. Why Don't Young Americans Want to Join?" *USA Facts*, November 7. usafacts.org/articles/military-recruitment-is-down/.

Waxer, Cindy. 2022. "What Generation Z Wants from Businesses." *SAP Original Research*, October 14. https://www.sap.com/sea/research/generation-z-behavior-explained.

Wingard, Jason. 2018. "Reverse Mentoring: 3 Proven Outcomes Driving Change." *Forbes*, August 8. www.forbes.com/sites/jasonwingard/2018/08/08/reverse-mentoring-3-proven-outcomes-driving-change/?sh=78eea0f88b51.

Winkie, Davis. 2022. "The Army's Pre-Boot Camp Boot Camp Is Likely to Expand." *Army Times*, October 11. www.armytimes.com/news/your-army/2022/10/11/the-armys-pre-boot-camp-boot-camp-is-likely-to-expand/.

Wytsma, Ken, and A. J. Swoboda. 2018. *Redeeming How We Talk: Discover How Communication Fuels Our Growth, Shapes Our Relationships, and Changes Our Lives*. Moody Publishers.

Chapter 10

Exploring New Frontiers of Discipleship for African-Muslim Contexts

Joel W. Wright

Introduction

This is the story of a persecuted but faithful pastor and chicken farmer from East Africa who is responsible for a large number of new believers of Muslim-background (BMBs) coming to faith in Jesus. After decades of struggle in an Islamic community, a persistent Christian community of faith is taking new root, gaining local respect and confidence together with other churches. During the middle of 2023, through the grace of God and in on-going teamwork with this author, this local pastor baptized more than 153 BMBs. Imams and their wives were included in the total baptisms. New paradigms are proving effective for both evangelism and discipleship, expanding new frontiers for the African-Muslim context.

The background to this story begins over a decade ago, when Pastor "Hezekiah" (his name has been changed for security's sake), after serving in a successful first pastorate, was called with his wife and family to pastor a suffering and "dead" local church. This church had been closed for over a decade because of intense persecution. The location is majority Islamic; the three previous pastors of Hezekiah's new church were each martyred in sequence in the 1990's. The church property was abandoned due to martyrdom and local persecution. Many of the congregation had scattered; through persistent prayer there remained a few house church believers including widows.

Despite this background, in 2015 Pastor Hezekiah heard the clear call from Jesus to reopen the church. Slowly and cautiously the church was reopened, repaired, and returned to ongoing services for worship, Bible study, and prayer. Since assuming leadership, Hezekiah has bravely survived three attempts on his own life, with pressure continuing to this day.

God allowed my own personal background to intertwine with Pastor Hezekiah's. As a forty-year missionary veteran, with twenty years of experience as a seminary Bible teacher in Brazil, I had the privilege of mentoring several African students for their master's theses. I had discovered at that time the important themes of reconciliation and brotherhood in the story-form of the Patriarchs (especially Joseph) as well as African connections found in the narratives. In 2018 I was invited to preach and teach in East Africa. Through these renewed African connections local teamwork began to flourish in exploring together new biblical and theological distinctives that over time contributed significantly to Muslims discovering their Messiah.

Initial headway came through community projects, widow care, childhood education, and hospitality. A newly developed "African Theology," that included the Patriarchal stories, caught the attention of local mosques, opening discussions on comparative texts relating to the names of Abraham, Isaac, Ishmael, Jacob, and Joseph, and their wives (Sarah, Hagar, and Asenath) and their sons (Ephriam and Manasseh). The culmination came in June of 2023 when Pastor Hezekiah was asked to teach the Joseph story in the local mosque. His brave but competent presentation allowed for a follow-up presentation on Christ as Messiah. As a result, hundreds of BMBs transitioned to faith together and are now a part of a new kingdom network that spans into other countries.

Upon such rapid kingdom expansion, we asked God together through days of prayer: "Now what shall we do?" Community discipleship was necessary, immediate, and widespread. Fatwas were proclaimed against some; others lost their family connections and inheritance. Homes were burned, jobs were lost, and children were forced out of schools. A number of leaders and their families needed to move out of the city and remain in hiding to secure their lives. Others resolved to remain quietly "under cover" with extended families and remain in current roles until there was some resolution to the difficulties.

In seeking to answer the question, "Now what shall we do?"—I began to evaluate resources for BMB's: comparing various ministries, consulting qualified books and researching on-line resources. Arising from prayer on the third day, the Lord's presence and voice tenderly said: "Why don't you use *me*?" Quickly recalling the words of Jesus from Matthew 5–7 on prayer, fasting, and giving, I made a connection with Islam's Five Pillars of faith and essential practice. I thought: "The name of Jesus is already respected in the Quran and by Muslims worldwide. Why not disciple Muslims with the very words of Jesus?"

The answers to this question are found in the remainder of this chapter.

Discipleship Through the Words of the Messiah

The fruit of this connection resulted in a twelve-week discipleship program crafted from the very words of Jesus himself, largely taken from the Sermon on the Mount found in Matthew 5–7. The text, of course, is acclaimed by many as Christ's finest expression of kingdom values, faith, and practice (see, for example, Stott 1978; Jenkins, Jenkins, and Huffman 2022; Wright 2024).

The program is titled, *God Is Great and Full of Mercy and Compassion*. It is a twelve-step discipleship process and approach specifically designed for the African Islamic context. In this title we highlight the greatness of God's nature and grace, couched with the glorious pragmatics of kingdom values and eternal promises. For an Arabic-sensitive or BMB audience, however, the "Twelve Pillars" were chosen to reflect the nomenclature of the Five Pillars of Islam for essential faith and practice.

The logistical aspect of the discipleship process was a united and tight-knit network held together through trusted Zoom and house-churches. In the "scattering" of the saints (cf. Acts 8:4), a new house-church network now spans loosely across the entire country, as well as over the borders. The results are multiplying disciples in new contexts, superseding linguistic barriers, and reaching formerly unengaged unreached people groups (UUPGs).

Our story here is one of modern-day polycentric missions: *beyond frontiers* and *from everyone to everywhere* (Yeh 2016, 2024; Hedinger and Wiseman 2024). Zoom meetings throughout 2020–2024 proved useful for global multi-site discipleship. New church members and new believers were strengthened together, while leaders helped arrange house churches and discipleship events. Altogether, partnerships with Pastor Hezekiah and other regional leaders in the area over the last two years has resulted in over one thousand baptisms taking place, including 250 BMBs.

Foundations for Breakthrough: A Contextual Approach Using Islamic Nomenclature with Biblical Texts Favoring Africa

As part of the initial evangelistic process, growing discussions occurred over common elements between biblical and qur'anic texts. In addition, common elements of both Arabic and African cultures were utilized in the discipleship program. Important qur'anic texts that were highlighted included: the Suras of Jonah (*Yunus*, Sura 10); Joseph (*Yusuf*, Sura 12); Abraham (*Ibrahim*, Sura 14); and Mary (*Maryam*, Sura 19) (Parshall 2002; Greenman 2012; Kombo 2012). A growing respect for the patriarchal narratives set the stage for group presentations on Messiah Jesus. Remarkably, in Islam Jesus is heralded as "The Messiah" (*al-Masheeh*, Sura 3:45). The term *Īsā al-Masīḥ* presents Jesus (*Isa*) as the "*Masih*" or "*Al-Masih*" nearly a dozen times in the Qur'an (Sura 4:171–172; 5:17; 5:72–75; and 9:30–31). Jesus's titles and attributes thus formed the foundation for prioritizing the very words of Jesus in the Gospels for the discipleship process.

In special regard to Jesus, it was noted that ninety-five verses mention Jesus (Isa) either in name, title, or attribute. Titles include: "Word" (*Kalima* or *Kalimat Allah* as in Sura 3:39, 45, 48; 4:171; 5:46, 110); "Jesus, Son of Mary" (*Isa Ibn Maryam* as in Sura 2:87, 253; 3:45; 4:157, 171; 5:17, 46, 72–78, 110–116; 9:31; 19:34; 23:50; 33:7; 43:57; 57:27; 61:6, 14); "Pure Boy" and "Without Sin" (Sura 9:19–21, 29, 35, 88–92; 19:19); "Sign for Humanity" or "A Mercy from Us" (*Ayah* as in Sura 20–26; 21:91; 23:50; 43:61); "Honorable" or "nearest to God" (*Wajih*, Sura 3:45); and "a Spirit from Him," in other words, from the Almighty (*Rūḥ minhu*, Sura 4:171) (Parinnder 2013; Bennett 2022).

In the growing community dialogue of Pastor Hezekiah with local Islamic clerics, the African connection of Joseph with Asenath (Gen 46:20) proved especially significant. Their sons, Ephraim and Manasseh, unmentioned in the Qur'an, were born on African soil and form an integral part of the original covenant under Jacob/Israel (Gen 48:1–16). The words of Israel's founder to his African-born grandsons still echo significantly today for the African context: "Ephraim and Manasseh will be mine, just as Reuben and Simeon are mine … Bring them to me so I may bless them" (Gen 48:5, 9). These biblical details, and others, sparked the interest of many African Muslims, given that Sura Yusef (Sura 12) is one of the most respected and beloved narratives. The Muslims' love and respect for Joseph proved captivating through the richly detailed biblical narrative (Gen 37–50).

Through investigative reading of the Torah, many precious and important elements came to further light, opening hearts and minds of many Muslims all the more in confidence of the biblical text. Amazing for them to hear and ponder, for instance, was the offer of Judah's own life on behalf of Benjamin (Gen 44:33). Here in our biblical narrative, we have the principle that "love breaks open" the story, leading Joseph to tears (Gen 45:1). More Muslims here might gain insight as to the nature and power of love. As Jesus is the "Lion of the Tribe of Judah" (Rev 5:5), one sees the prototype of Jesus in Judah's offer, pointing directly to the Messiah, the fulfillment of the Patriarchs.

Advantages of Islamic Cultural Inroads and African Theology

The advantages of this contextualized approach with BMBs, using the Patriarchal narratives and the words of Jesus in this twelve-week discipleship program, include the following:

- **Authority**: Opens biblical texts as primary sources rather than introducing unknown authors.
- **Trust**: Builds upon the authoritarian nature and high respect for the Patriarchs and Jesus as Messiah already found in the Qur'an.
- **Common Nomenclature**: Takes advantage of broader Islamic nomenclature (Jesus as *Kalima*—the "Word" or "Command of God"). We then might ask: "If Jesus was Word, then what are his words or commands?"
- **Application**: Matthew 5–7 makes ready application for life and practice. The words of Jesus are backed by paradigms of Christ-like character. Persistence, prayer, fasting, giving, purity, and so on, are all elements which new believers can and should attempt to emulate and/or put into practice.
- **Hermeneutics**: Hermeneutically, uniting the words of Jesus with Old Testament foundations allows for the whole Old and New Testament narrative to fit into one larger, more seamless whole (Wright 2018).
- **Integration and Adaptation**: Allows for expanded discussion. Welcomes parallel use with other resources of faith. Such

integration corresponds closely with the very words of Jesus: "I have come to fulfill, not destroy" (Matt 5:17).
- **Technology**: Strengthened by the use of technology, allowing for creative partnerships, global networks, media, and worship.

In summary, then, the discipleship process of these BMBs followed naturally as an outgrowth of earlier Islamic convictions and loyalties. The "fishing net" of harvest was full as the group transitioned together towards messianic faith. Comradery helped as questions were treated in mutual discipleship and guidance together. New believers helped others continue in their progression towards Jesus.

We now ponder the very words of the Messiah in Matthew 5–7 through the *God Is Great and Full of Mercy and Compassion* twelve-step discipleship process.

An Overview of the "Twelve Pillars of Jesus"

While rereading Matthew 5–7 with "Islamic eyes" we hope to encourage new frontiers with BMBs. The Sermon on the Mount is progressive and seamless, building one element upon another. Foundational elements of the kingdom of God flow together towards personal character, perseverance, kindness, forgiveness, personal ethics, and morality. We are led into the pragmatic but necessary details of marriage, prayer, and finance, ending in secure eternal hope.

Comparison and contrast of Jesus's teachings can easily be made with Islam's Five Pillars and the Six Articles of Faith (Khattab 2016). This includes the *Shahadah* (confession of faith in one God and Muhammad as Prophet) as the first pillar. This is followed by the second through fifth pillars: *Salah* (praying five times a day); *Sawm* (fasting from dawn to dusk during the month of Ramadan); *Zakah* (giving or paying an alms-tax); and *Hajj* (journey to Mecca).

The "Twelve Pillars" of Jesus follows the larger flow of Matthew 5–7. British theologian John Stott, in his own study entitled, *The Message of the Sermon on the Mount* (1978), also notes that the Sermon contains twelve chapter sub-divisions of the biblical text, similar in some regards to the Twelve Pillars here for our purposes. Stott develops the twelve sub-divisions with such titles as: "A Christian's Character" (5:3–12); "Christ, the Christian and the Law" (5:17–20); and "A Christian's Righteousness:

Fidelity in Marriage and Honesty in Speech" (5:31–37). He places the twelve sub-divisions with an Introduction (5:1–2) and a Conclusion (7:28–29). Overall, these topics all proved highly applicable to Muslims suffering local persecution. Many needed orientations on pragmatics of marriage and emotional health amid stresses and social confusion.

What follows are some of the specific uses of Matthew 5–7 as the Twelve Pillars of Jesus. Notice that the twelve steps build on one another as well as the use of other corresponding Scriptures found outside of the Sermon itself.

1. God (Matt 5:1–12) / Jesus's Orientation as to How to Pray to God (Matt 6:9)

The larger representation of God in the Sermon on the Mount is that of God as *Father*. Jesus offers us, in contrast to Islam, the comforting image of the Almighty not only as sovereign and powerful, but also as deeply relational, intimately attentive, and lovingly kind. One dozen verses utilize the motif of the fatherhood of God (vv. 5:16, 45, 48; 6:1, 4, 6, 9, 14, 18, 26, 32; 7:21).

God is great in that he addresses each of us in our personal worlds of daily concern. There are parallels with the later Qur'anic refrains: "God is All-Forgiving, Most Forbearing" (Sura 2:225); "God is All-Bountiful, All-Knowing" (Sura 2:261); and "God is All-Seeing" (Sura 2:237, 265). With such connections at the outset, we can draw from the deep respect Muslims have in their hearts for the Almighty. For this reason, we have entitled our twelve-step series "God Is Great and Full of Mercy and Compassion." In the Beatitudes, God is already known through the foundation of love and grace, not fear.

We must pause here to consider the difficult topic of the Trinitarian nature of God. We found much encouragement from the Hebraic Scriptures, the very Torah of Moses. The use of Genesis 1:1 (God as *Elohim*) gave us a foundation for new understandings of the divine, both in nature and in attribute. This approach follows the Qur'anic charge to follow Torah and the *Injil* (Gospels), as the "People of the Book" (Sura 3:99).

We must strongly assert there is no God but one (Deut 6:4–5), answering criticisms of polytheism (Sura 3:95). The use of *Elohim*, however, utilized some 2,500 times in the Hebrew Scriptures, opens numerous doors both theologically and intellectually to a Tripartite formula. The term *Elohim* is the plural form of the title *God* (lit. *gods*). With its verbal construct, however, the word speaks to the Almighty in singularity. This is the "Many as One" or perhaps more theologically, the "God of Love." Contrasting with *Allah* as singularity, then, God is as a "Unity of One" or even a "Community of One." We followed standard Christological defense using the *Ehad* of Deuteronomy 6:4–5 with Genesis 2:24.

To further explain the Triune Godhead, we took refuge in various illustrations from nature. From the whole of nature, the largest to smallest, we witness reality as "complexity into unity." The atom, for example, is a composition of subatomic particles—protons, electrons, and neutrons—flying in quantum dance.

This God thematic was initially bold on our part. Yet these relational aspects of the Fatherhood of God and God as love—all seemed to initially work, calming the minds and hearts of these Muslim believers. The new Christ-followers did not abandon their new faith. We found favor as we moved on to development of Jesus as the "God with Us" (*Immanuel*) theme. God gave grace through his word; faith took further root.

2. Jesus on the Mountain and the Message of Salvation by Grace (Matt 5:1–3)

Soteriology and Christology are immediately seen in the opening of Matthew 5:1–3. Christ echoes the Old Testament Law given at Sinai (Exod 19–20), himself as the fountain of divine revelation as he goes up on the mountain to teach. The nature of the Godhead is already soon given as Christ proclaims: "You have heard it said, but I say to you" (see Matt 5:21–22). To declare divine law is to declare divinity itself, authority from heaven (7:28, 29).

The good news of the kingdom of heaven however is made open to us as we come to God "poor in spirit," confessing our sin and poverty before him and receiving grace. Personal salvation (soteriology) is immediately in view: "Blessed are the poor in spirit for *theirs* is the kingdom of heaven" (Matt 5:3, emphasis added). These remarkable words speak of grace, that we come to God as we are: needy, broken, humble, sinful, repentant, asking for grace from the Holy God.

The promise of eternal life is made open to those who are not righteous by their own righteous deeds and hard work. The condition for salvation comes from the loving nature of God himself, much as happened with Isaiah when his own lips were cleansed for service by a gift from heaven (Isa 6:1–7).

Space considerations limit our discussion, but much more time can be taken here as to Christology. Christ's own baptism (Matt 3) can be utilized to speak of the triune Father, Son, Spirit. Matthew 4 provides an intense witness of divine power from on high. John 1:1–18 and the numerous declarations of "I Am" in the book of John can be employed here as well, confirming one testimony after another. The virgin birth and messianic titles of Jesus in the Qur'an also open the door for expansion—for example, comparing Matthew 1 and 2 with Sura 19, Sura *Mariam* (Mary).

We thus presented Jesus boldly as God incarnate, using the example of sunlight as an expression to earth of the nature of sun: just as earth needs to absorb the gift of light from above, so each believer needs to "receive Christ" for salvation and his Spirit for empowerment (John 1:12; 20:21, 22).

3. The Holy Spirit and the Transformed Life (Matt 5:13–20)

While the Holy Spirit is not specifically addressed in Matthew 5–7, the baptism of Jesus in Matthew 3 shows the importance of the Spirit of God upon the messianic calling. The empowerment of Christ for life and ministry through the Spirit establishes a paradigm for our own transformed life. Christ calls us to be the "light of the world" and the "salt of the earth." But this cannot be in toughened self-determination, but rather, like Jesus, through Spirit-filled transformation.

BMB's are thus already encouraged at the outset as to the fullness of life under the Godhead of the true Almighty, Elohim: loving Father, incarnate Son, and empowering Spirit.

4. Living Life with Kingdom Values (Matt 5:3–12, 20)

The fullness of the Beatitudes are explored here, the foundation to a transformed life and living out the fullness of the kingdom. Jesus follows Old Testament law in offering his new covenant law as the way of blessing (see Deut 11:26–29; 30:1, 19; 33:1; Jer 33:31). The "nine beatitudes," or "twelve blessed" elements, speak to the new way of living for new believers. The "twelve blessed" elements can be identified and listed in order:

- "Blessed are the poor in spirit" (5:3).
- "Blessed are those that mourn" (5:4).
- "Blessed are the gentle" (5:5).

- "Blessed are those who hunger and thirst for righteousness" (5:6).
- "Blessed are the merciful" (5:7).
- "Blessed are the pure in heart" (5:8).
- "Blessed are the peacemakers" (5:9).
- "Blessed are those who are persecuted for the sake of righteousness" (5:10).
- "Blessed are you when people insult you and persecute you" (5:11).
- "[Blessed are you when people] falsely say all kinds of evil against you because of me. Rejoice and be glad for your reward in heaven is great" (5:11–12).

Mourning involves inner emotional life, repentance over one's own sin, but also concern for the ongoing suffering of others. Personal motivations and endurance in the sight of persecution is addressed, all very pertinent topics for those coming out of Muslim contexts. Peacemaking, too, is a task for new believers, following the nature of God, the way of peace and reconciliation. Contrasts to Islamic jihad can be lightly employed or touched upon here, but perhaps not heavily discussed. Better to focus on the life of Christ and models of the suffering Savior.

5. Community/Worship (Matt 5:21–26)

In this section of Matthew 5, Jesus opens the door of the discipleship process in relationship to his followers in community. He applies the murder element towards the broader roots or heart of the issue (Exod 20:13), as well as to its effect on society.

Moral law internally broken (anger) impacts the need for personal reconciliation (society). This upholds the Mosaic vision of the Old Testament in the tripartite moral law/civil law/ceremonial law of the whole of the Exodus/Deuteronomic texts. While the "forms" of law may differ, the "essence" remains. As subjects of a larger kingdom, we need to "leave our offering at the altar" and apply ourselves towards a community of faith, worship, and witness together.

To that end, new believers are encouraged toward communal reconciliation. Worship at the temple is also mentioned by Jesus here, speaking to a pattern of communal celebration as part of regular life and practice.

6. Marriage (Matt 5:27–32)

Upholding the highest standards of conjugal relations, Jesus speaks to purity of mind. Jesus is radical and strong, perhaps with a shade of humor, in his use of hyperbolic language: "Better to pluck out one's eyes, than lose one's soul to hell" (5:29).

It was at this point that we in our discipleship series entered necessary and lengthy discussions as to the Old Testament and patriarchal polygamy. The Old Testament narratives are descriptive and not normative. As to the perversions and their consequences we see jealousy, rivalries, and ongoing familial disputes, even murder. In this we see the unraveling of society and the demise of whole nations.

Much grace and balance were needed here in our discipleship process as Imams often have numerous wives. Our counsel at this time was to "come as you are" in a posture of humility and seeking wisdom from above for each family network. Women were not to be initially "cast away," but rather encouraged to maintain compassion as sisters one with another. We encouraged each family unit to make it all a matter of prayer, seeking the counsel of the Spirit. For some, there may be a release of some women to pursue a more monogamous relationship, especially in the situation of older men with younger women.

In the end, we took the time for ongoing dialogue and the hearing of one another. We allowed for limited permissions ("come as you are") balanced with the New Testament normative ideal. Jesus reasserts elsewhere: "How was it at the beginning?" (Matt 19:3–12). Without denigrating the founder of Islam, we highlighted the highest of moral behavior of our Messiah. Jesus himself took no wife, and treated women with utmost respect, showing absolute self-control.

7. Growing in Character (Matt 5:33–48)

The kingdom of God is not without law. We need to be ethical in our behavior and faithful in our speech (5:33–37). We must go the extra mile (5:41). We must love our neighbor and pray for those who persecute us, even enemies (5:43–47). As children of God, we aim to grow in faith, seeking the "perfect" (mature, complete; 5:48).

Jesus here speaks of the selfless, self-giving nature of the Almighty. God gives the rain and sunshine. We too need to be marked by ongoing grace among neighbors, with humility in our overall relationships.

Many applications could be made here in terms of fatherly roles, protection of women, children-rearing, and community care. We avoided negativity as to the lifestyle of Mohammed, even as we highlighted Christ's own model for life and service.

8. Giving (Matt 6:1–4)

Christ exemplified deep compassion for the multitudes: in healings, miracles, and provisions. Likewise, we are merciful and compassionate, nurturing community care.

Sessions eight, nine, and ten now easily flow in parallel to the second, third, and fourth pillars of Islam. Jesus says to beware of practicing your righteousness to be noticed by men. We give to honor God, knowing that what is done in secret will have the Father's reward.

In contrast to seasonal times of Ramadan, giving is ongoing, it is spontaneous. It is a personal release of kingdom power: "do not let your left hand know what your right hand is doing" (6:3). Jesus speaks to our quick and responsive freedom before God. We give as we see the need.

9. Prayer (Matt 6:5–15)

Much could be said here as to Christ's magnificently simple but profound guide, largely known as the Lord's Prayer.

In our Savior's orientation, Jesus does not demand regular prayers five times daily, nor obligatory visits to mosques. Neither must we go on Hajj to specially meet with the Almighty. Jesus teaches us to seek God out in private conversation in the regular intimacy of our own inner sanctums.

Like a child who has ongoing access to the Father, we do not need meaningless repetition, nor obligatory calls to remind us to pray. We have freedom to seek God anytime and anywhere, in the time of personal need and at the leading of the Holy Spirit.

In our prayer life, we seek God's own "kingdom come." This is not primarily a geographical locality; but rather in transformed lives and inner hearts, working justice and righteousness on earth. "Daily bread" speaks to personal needs, our necessity for manna from heaven.

Forgiveness speaks to the refrain of kingdom love, reminding us of model forgiveness and faith. Biblical story-forms on forgiveness include models like Joseph (Gen 50:17–21), Stephen (Acts 8:60), and Jesus (Luke 23:34).

We pray as well to avoid the traps and temptations of the evil one's designs against us. We finish prayer with seeking God's victory and praise, aligned with his purposes for daily life.

10. True Religion (Matt 6:16–18)

Jesus gives us the paradigm of fasting as normative for believers, but not for human show. As we seek God in secret, we will have victorious reward. The Muslim is thus freed from mandatory annual "Ramadan."

Jesus began his own ministry in fasting, still a model for current practice. Muslims enjoy knowing that our Messiah fulfilled a complete forty-day testing of absolute Ramadan to begin his ministry. He went without food altogether! Jesus showed the perfect model of faith in a time of intense trial, denying the temptations of Satan. In the end, he was strengthened by angels of God (Matt 4:1–11).

Like Jesus at his baptism and subsequent desert experience, however, we must be Spirit-led. As the Spirit might periodically or even regularly guide us into fasting, we are to seek God in times of highest priority, even above food. We set aside all else as we seek Jesus's personal direction and strength.

11. Emotional Life/Worry and Finance (Matt 6:19–34)

Jesus continues elaborating kingdom vision on personal needs, worry, and finance. The answer for it all lies in the heart: trusting in the love of the Father and restoring priorities towards that of the eternal kingdom (6:19–34). As we seek God, heaven will remain concerned for our personal needs: "But seek first his kingdom and his righteousness, and all these things will be added to you" (6:33).

Beautiful words from the Savior flow at this point, reminding us of God's ongoing care. God is concerned for the smallest of sparrows and feeds them (6:26). And if the flowers of the fields are clothed with glory above that of Solomon (6:29), how much more shall then we be clothed in final glory as well? Oh, have faith! (6:30).

We are not to "store up" treasures on earth; rather we are to invest our finances for kingdom purposes (6:19–21). We cannot have two masters: it is either God or money (6:24).

12. Final Hope (Matt 7) and the Rock upon Which Our Lives Stand (Matt 7:25).

The crescendo of the words of Jesus now rises like a mighty wave. Jesus ends his discourse with an authoritative final summary and closing call to discipleship. It is a call to decision and ongoing commitment, that of secure eternal promise. The commands of Matthew 6 now flow into Matthew 7, uniting God's kingdom purposes with our final hope (6:33–7:29):

1. Seek first his kingdom and his righteousness (6:33) and all will be added.
2. Do not worry (6:25, 31, 34).
3. Do not judge others (7:1).
4. Take out the log (7:5).
5. Do not give what is holy to dogs, nor place pearls before swine (7:6).
6. Ask and it will be given (7:7–8). In asking, we will receive.
7. Seek and you will find (7:7–8) In persistent seeking, we will find.
8. Knock and the door will be opened (7:7–8). We will be successful in this endeavor to seek and know God for the Father gives good gifts (7:7–11). Therefore,
9. Do to others (7:12). This is the summary of the whole law, living a life of outgoing love.
10. Enter the narrow gate (7:13). The invitation to the kingdom is open to all.
11. Be aware of false prophets and false religiosity (7:15–23).
12. The final secure hope: build on the Rock (7:24–27).

As our Savior started with the blessings of living out the new law (as a fulfillment of the old), Jesus now closes his Sermon on the Mount with a contrast like the "curses and blessings" of Moses (cf. Deut 11:26–28; 27–34). While Moses, however, went up to receive the law, Jesus goes up to speak of the new law. While Moses goes up on Mount Nebo and is buried, Jesus himself has fulfilled the law and ascended into heaven. Jesus now reigns as the pillar or Rock of our salvation (cf. 1 Cor 10:4).

Jesus speaks of two paths and narrow and wide gates (7:13–14). He speaks of knowing trees by their fruit (7:15–20). There are two multitudes, two destinies and the coming of the final Day of Judgement (7:22, 23). Given these final challenges, and yet secure hope in Messiah, we need to be careful to whom we owe our allegiance. Wolves and false prophets can be in sheep's clothing (7:15–20). The way of Jesus, however, is narrow, much like the way into the temple and beyond the veil. We live in conformity to new kingdom values: in peace, humility, grace, and love (7:21–23; cf. Matt 25:31–46). Blessed eternity awaits those who follow Jesus, our lives secure upon "the Rock" (7:25).

Conclusion: Towards New Frontiers and Global Impact

Matthew's narrative of Jesus's teachings on the Sermon on the Mount, found in Matthew chapters 5–7, contains many positive "new frontiers" for the discipleship of BMBs in East-African contexts, especially by using the "Twelve Pillars of Jesus" approach. Other Islamic and diaspora global contexts may benefit as well. We call upon all those who are working in similar Islamic and African contexts to seriously consider using the Sermon on the Mount for disciple-making movements elsewhere.

The numerous positive responses from those in East Africa, following the twelve-week discipleship program, proved to encourage us further along this path. As one BMB shared: "Thank you so very much. These studies on the words of Jesus have touched our hearts and minds like no others ever before. They have impacted us deeply. We will never be the same." May God continue to give us all new insights into how to use his word in ways that have maximum impact among Muslims throughout the world.

References

Bennett, Matthew Aaron. 2022. *The Qur'an and the Christian*. Kregel Academic.

Greenman, Jeffrey P., and Gene L. Green. 2012. *Global Theology in Evangelical Perspective: Exploring the Contextual Nature of Theology and Mission*. IVP Academic.

Hedinger, Mark, and Kate Wiseman. 2024. "Training for Polycentric Mission." *Evangelical Missions Quarterly* 60 (1): 31–34.

Jenkins, Amanda, Dallas Jenkins, and Douglas Huffman. 2022. *Blessed Are the Chosen: An Interactive Bible Study*. Vol. 2. David C. Cook.

Khattab, Mustafa. 2016. *The Clear Qur'an*. Book of Signs Foundation.

Kombo, James. 2012. "African Theology." In *Global Theology in Evangelical Perspective: Exploring the Contextual Nature of Theology and Mission*, edited by Jeffrey P. Greenman and Gene L. Green. IVP Academic.

Parinnder, Geoffrey. 2013. *Jesus and the Qur'an*. Oneworld Books.

Parshall, Phil. 2002. *The Cross and the Crescent: Understanding the Muslim Heart and Mind*. InterVarsity Press.

Stott, John. 1978. *The Message of the Sermon on the Mount*. InterVarsity Press.

Wright, Christopher. 2018. *The Mission of God: Unlocking the Bible's Grand Narrative*. IVP Academic.

Wright, N. T. 2014. *The Lord and His Prayer*. Eerdmans.

Yeh, Allen. 2016. *Polycentric Missiology. 21st Century Mission from Everyone to Everywhere*. IVP Academic.

Yeh, Allen. 2024. "What is Polycentric Mission?" *Evangelical Missions Quarterly* 60 (1): 8–12.

Chapter 11

The Urbanization of the Mission Frontier

John E. White

Introduction

Where are the frontiers of mission today? Certainly, there are many important frontiers that should be considered and addressed by the missionary community. These frontiers include missions to the massive numbers of people migrating across the globe, missions to frontier people groups, missions employing a polycentric methodology, business as mission, and missions using different technologies to reach across borders and to connect with those interested in hearing the gospel in a virtual world.

Yet, despite the importance of each of these examples, and certainly numerous others, I believe that the most important, and certainly the biggest, frontier of mission today is global urban areas. By "urban" I mean a place characterized, *relative to the surrounding area*, by a dense and large population, a diversity of peoples, specialized and segmented communities, an intense and complex way of life and mindset, and hubs of concentrated influence, networks, and movement. Considering these urban areas, mission is strategic not just because of the large numbers of people in cities but also because of the people movements and connections into and between cities and the rest of the world.

Many leading missiologists and mission organizations believe that ministry to urban areas is vitally important for twenty-first century mission. Missionary leader and Professor Roger Greenway (2009, 559) declared that "Cities are the new frontier of Christian missions." From the Third Lausanne Congress on World Evangelization, the Cape Town Commitment stated that "Cities ought to lie at the heart of any 21st century strategy for global mission" (Hildreth 2014).

Tim Keller (2016), pastor and founder of the international Redeemer City to City ministry, proposed the simple formula, "Reach the city to reach your region and the world." And finally, David Smith, the missiologist and author on both global and urban mission, claimed that "Mission organizations have to place the challenge posed by an urban world at the very centre of their thinking and planning" (David Smith, email to author, November 13, 2019).

Unfortunately, despite these calls to focus more on global urban mission, the global mission community continues to largely ignore mission to urban areas. As a prime example of this, at the recent Fourth Lausanne Congress in Seoul, Korea, only one of twenty-five "Great Commission Gaps" was focused on urban communities. In the Lausanne plenary sessions, the only focus on urban mission was combined with mission to the workplace (Fourth Lausanne Congress, 2024). Although there certainly is a need to do more intentional ministry in workplaces, this is only a small part of the greater need for mission work in urban areas, as will be explained further in this paper.

I have been a missionary in Ukraine for the past twenty years, and I have seen the same "urbanization" of the mission frontier in Ukraine that is taking place around the world. The Ukrainian evangelical church was largely marginalized under communism, and thus, most evangelicals were poor and there were limits on the number of churches that could exist in a given area—usually only one registered church per city. Thus, when communism fell in 1991, bold evangelicals wanted to do mission work and church planting, so many left their cities (since each already had a church) and spread the gospel "to the ends of the earth" into the churchless areas of Siberia and across the former Soviet Union. But as interest in the gospel cooled down, evangelicals found that more and more of the people they needed to reach lived in cities.

I remember sitting in a meeting in the early 2000s as one Baptist leader shared that in Ukraine, 70 percent of the people lived in cities, but 70 percent of the churches were in villages. He proposed the challenge of doing more church planting in cities. Not much had changed by the 2010s when I was given a different challenge by leaders of an evangelical seminary to start a program to help train nationals for ministry and mission in cities. This Ukrainian leadership had realized that they needed new ideas and new methods to minister more effectively in urban areas. They were grappling with an urbanized mission frontier, as we all need to today.

Today's Biggest Mission Frontier

D. L. Moody had the foresight to see the growing importance of urban ministry at the end of the nineteenth and beginning of the twentieth century. Moody declared: "Water runs downhill, and the highest hills in America are the great cities. If we can stir them we shall stir the whole country" (Dorsett 2003, 236).

Although there have been great waves of urban development throughout history (DuBose 1978, 22) and periods in which urban areas have been influentially dominant, such as during the Roman Empire (Stark 2006, 60), only a small fraction of the world's population lived in cities up until the current period of urbanization (Mumford 1961, 29). In 1900, around the time that Moody gave his above insight, still only 10 percent of the world's population lived in cities. Yet through the twentieth century, the world has steadily become more urban, with the tipping point finally being reached in the early twenty-first century, when more than 50 percent of the population lived in urban areas. Thus, some have called the present time, "mankind's first Urban Age" (Burdett and Rode 2007, 8).

Today, the world is experiencing continued urbanization, with 56 percent, or almost 4.4 billion people, living in cities. Looking around the world, North America is 83 percent urban, Latin America and the Caribbean 81 percent, Europe 75 percent, Oceania 68 percent, Asia 51 percent, and Africa 43 percent. Urbanization is expected to increase to 68 percent by 2050, with the vast majority of this increase coming in Asia and Africa (UN-Habitat 2022, 9–10). The Urban Age Project predicts an even larger increase to 75 percent of the world population being urban by 2050 (Burdett and Rode 2007, 8). Clearly, more and more of the people that need to be reached for Christ are living or will soon live in urban areas.

What does this new urban mission frontier look like? Cities can now grow without limits, no longer needing walls or other means of protection as they once did. Before 1800, no city had a population greater than one million (Mumford 1961, 529, 540). Today, there are forty-four "megacities," each with populations greater than ten million (Demographia 2023). The Urban Age Project's research entitled "The Endless City" seems more and more appropriate each year (Burdett and Sudjic 2007).

Just as this urban mission frontier is extremely large, it is also extremely varied. For example, there are "global cities" like London, New York, and

Tokyo (to name just a few). These cities are command points for the world economy, where many finance and service firms are located and where much of the world's production and innovation takes place (Sassen 2001). Cities like these are connected to places all over the world, having influence far beyond their populations.

In contrast, many of the cities of the world have large slums where some of the poorest and neediest people in the world live. Slums often grow as people move into cites looking for hope in the form of jobs, education, or an escape from a bad situation back home. Failures of local governments to support these large influxes of people often lead to the growth of slums (Hall 2002, 467). Today, it is estimated that more than one billion people live in urban slums (Davis 2017, 23).

It is also important to note that this "endless city" stretches beyond formal urban borders taking another form known as "suburbs." Suburbs were meant to be a place of retreat from the city, an environment that could be more controlled, and thus, safer and more relaxing (Mumford 1961, 492–94). However, over time, suburbs have become more and more like the cities from which they were spawned, essentially becoming "centerless" cities that have many of the same characteristics and problems as urban areas (Conn 1994, 136).

This new urban age brings with it many challenges, including social, economic, and environmental ones (Burdett and Rode 2007, 8). Philip Jenkins (2011, 117), professor of history and religious studies, pragmatically forecast that "Rich pickings await any religious groups who can meet the needs of these new urbanites, anyone who can at once feed the body and nourish the soul." This is, indeed, a great opportunity for missions. One of the most important parts of this larger task is the opportunity in cities to minister to least reached peoples, or ethnolinguistic people groups that are less than or equal to 5 percent Christian adherent and 2 percent evangelical (Joshua Project n.d.).

Urbanized Least Reached Peoples

Another reason that the mission frontier has been "urbanized" is that many of the least reached peoples in the world are moving to cities. Today there are massive movements of people, with an estimated 281 million international migrants and 89 million displaced persons (including refugees) (McAuliffe and Triandafyllidou 2022, 3–4). Millions of these people are moving into cities. In fact, more than half of the refugees in the world are based in cities (Crane 2022, 275). And of those moving into cities, some of these are from least reached peoples.

Ray Bakke (1997, 117) described the change that is happening by declaring, "Cities have replaced the nations. Yesterday, cities were in the nations; today all the nations are in our cities." Unfortunately, the mission community has been slow to respond to this change, continuing to consider "real missionary work" to be work in remote and tribal areas (Thompson 2011, 16). Yet, today, missions to least reached peoples can be done in many cases by simply "crossing the streets of the world's cities" (Bakke 1997, 13). And therefore, as Roger Greenway (2009, 563) challenged, "The migration to cities is so large that it must have a divinely-ordained, redemptive purpose behind it. How shall we respond?"

As least reached peoples move into cities, the missionary task is becoming both easier and harder. Paul Bendor-Samuel (2020, 191–92) described the way that least reached peoples are being changed as they are urbanized:

> The "least reached" no longer exist primarily in neat, geographically located "people group" clusters. Not only are they dispersed widely through migration and urbanisation, vast numbers of least-reached communities are found in contexts where the church exists, and may even be strong, yet these communities remain distant to the gospel due to all kinds of frontiers, many of which are now primarily intellectual, social, and ethical.

Despite these difficulties, least reached peoples that are largely closed to the gospel in their home countries and villages are often more open to the gospel when they migrate to cities. They have a great desire to build new relationships (Johnstone and Merrill 2015, 19). They are exposed to new ideas and rapid change. Migrants' relationships with their families and traditional networks usually remain on some level, but in many cases, they have more freedom to explore new ideas and/or their new faith can positively impact their families and networks back home. This openness is typically only true for a limited period of time after moving, perhaps for up to five years before they become more settled (Thompson 2011, 17). So, there is a significant, urgent need for mission work among urban migrants, especially when they first arrive in cities.

Ministry to urbanized least reached peoples can be a complex task, as multiple and hybrid cultures are often involved (this will be discussed more below). Incarnational and contextualized ministry is vitally important, yet the missionary must be constantly learning as the cultures themselves are often changing as they interact with many other cultures and influences in cities.

As Jenkins alluded to above, holistic ministry is very important to many people moving into cities. Many least reached peoples, and especially refugees, have few resources and sometimes face many obstacles in the way of finding good work and housing. Ministry that offers employment or housing help can be an effective way to build relationships and share the gospel. Legal help can be important as well in order for immigrants to be able to stay in the country and get better work. These kinds of ministries can help migrants avoid more desperate alternatives, like trafficking or other forms of crime.

Another point to consider is that when least reached peoples come to a new city, the barriers that existed between different groups in their homelands may no longer be as formidable. When multiple peoples migrate to a new city, Christians from one culture can sometimes effectively reach peoples from a near culture with the gospel (Clayman 2014, 17).

There are many examples of Christian diaspora, notably African (Hanciles 2008) and Chinese (Hattaway 2003), who want to share the gospel in a new city and new culture, but they may need help adapting to the new context (interview with Jared Looney, April 17, 2020). A great example of this has occurred in the city of Boston, which has undergone a "Quiet Revival," with the number of churches doubling from three hundred to six hundred since 1969. As many white churches fled to the suburbs, immigrants from Puerto Rico, Brazil, and Korea (in addition to those from many other nations) planted new churches and did outreach among the broader Boston community, as tracked and supported by the Emmanuel Gospel Center (Swartz 2020, 263–75). Even urban refugee churches can become catalysts for sharing the gospel with other refugees and with the rest of the city, ministering both to people's physical and spiritual needs (Crane 2022, 290).

Many least reached peoples moving into cities come from countries that allow little to no access to Christianity (Crane 2022, 289). But, when urban least reached people turn to Christ, they are often open to trying to reach their friends and family back home. Sometimes, even non-Christian immigrants can bridge the gap to their homelands, offering to help their Christian missionary friends make contacts there. Although many migrants to cities are needy in their new locations, there are some who are significant influencers back in their home countries and villages (Clayman 2014), even on the same level with village leadership (Wayne Denny, email to author, August 1, 2020; Kane 2011). Ministries of mercy to urban migrants can lead to ministries of influence in other lands, even lands that are traditionally more closed to the gospel.

In Ukraine, most of the native people groups would not be considered least reached. However, the cities of Ukraine have attracted people from many different countries as they pursue education and business opportunities. In these urban contexts, we often see an openness among these immigrants (some of whom are from least reached peoples) to new ideas and to the gospel. One interesting method of connecting with these immigrants is international church ministry, which allows immigrants to come together and hear the gospel in a common language, often English. For an immigrant looking for paths to success, speaking English and connecting with other internationals is very attractive. In urban contexts, we can offer something even more attractive and meaningful—the gospel.

Finally, one other important factor for ministry to urban least reached peoples is the generation of the immigrants. Often first-generation immigrants choose to not integrate significantly into their new culture, and what is written above generally refers to them. Second-generation immigrants tend to integrate more into the host culture, but not 100 percent. They often have more of a "third culture" mentality (like Third Culture Kids or TCK's), often bonding with other "third culture" people more than people in their parents' culture or the new host culture (interview with Nate Scholz, February 21, 2020). These second-generation immigrants can struggle with identity issues (Hiebert and Meneses 1995, 285).

Thus, missionaries (and their kids!) who are used to living between cultures themselves may have much in common with second-generation immigrants, but reaching this group will be very different than reaching their parents, with their heart language and culture differing significantly. Missionaries in urban diaspora contexts must constantly learn about the people around them and be aware that they are constantly being pulled by multiple influences and are in a state of flux.

Diverse and Hybridized Urban Communities

Urban areas tend to develop diverse and hybridized communities that form around many factors in addition to ethnicity, including social, economic, and professional factors. These communities do not fit traditional categories for least reached peoples or unreached people groups, either due to being mixed ethnolinguistic groups or due to forming their identity around non-ethnolinguistic factors. Yet, many of these communities have little to no gospel witness. Often, we lack data about the number of Christians or amount of gospel witness that these urban communities have.

First, let's consider mixed ethnolinguistic urban communities, or hybridized communities. Typically, cities grow more through an influx of people than through internal growth. Thus, there is a continual mixing and clashing of cultures, which leads to the creation of new hybrid cultures. As Sadiri Joy Tira (2020, 19) shared, "The Filipino people are a wonderful example of hybridity as evident in their multiracialism and multiculturalism, resulting from centuries of migration into and out of the geographical crossroads that are the Philippine islands."

Hybrid cultures tend to reflect a combination of fusion, two-ness, and displacement. In other words, a given hybrid culture will fuse some elements of different cultures together, creating something new. Two-ness can be seen as some elements originating from other cultures remain in a hybrid culture, each being believed or done at the same time, even if contradictory. Finally, hybrid cultures can have areas of displacement, or otherness, in which they don't feel at home in any one community. Thus, hybrid cultures have identities that can be shifting and even plural, which goes beyond typical notions of diversity (Rodriguez 2021, 139–44). Missionaries must continually dialogue with those in hybrid cultures to relate to them and minister in them appropriately.

Now, let's consider communities that form around socioeconomic factors. There are many levels of social organization, including government, business, family, and recreation, among others (Hiebert and Meneses 1995, 264–65). Sometimes even geographic factors play a role in the formation of urban communities, as Bakke with Hart (1987) noted the role that networking can play, and Sampson (2012) showed the importance of the "Neighborhood Effect."

Within these various factors and levels, urban communities exist, both rich and poor, as mentioned in a previous section. These diverse urban communities grow alongside one another.

> Simultaneous with the growth of urban poverty has been an almost equally large expansion of the professional-managerial-executive and "creative" class, a largely neo-liberal elite that is having a particularly influential effect on shaping the city-building process. This has led to the emergence of a new dualism in the world's major cities, quite different from the older division between industrial bourgeoisie and urban proletariat. (Soja and Kanai 2007, 65)

Yet, urban communities are "complex, fragmented and multilayered" and should not be understood dualistically, as just rich or poor (Soja and Kanai 2007, 65). Categories such as "influencers" and "poor" or "needy" can be helpful in describing large groups of people, but individual urban communities are much more nuanced and require research to understand and to minister to well.

We should now address the question, how "reached" are these urban communities? In most cases, we don't have definitive statistics. In general, Christians' influence in the global urban public square has been diminishing. In many cities, people are increasingly suspicious of organized religion, often considering it to just be "cultural residue from past societies" (Peters 2018, 32). In some parts of the world, Christians have never had much urban or public influence. This has certainly been true in Ukraine, where evangelical Christians have virtually always been oppressed up until Ukrainian independence in 1991. But in places like the US, influential Christians chose to leave the cities for the suburbs in the 1960s–1980s, leaving a "tremendous vacuum" of Christian witness (Thompson 2011, xix).

Lacking a significant influence in urban areas for so long, it has become very difficult for Christians to make inroads into cities. As R. Drew Smith (2018, 11–12) explained,

> A growing proportion of the global population resides in urban spaces, even as the intensity and dynamism characteristic of those spaces has been multiplied by technologies that have facilitated vastly increased communications, information gathering, and social intersectionality. Given the intensifying nature of these

urban dynamics, Christian ministries have struggled to account for urbanization's growing force, complexities, and reach—and to formulate theologically and sociologically appropriate responses.

This struggle to gain influence and connect with people in cities has been one of the biggest issues that the evangelical church in Ukraine has faced. Since evangelicals were oppressed under the Russian Empire and the Soviet Union, nearly all evangelicals were poor, and as a result, only had access to ministry among the poor. Since the country gained independence, Ukrainian evangelicals in urban areas have struggled to do effective ministry among influencers and in the public square. Providentially, the war with Russia has offered more opportunities for Ukrainian evangelicals to influence society as they have filled large public needs, serving through chaplain and trauma ministries, and offering shelter to displaced people.

Tim Keller, founder of one of the most successful global urban ministries, Redeemer City to City, admitted as well how little impact Christians presently have in cities. But even so, there is still hope for unreached urban communities. He shared:

> Protestant (evangelical) Christians are the least urban religious group and thus have the least impact culturally. Three kinds of people here affect the future: a) elites, b) new immigrants, c) the poor. The single most effective way for Christians to "reach" the US would be for 25% of them to move to two or three of the largest cities and stay there for three generations. (Keller, 2016)

Keller's advice is sound, and something that we should seriously consider for frontier mission. Also, we might add one more kind of people to Keller's list: young people. Certainly, this next generation of adults and leaders will affect the future of cities, and consequently, the world.

We should consider the amount of gospel witness among the urban poor as well. Bendor-Samuel (2020, 192) pointed out the lack of missionaries and national workers in urban slums:

> While accurate figures are difficult to obtain, in 2014 Todd Johnson and his colleagues estimated that fewer than 1 in 500 Christian foreign missionaries are working in slums, 1 in 10,000 national workers works in slums in their own countries, and the vast majority of these missionaries and workers live outside the slums.

Unfortunately, this lack of missionary work in slums is not surprising considering the difficult conditions which discourage families from moving there and certainly lead to many deciding to leave due to health problems and other dangers.

Considering these diverse and hybridized urban communities that fall outside of lists of least reached and unreached peoples, we must rethink our priorities for mission and focus more effort on the urbanized mission frontier. So many people in cities remain unengaged by the church and desperately need the gospel preached in a way that will connect with them.

Connections from Cities to the World

Finally, ministry in cities can facilitate bringing the gospel to far-flung mission frontiers all over the world by leveraging the connections between cities and other regions, both near and far. These connections can be seen in various forms, but often they are characterized by the term "globalization."

Urbanization, industrialization, and globalization have been tied together in driving the growth of cities since the Industrial Revolution (Soja and Kanai 2007, 63). Despite some critics who say that the influence of globalization is diminishing, multiple studies show that the connections of globalization continue (Bacchus 2023). Statistically, the global merchandise trade hit a record high in 2022 in both nominal value ($25 trillion) and volume. DHL's "Global Connectedness Index," which examines trade, capital flows, information, and migration, reported that 2021 nearly reached the all-time high set in 2017, with 2022 projected to go even higher (Altman and Bastian 2023; Lincicome 2023). Despite the end of the era of "hyperglobalization" in 2008 and the two global crises of the pandemic and the war in Ukraine, "interdependence still rules" (Bremmer 2022; Lincicome 2023).

In considering how these connections can be avenues for the gospel, we need look no further than the ministry of the Apostle Paul to the cities of the Roman Empire. Paul spent most of his time doing ministry in cities. One could argue that at this time, the whole world was a mission frontier, and yet, Paul focused on large, influential cities. On his second missionary journey he spent most of his time in Corinth, one of the largest cities in Greece. On his third missionary journey, Paul spent three years in Ephesus, the largest city in Asia Minor (Thompson 2011, 16–17). Then, he traveled to

Rome, the largest and most influential city of the Roman Empire. According to Romans 15:18–23, Paul felt his work was done since he expected that the churches that he planted in major cities would actively minister to the regions surrounding those cities. It appears that Paul's strategy was effective since sociologist Rodney Stark (1996, 6) estimated that Christianity grew at a rate of 40 percent per decade for its first several centuries.

So, in that vein, we should also consider how reaching cities will help us reach the world today (as Tim Keller put it above). The connections between cities and the world are even stronger now than they were in Paul's time. Ray Bakke (1997, 168) called cities "both magnets, drawing the nations into them, and magnifiers, broadcasting the gospel out into the hinterlands."

Today, cities are the seats of power for government, media, business, education, and health care. Cities are places where many nationalities and ethnic groups come together. People are becoming more and more connected to one another through the products of cities that are spread through the forces of urbanization and globalization. Technology, entertainment, the arts, and literature all connect people to the cities where these products are created and developed. As cities go, so goes the nation (Thompson 2011, 17).

There are numerous examples of ministries that have spread through these various connections. Faith and work ministry (which has many advocates today, including Redeemer City to City), religious dialogue (for example, Christians dialoguing with Muslims in Europe), and many kinds of counseling ministry (for example, in Ukraine many kinds of counseling are spreading from cities into the country, from trauma counseling to art therapy to counseling children and adolescents) are known around the world.

Ministries to migrants and immigrants can connect with many people outside the city as well. For example, an urban community center can affect many migrants and immigrants who use its services. The impact from the community center can be felt in far-flung places as those migrants and immigrants return home, send money home, or call more family and friends to come to the city. Similarly, multicultural churches can have an impact on their congregants' family and friends far away from the city. They can be strategic in reaching the nations, both in the city by creating a safe place for different ethnicities, and beyond by creating a hub for networks to different nations (McIntosh and McMahan 2012, 180).

Technology is another important means of connecting the city to the world as it cuts through national borders, creating links and networks (Conn and Ortiz 2001, 214). Some examples of the missionary use of technology that spreads from cities are Bible applications, Christian music, and Christian movies. Technology can also be a tool for community building (for example, cell phones, email, WhatsApp, Zoom, etc.), but it can't be relied on as an alternative to face-to-face interactions (Bergquist and Crane 2018, 314).

Technology can be a means for education in both distance and face-to-face learning (Baker 2009, 39). At Ukrainian Evangelical Theological Seminary, we have used technology in many forms in order to keep our education programs going during COVID-19 and the war with Russia. Using Zoom has allowed us to work with teachers and students across Ukraine and in other countries. Sharing resources through Moodle has allowed us to equip people in ministry in Ukraine and beyond. What we can offer in the city of Kyiv is quickly available to our students in other cities like Kharkiv, Lviv, Odesa, Paris, Accra, and Nairobi.

Finally, it is important to note that young people tend to be especially connected to the products of the city both through technology and media. Linhart and Livermore (2011, 192) gave some examples from Asia:

> Like their Western counterparts, Asian youth are mediavores and technoids—media and technology influences every area of their lives. Their perspective is Western, their fashion is Japanese, and their language is Korean. Materialism spurred on by the media is rampant: Japanese youth choose style over comfort in a need to conform, "little emperors" of China are indulged with "an increasing amount of discretionary spending income," middle-class and upper-middle-class Indian youth are more prone to materialism compared to lower-middle and lower-class youths who deal more with an inferiority complex.

Making connections through technology and media can be useful for ministry to youth as well.

All these connections from cities, whether through personal networks or technology, reflect relational networks, and these are means through which the gospel can flow (Hall with Hall and Daman 2010, 253). And thus, ministry on the urban mission frontier can help missionaries reach other mission frontiers through these relational networks.

Conclusion: Future Directions of Mission

The urbanization of the mission frontier means that cities should be a major focus of new missionary work in the twenty-first century. The sheer numbers of people moving to cities should motivate more global urban mission. Furthermore, cities provide a platform for ministry to least reached peoples, offering greater access and openness than can be found in many peoples' home countries and villages. Cities also produce diverse and hybridized communities that represent new mission frontiers. Finally, connections from cities to the rest of the world make cities strategic since mission in the city can yield fruit both in urban areas as well as around the world through relational networks. As Ray Bakke noted, the nations have really come to the cities, and more and more people that need to hear the gospel are in or closely connected with cities. How will we respond to the new reality of the urbanized mission frontier?

References

Altman, Steven A., and Caroline R. Bastian. 2023. "The State of Globalization in 2023." *Harvard Business Review*, July 11. https://hbr.org/2023/07/the-state-of-globalization-in-2023.

Bacchus, James. 2023. "In the Rush to End Globalization, We're Missing Critical Points." *The Hill*, January 31. https://thehill.com/opinion/finance/3837548-in-the-rush-to-end-globalization-were-missing-critical-points/.

Baker, Susan S. 2009. "Globalization: How Should Mission Respond?" In *Globalization and Its Effects on Urban Ministry in the 21st Century*, edited by Susan S. Baker. William Carey Library.

Bakke, Ray. 1997. *A Theology as Big as the City*. IVP Academic.

Bakke, Ray, with Jim Hart. 1987. *The Urban Christian*. InterVarsity Press.

Bendor-Samuel, Paul. 2020. "Epilogue: Called to Undivided Witness." In *Undivided Witness: Followers of Jesus, Community Development, and Least-Reached Communities*, edited by David Greenlee, Mark Galpin, and Paul Bendor-Samuel. Regnum Books.

Bergquist, Linda, and Michael D. Crane. 2018. *City Shaped Churches*. Urban Loft Publishers.

Bremmer, Ian. 2022. "Globalization Isn't Dead: The World Is More Fragmented, but Interdependence Still Rules." *Foreign Affairs*, October 25. https://www.foreignaffairs.com/world/globalization-isnt-dead.

Burdett, Ricky, and Philipp Rode. 2007. "The Urban Age Project." In *The Endless City*, edited by Ricky Burdett and Deyan Sudjic. Phaidon Press.

Burdett, Ricky, and Deyan Sudjic, eds. 2007. *The Endless City*. Phaidon Press.

Clayman, Chris. 2014. "Reaching the Nations Through Our Cities," *Great Commission Research Journal* 6 (1): 6–21.

Conn, Harvie M. 1994. *The American City and the Evangelical Church. A Historical Overview*. Baker Books.

Crane, Michael D. 2022. "Refugees in the Urban Wilderness: Plight of Refugees in Landing Cities and Opportunities for Response." In *Migration, Mission, and Ministry: An Introduction*, edited by Robert Chao Romero and Stephen Burris. Urban Loft Publishers.

Davis, Mike. 2017. *Planet of Slums*. Verso.

Demographia. 2023. *Demographia World Urban Areas*. 19th annual edition. http://www.demographia.com/db-worldua.pdf.

Dorsett, Lyle W. 2003. *A Passion for Souls: The Life of D. L. Moody*. Moody Publishers.

DuBose, Francis M. 1978. *How Churches Grow in an Urban World*. Broadman Press.

Fourth Lausanne Congress. 2024. "Programme Schedule." https://congress.lausanne.org/schedule/.

Greenway, Roger S. 2009. "The Challenge of the Cities." In *Perspectives on the World Christian Movement*, edited by Ralph Winter and Steven C. Hawthorne. 4th ed. William Carey Library.

Hall, Douglas A., with Judy Hall, and Steve Daman. 2010. *The Cat & the Toaster: Living System Ministry in a Technological Age*. Wipf and Stock.

Hall, Peter. 2002. *Cities of Tomorrow*. 3rd ed. Blackwell.

Hanciles, Jehu J. 2008. *Beyond Christendom: Globalization, African Migration, and the Transformation of the West*. Orbis Books.

Hattaway, Paul. 2003. *Back to Jerusalem*. InterVarsity Press.

Hiebert, Paul, and Eloise Meneses. 1995. *Incarnational Ministry: Planting Churches in Band, Tribal, Peasant, and Urban Societies*. Baker Books.

Hildreth, Paul. 2014. "Commitment to the City: Responding to The Cape Town Commitment on Cities." *Lausanne Movement*, March 12. https://lausanne.org/content/lga/2014–03/commitment-to-the-city-responding-to-the-cape-town-commitment-on-cities.

Jenkins, Philip. 2011. *The Next Christendom: The Coming of Global Christianity*. 3rd ed. Oxford University Press.

Johnstone, Patrick, with Dean Merrill. 2015. *Serving God in Today's Cities: Facing the Challenge of Urbanization*. GMI.

Joshua Project. N.d. "Definitions." https://joshuaproject.net/help/definitions#least-reached.

Kane, Ousmane Oumar. 2011. *The Homeland is the Arena: Religion, Transnationalism, and the Integration of Senegalese Immigrants in America*. Oxford University Press.

Keller, Tim. 2016. "A Theology of Cities." *Cru*, February 23. https://www.cru.org/us/en/train-and-grow/leadership-training/sending-your-team/a-theology-of-cities.html.

Lincicome, Scott. 2023. "Globalization Isn't Going Anywhere." *Cato Institute*, September 12. https://www.cato.org/publications/globalization-isnt-going-anywhere.

Linhart, Terence, and David Livermore. 2011. *Global Youth Ministry: Reaching Adolescents around the World*. Zondervan.

McAuliffe, Marie, and Anna Triandafyllidou, eds. 2022. *World Migration Report 2022*. International Organization for Migration.

McIntosh, Gary, and Alan McMahan. 2012. *Being the Church in a Multi-Ethnic Community*. Wesleyan Publishing House.

Mumford, Lewis. 1961. *The City in History. Its Origins, Its Transformations, and Its Prospects*. Harcourt, Inc.

Peters, Ronald E. 2018. "Urban Conceptualizing in Historical Perspective." In *Urban Ministry Reconsidered: Contexts and Approaches*, edited by R. Drew Smith, Stephanie C. Boddie, and Ronald E. Peters. Westminster John Knox Press.

Rodriguez, Martin. 2021. "Hybridity, Borderlands, and Paul Hiebert: A Latinx Missiologist Reexamines Critical Contextualization." In *Advancing Models of Mission*, edited by Kenneth Nehrbass, Aminta Arrington, and Nancy Santos. William Carey Publishing.

Sampson, Robert J. 2012. *The Great American City: Chicago and the Enduring Neighborhood Effect*. University of Chicago Press.

Sassen, Saskia. 2001. *The Global City: New York, London, Tokyo*. 2nd ed. University Press.

Smith, R. Drew. 2018. "Introduction." In *Urban Ministry Reconsidered: Contexts and Approaches*, edited by R. Drew Smith, Stephanie C. Boddie, and Ronald E. Peters. Westminster John Knox Press.

Soja, Edward, and Miguel Kanai. 2007. "The Urbanization of the World." In *The Endless City*, edited by Ricky Burdett and Deyan Sudjic. Phaidon Press.

Stark, Rodney. 1996. *The Rise of Christianity: A Sociologist Reconsiders History*. Princeton University Press.

Stark, Rodney. 2006. *Cities of God: The Real Story of How Christianity Became an Urban Movement and Conquered Rome*. HarperCollins Publishers.

Swartz, David R. 2020. *Facing West: American Evangelicals in an Age of World Christianity*. Oxford University Press.

Thompson, John L. 2011. *Urban Impact: Reaching the World Through Effective Urban Ministry*. Wipf & Stock.

Tira, Sadiri Joy. 2020. "Preface: Hybridity, Diaspora, Missio Dei." In *A Hybrid World: Diaspora, Hybridity, and Missio Dei*, edited by Sadiri Joy Tira and Juliet Lee Uytanlet. William Carey Publishing.

UN-Habitat. 2022. *World Cities Report 2022: Envisaging the Future of Cities*. United Nations Human Settlements Programme. https://unhabitat.org/world-cities-report-2022.

Chapter 12

St. Paul Hiebert's or Ours?
New Frontiers in Missionary Anthropology and the Advancement of the Great Commission

Anthony Casey

Can the Great Commission be completed without the social sciences? In other words, could first century Christians legitimately have completed the Great Commission, or did we need two thousand years of development to get to our current understanding of what a people group is in relation to what we mean by fulfilling the Great Commission? There has been a history of tension between theological understandings of mission and the interface of the social sciences in how we conceive of the Great Commission. Yet, the two are inextricably linked in the modern practice of missions. This chapter raises questions as to whether our current understanding and definition of people groups matches the reality of the world today, particularly in light of the prevalence of the modern diaspora. Paul Hiebert and others pioneered the field of missiology, but is it time for another generation of Hieberts and Hesselgraves for the continued advancement of the Great Commission?

People Group Theory Drives Modern Missions

People groups are the driving factor in how most missiologists and mission agencies conceive of missions strategy. Picture the Global Status of Evangelical Christianity (GSEC) map with its Christmas tree lights of red for unreached, yellow, and green, representing the *panta ta ethne* ("all nations" or "all people groups") of Matthew 28:19 (GSEC, IMB Global Research). These dots represent people groups, broadly defined as socio-linguistic constructs through which the gospel can travel without encountering significant barriers or hindrances (Moreau, et al. 2004, 43). The very language of this definition—socio-linguistic constructs—comes out of the social sciences. If it is our aim to make disciples of all the socio-linguistic groups of the world in order to complete the Great Commission, we need to know how many people groups there are in the world.

How Many PPGs Exist?

Over time, but primarily in the past fifty years, many have tried to answer the question of how many people groups there are, but wildly divergent numbers have been put forth. The IMB, with their global research division, lists 12,111 (Reports, IMB Global Research). The Joshua Project, specializing in people groups research, suggests 17,000 (Joshua Project). Others have listed as many as 24,000. Where do these numbers leave us with the Great Commission? We cannot agree on how many people groups there are, or even how we might actually know. The Ethnologue lists over 7,100 spoken languages in the world, with this number changing regularly (Ethnologue). Add to that at least 300 signed languages. As sign language develops in additional languages, do more people groups come into existence, further expanding the Great Commission? Such are the difficulties with identifying a number.

Furthermore, peoples are on the move today. They are going everywhere from everywhere. Urban centers are diverse. Diaspora is front and center in global politics, and more recently in my own specialty of diaspora missiology. What happens when a group moves from their homeland to a new place with different social and linguistic influences? If people groups are socio-linguistic constructs, do they deconstruct in new socio-linguistic settings? Immigrants make decisions about what language to use and which cultural identity to put forth in new settings. They often ask who they even are anymore. In these instances, which are many, our tidy definition of a people group as a static, bounded entity becomes fuzzy and messy. I lived in Kuala Lumpur, Malaysia (pop. 9 million) and I loved the diversity, complexity, and chaotic nature of a true multi-ethnic society, but it continually called into question the sufficiency of a traditional understanding of a people group and what it means to "complete" the Great Commission.

What Does It Mean to Be Reached?

Though increasingly contested, modern missiologists have used the 2 percent threshold of evangelical Christianity to identify a people group as "reached." Where did this number come from, particularly if it seems to be *the* driving factor in determining reached from unreached? It came from the social sciences. Sociologists and economists have identified what they call the "tipping point"—that is, at what point does a new idea gain enough acceptance in a society that it crosses a threshold and begins to spread more readily throughout the whole of society? The tipping point focuses on receptivity. Every society has early adaptors, but when does something move from the fringes to the center of social acceptance? Probably once around 20 percent of a group accept a new idea. Some years ago, missiologists were reflecting on the tipping point and determined if we have to reach 20 percent of twelve thousand people groups, we will never complete the Great Commission. After discussion, the sociological principle of 20 percent was reduced to 2 percent when applied to unreached people groups, thus defining one of the most influential markers of Great Commission fulfillment (cf. Sills 2010, 105–28).

Today, nearly everything we do in the conceptualization and engagement of the Great Commission comes from the last seventy years of the social sciences. Our definition of people groups, our methods for counting them, and what constitutes a group being reached in regard to completing the Great Commission are all influenced, if not defined, by modern social science. Our definition does not come specifically from the Scriptures, nor from two thousand years of missions history, but from the past fifty to seventy years of the social sciences.

Historical Awareness of People Groups

If missiology is so heavily influenced by recent social science theory, how did people go about the missionary task throughout history? There is a bit of natural intuitiveness that people had that can be seen in Acts 2 when they encountered different languages. People realized others spoke different languages and had different cultural backgrounds and contextualized the gospel appropriately, even in the New Testament (Flemming 2005). In the 300s, Patrick of Ireland clearly understood the unique cultural and linguistic barriers of the Miliuc peoples with whom he lived (Hunter 2000). Around the same period, the Goths were primarily engaged through a translation of Scripture so they could encounter God in a way they could understand (Smith 2015, 379). There are many examples in the intervening centuries, but clearly William Carey understood the complexities of peoples living in India, probably the most culturally and linguistically diverse place in the world. Hudson Taylor in the late 1800s said "in all things but sin, Chinese"—

in clear contrast to the extraction model of missions used by many of his European counterparts. Taylor provides an example of modern missiology where we do not want to import outside cultural and linguistic constructs of Christianity to the nations.

Clearly, even in the nineteenth century and prior, there was some understanding of socio-linguistic boundaries and barriers of peoples around the world. But it was not until the 1974 Lausanne Conference on World Evangelization that Ralph Winter dropped a missiological bombshell on our idea of how we go about completing the Great Commission. It was here that our current understanding of *panta ta ethne* began to be the driving force in modern missions.

Social Science Leads to the Rise of Missiology

As I looked more closely into the background of Ralph Winter, and others of his era that became so influential in our understanding of the Great Commission, I noticed several fascinating commonalities. I have compiled a list of the major players in the development of modern missiology, where they went to school, when, and the focus of their degree. This list, found below, is not exhaustive, and credentials were identified via author biographies, obituaries, school websites, and other interviews and publications.

- Donald McGavran, PhD in Anthropology, Columbia University, 1936
- Ken Pike, PhD in Linguistic Anthropology, University of Michigan, 1942
- Eugene Nida, PhD in Linguistic Anthropology, University of Michigan, 1943
- Ralph Winter, PhD in Anthropology, Cornell University, 1940s
- William Smalley, PhD in Linguistic Anthropology, Columbia University, 1956
- Jacob Loewen, PhD in Linguistic Anthropology, University of Washington, 1958
- Charles Kraft, PhD in Anthropological Linguistics, Hartford Seminary, 1963

- Alan Tippett, PhD in Anthropology, University of Oregon, 1964
- Dan Shaw, PhD in Anthropology, University of Arizona, 1968
- Donald K. Smith, PhD in Linguistic Anthropology, University of Oregon, 1969
- Michael Rynchevich, PhD in Anthropology, University of Minnesota, 1972
- Peter Wagner, PhD in Social Ethics, University of Southern California, 1977
- Miriam Adeney, PhD in Anthropology, Washington State University, 1980
- Darrell Whiteman, PhD in Anthropology, Southern Illinois University, 1980
- David Hesselgrave, PhD in Cross-Cultural Communication, University of Minnesota
- Paul Hiebert, PhD in Anthropology, University of Minnesota
- Sherwood and Judy Lingenfelter, PhD in Anthropology, University of Pittsburg
- Duane Elmer, PhD in Education, Michigan State University
- George Hunter, PhD in Intercultural Communication, Northwestern University
- Enoch Wan, PhD in Anthropology, SUNY system
- Bob Priest, PhD in Anthropology, University of California-Berkeley, 1993

Nearly everything we know and use today in missiology, linguistics, and intercultural communication related to our conceptualization of people groups and the Great Commission was pioneered by those on this list. Nearly every one of them has a PhD in the social sciences from a secular university. Obviously, missiology did not exist as a discipline to be studied, so these men and women pioneered the field. What they brought to the table was insight into the socio-linguistic construction of the world as it pertains to understanding, identity, receptivity, rejection of the gospel, and barriers to the advancement of the Great Commission.

The majority of these missionary social scientists were then hired by evangelical schools and seminaries like Biola University, Fuller Seminary, Trinity Evangelical Divinity School, and so on. They taught in seminaries the second generation of missiologists, one step removed from cutting edge social science research. That generation then taught me, the third generation of missiologists, two steps removed from frontier social science research. My PhD supervisor at the Southern Baptist Theological Seminary was David Sills, himself supervised by Enoch Wan at Reformed Theological Seminary, who had graduated with a PhD in anthropology from SUNY. I now teach fourth generation budding missiologists, yet another generation removed from a fresh infusion of anthropological research and insight.

My Own Journey in Diaspora Missiology

My own journey sheds light on the point I am attempting to make. In 2009 I began a PhD in missiology at the Southern Baptist Theological Seminary in Louisville, Kentucky. I had worked with some of the twelve thousand resettled refugees in Louisville for a number of years. I had gone to college in Wisconsin where there were Hmong, Lao, and Vietnamese resettled after the Vietnam War, now living forty years on with multiple generations having grown up in the United States. I was fascinated with how people in these diaspora settings understood themselves, navigated new cultural systems, and interacted in multiple and newly learned languages. It seemed to me that depending on peoples' backgrounds, they took a different approach to identity in diaspora.

My dissertation focused on ethnic, linguistic, and religious identity in multi-cultural urban diaspora settings. The Southern Baptist Theological Seminary had one of the best theological libraries in the country, yet it did not help me much in my dissertation. For the literature review and theoretical interaction, I spent most of my time in the University of Louisville library because of their long tradition of programs in anthropology and sociology. I needed scholarly works on ethnic identity, urban anthropology, and immigration that could be applied to gospel engagement. At that time, few missiologists had written anything in those areas. Diaspora missiology was just getting going. The majority of my dissertation research came from so-called secular insights in urban anthropology and my field research with refugees. My seminary was a wonderful experience and was so helpful in a thousand ways that I would never take back, but I had to create a bit of my own path to explore this budding field of diaspora missiology and immigrant cultural identity.

As I was reading, I came across Michael Rynkiewich (PhD in anthropology, University of Minnesota, 1972) who had just retired from Asbury Theological Seminary. Rynkiewich does not mince words when he writes, "The result is that missiology, as it is taught in colleges and seminaries now, tends to be based on an outdated anthropology that is recommended to potential missionaries for a world that no longer exists" (Rynkiewich 2011, xii). This statement was shocking to me, yet not out of touch with what I was encountering as I worked on my dissertation. Rynkiewich goes on to suggest this is not Paul Hiebert's world. Yes, Hiebert pioneered anthropological insights in missiology in the 1970s, 80s, 90s, and so on. But now it is 2010 (2025 today!) and the world is a different place.

When I read third and fourth generation missiologists, they were citing Hiebert and Hesselgrave. Where is the new insight, particularly in diaspora, ethnic identity, and multi-cultural settings? Could it be that our current understanding of people groups comes from the 1970s where we thought of them as tidy silos with impermeable boundaries that remained in place, even in diaspora settings? Modern social science research seems to say that is not the case at all. Ethnic boundaries might become porous, or semi-porous. People operate under a variety of social and linguistic identities depending on the social context. Multi-cultural interaction created something that was not a nice, tidy people group identity.

I was reading missiologists who were writing that unreached people groups around the world were difficult and dangerous to reach. But peoples today are on the move! We *can* engage and reach them here in a diaspora setting. There are up to 365 people groups living in North America (Global Gates) that we can engage and basically check off the list on the GSEC map and move closer to the completion of the Great Commission. In response, I started to ask the question "Yes, but are they the same people in a diaspora setting?" and I had no easy answer to that.

The State of Things Today

This dilemma seems to be the state of things today. During my PhD, I was part of a team invited by the IMB to help their newly formed Diaspora

Affinity team make sense of their experiences in London, England—that beautifully glorious complex, chaotic mixture of people from everywhere. The IMB had moved seasoned missionaries from the Americas who had been successful in their relatively monocultural, monolinguistic settings to London with hopes to reach and mobilize diaspora Latinos to engage UPGs in London, mainly from Islamic backgrounds. After a few years, things were not going well and they were not sure why. Our team spent a lot of time in the back alleys of London talking to Bengalis, Afghans, Somalis, and others and wrote up an eighty-five-page description, summary, analysis, and recommendations for ministry in this unique context. The missionaries, while good and godly folk, found their training in a monoethnic context was not sufficient for understanding the complexities of the urban, diaspora setting in which they now lived. They are not alone. I have seen these scenarios play out repeatedly as I have helped pastors, church planters, and missionaries understand their communities on four continents.

So where are we with regard to completion of the Great Commission? Do we need another round of first-generation social science PhDs in the model of Hiebert and Hesselgrave for us to advance the Great Commission in light of immigrant, diaspora realities and fuzzy people group identities? What can the social sciences do for us today in light of current missiological practice? Let me be clear that we do not need only the social sciences. A solid theological foundation should always be at the core of church planting and the Great Commission. Biblical definitions and boundaries around matters such as what is the gospel, sin, salvation, redemption, a disciple, a church, and so on are ultimately decided not by cultural expression, but by the authority of Scripture. Yet, these timeless truths that transcend culture still have their expression in and through culture, so there is also the need for deep cultural understanding. There are several areas I have observed in recent years in which a new infusion of social science research can be of help.

Qualitative Research

Qualitative research and ethnographic skills are at the heart of many intercultural studies PhD programs. Additionally, many papers presented at EMS use qualitative methods as their theoretical model for understanding a community. However, I am afraid that the depth and accuracy of many of these projects are not what they should be. Many seminaries have little in the form of coursework to adequately prepare students to undertake a qualitative project. Many seminary professors do not feel competent to teach such classes because they themselves do not have the qualitative background from their own seminary training.

Furthermore, there is little good literature available for missions-oriented qualitative research. The thematic analysis portion is especially lacking in many books (See Gilbert et al. 2018). I wrote the book I wished someone else had written in an attempt to address these issues as I have worked with doctoral students at a number of institutions over the years (Casey 2020). True qualitative methodologists just do not seem to exist in broader missiology today, whether in books, the classroom, or on the field. Perhaps a new batch of thoroughly trained social scientists would help the research that is currently being done to be done better.

Linguistics

If people groups are socio-linguistic constructs, a deep understanding of linguistic identity is essential. What happens in places like the Amazonian basin or Indonesia where small tribal languages are going extinct, morphing, or becoming pidgin languages mixed with a national language? If a language disappears, does that people group disappear? Do two people groups become one with the dropping of the linguistic divide of a socio-linguistic group? Many seminarians and missiologists have little to no training in linguistics. Bible translation is left to one or two specialist entities, or increasingly, to AI (Barger 2024). These are other issues altogether, but for me, the question remains: Does our current definition of people groups, how many there are, and what does it mean to complete the Great Commission hold up with the rapidly changing linguistic realities of the world and diaspora?

People Group Theory

Much of this paper has raised issues related to people group theory. Many of these issues may be unsolvable. Yet, for most of my academic career I have heard conversations and reservations about how we understand people groups. Many are unsatisfied with the current state of the GSEC. Books need to be written exploring these issues in light of a globalized, postcolonial, diaspora world. The question is, who can write such a book? It would take someone with a unique background and training. Perhaps it is time for a new batch of missionary anthropologists to take on these issues.

The Way Forward

I certainly do not have the answers to all the questions that I raise in this chapter, but I want to put something in writing as a formal starting point for the conversation. I hope others will reflect, challenge, and build on what I propose here. I pose three further questions that may open a way forward as we consider the Great Commission in the modern world.

Is Seminary Enough?

I went to seminary, for a long time! It was a wonderful experience. But, is seminary enough to prepare missionaries and missiologists (which can be different entities) for advancing the Great Commission in the modern world? At places like EMS, I have heard for a number of years now many missiologists questioning the value of seminary training for these issues. Some are directing students away from seminaries and into university settings for social science PhD training. I have heard certain denominational seminaries spoken of poorly with regard to their perceived equipping for missions in the modern world. Seminary can be enough, and is enough, for the majority of people. Yet, many seminaries could do a better job of equipping and enabling students in the socio-linguistic side of the Great Commission.

Should Seminaries Hire Social Science PhDs?

To my knowledge, my own denomination, the Southern Baptist Convention, has not hired missions professors with PhDs in the social sciences at their seminaries. I do know of several others such as Biola University and Trinity Evangelical Divinity School that have explicitly hired these kinds of PhDs. Their job posts clearly stated they wanted a social science PhD, along with an MDiv or other theological degree. These schools have a hard time finding candidates that have sound theological convictions, believe in the inerrancy, authority, and sufficiency of Scripture, and a PhD in the social sciences.

In private conversations, professors and chairs at some of these schools told me they do not want to hire graduates with PhDs from seminaries to teach in their programs. They believe many seminaries are teaching outdated, unhelpful, 1970s anthropology in their doctoral programs that is not sufficient for today. While I am sympathetic, I have asked the question of what are you trying to produce in these programs? Who are you actually training, and in what? In my view, some of these programs hold anthropology as superior to missiology. I asked one chair, "Are you training missionaries or 'interculturalists' as you continue to put it?" And interculturalists only because that school did not offer a PhD in anthropology.

The first generation of missiology professors like Hiebert and Hesselgrave, those who pioneered missiology as a discipline, described themselves as missionary anthropologists. They cared first and foremost about the Great Commission. They used their training in anthropology *for* the advancement of the Great Commission. Their many books prepared missionaries. I am afraid that some of today's anthropology PhD-holding professors in some of these institutions care more about anthropology for its own sake rather than for bringing clarity to the task of missions. Should evangelical schools hire anthropology PhDs for their missions programs? Maybe. But they must be the right kind of people, in the vein of Hiebert and Hesselgrave, and not many of those people exist.

Should You Do a PhD in Social Science?

As I worked on my dissertation and struggled to find adequate academic resources related to diaspora and urban multiculturalism, I seriously considered transferring out of seminary and into a state university for anthropology. I talked with several schools and even visited one for an interview for their program. It was interesting to see their perception of me, coming from a Baptist seminary. Was that good, bad, indifferent? For some schools that was fine, for others, not so much. One school did not have anthropology but had medical sociology. I told them I might be interested in researching cultural constructions of health among former Hmong refugees in Wisconsin. They thought that was great. My interest in diaspora communities matched with these schools' focuses, though I planned to use my research for ministry application. In the end, I stayed at my seminary.

But, what about those not yet in a doctoral program? Should they go the anthropology route? In short, no. In general, our seminaries do a great job of preparing missionaries. For most, this training is more than enough. Yet, for a select few, a social science PhD is appropriate. There are several considerations for those contemplating this route: (1) There is a job market for evangelical social science PhDs. Many schools have told me they cannot find such graduates so if you are one, you all but have a guaranteed job somewhere. (2) These PhD programs are about fit. Do your research interests match those of their professors? You will likely have to back away from clear Christian application and isolate out some issue to study more deeply. In contrast, many seminary PhD programs accept students with any number of broad missiological interests. (3) There are Christian anthropology professors at several state universities with whom you may study. However, in many instances it will be difficult to maintain a Christian identity in your program. You need to be comfortable keeping quiet at times and navigating systems that clearly do not share your worldview and values. (4) These programs are often longer than seminary PhD programs. You may need to move to a new cultural context, possibly learn a language, and undertake two or more years of fieldwork after completing several years of coursework. Many of these programs will not accept a master's degree from a seminary so you may need to do another MA on the way to the PhD.

In short, a state university PhD program is not advisable for most people. But, as much of this chapter argues, there is a need for a new batch of missionary anthropologists with the right mix of skills, background, and experience.

Conclusion

I do not have all the answers as to the question: Do we need a new batch of social science PhDs to advance the Great Commission? However, in my own field of diaspora missiology, I have seen the complexities of immigrant ethnic identity, linguistic drift, urban multiculturalism, and so on, blow apart our nice, neat, bounded definition of people groups. Without question, immigration changes people. But how, and to what extent, and are we still reaching "their" people group in the diaspora setting? The core of the Great Commission and modern missions strategy is *panta ta ethne*—all the peoples of the world—yet how many are there and how do we know? We cannot know what we do not yet know. Maybe it is time for a new infusion of the social sciences with new insights like those who pioneered missiology in the late 1900s. Ultimately, we need St. Paul Hiebert's methods *and* ours for missions in the modern age.

References

Barger, Don. 2024. "How AI Assists in Global Bible Translation." *The Gospel Coalition*. https://www.thegospelcoalition.org/article/ai-bible-translation/.

Casey, Anthony F. 2020. *Peoples on the Move: Community Research for Ministry and Missions*. Wipf and Stock.

Ethnologue. https://www.ethnologue.com.

Flemming, Dean. 2005. *Contextualization in the New Testament: Patterns for Theology and Mission*. InterVarsity Press.

Gilbert, Marvin, Alan Johnson, and Paul Lewis, eds. 2018. *Missiological Research: Interdisciplinary Foundations, Methods, and Integration*. William Carey Library.

Global Gates Database. https://globalgates.info/resources/priority-matrix.

Hunter, George. 2000. *The Celtic Way of Evangelism: How Christianity can Reach the West Again*. Abingdon Press.

IMB Global Research GSEC Map. https://www.imb.org/research/maps/.

IMB Global Research People Group Assessment. https://www.imb.org/research/reports/.

Joshua Project. https://joshuaproject.net.

Moreau, Scott, Gary Corwin, and Gary McGee. 2004. *Introducing World Missions: A Biblical, Historical, and Practical Survey*. Baker.

Rynkiewich, Michael. 2011. *Soul, Self, and Society: A Postmodern Anthropology for Mission in a Postcolonial World*. Cascade.

Sills, David. 2010. *Reaching and Teaching: A Call to Great Commission Obedience*. Moody Publishers.

Smith, Ebbie. 2015. "Introduction to the Strategy and Methods of Missions." In *Missiology: An Introduction to the Foundations, History, and Strategies of World Missions*. 2nd ed. Edited by John Mark Terry. B&H Academic.

Contributors

Larry W. Caldwell is chief academic officer, dean, and professor of intercultural studies and Bible interpretation at Kairos University in Sioux Falls, SD. Before this, he and his wife Mary served as missionaries with Converge for twenty-one years in Manila, Philippines. During that time, he was academic dean and professor of missions and Bible interpretation at Asian Theological Seminary and also served as director of the doctor of missiology program at the Asia Graduate School of Theology. He has authored many books, including *The Bible in Culture, Missions and You!*, and *Doing Bible Interpretation!* He and Mary have four adult children and four grandchildren.

Anthony Casey (PhD, Southern Baptist Theological Seminary) is associate professor of intercultural studies at Grace College and Seminary in Warsaw, IN. He has conducted qualitative research on four continents and ministered cross-culturally for fifteen years in a variety of contexts, particularly in diaspora settings. He is the author of *Peoples on the Move: Community Research for Ministry and Missions* and *Church Planting among Immigrants in U.S. Urban Centers: The Where, Why, and How of Diaspora Missiology in Action*.

Andrew Feng's (ThM, Dallas Theological Seminary) motto is to be an Authentic Advocate, Break Bottlenecks, and Catalyze Collaboration. As an advisor for Indigitous, he consults with nonprofits on global strategy and strategic partnerships to drive collective impact. Passionate about young adults, he ideates with emerging leaders to use their gifts beyond the church walls. Before ministry, he studied at USC, worked at Yahoo, and consulted for KPMG. He and his wife served abroad for five years, during which they adopted their son with special needs. With a deep heart for the next generation, Andrew continues to mentor young leaders through Indigitous, equipping them for kingdom impact.

Contributors

Todd M. Johnson (PhD, William Carey International University) is the Eva B. and Paul E. Toms Distinguished Professor of Mission and Global Christianity and co-director of the Center for the Study of Global Christianity at Gordon-Conwell Theological Seminary. Johnson is Research Associate at Boston University's Institute for Culture, Religion and World Affairs, and is leading a research project on international religious demography. He is co-author of the *World Christian Encyclopedia* (2nd and 3rd editions), co-editor of the *Atlas of Global Christianity*, and series editor (with Ken Ross) of the ten-volume *Edinburgh Companions to Global Christianity* series. He is co-editor of the *World Christian Database* and the *World Religion Database* (Brill).

Kyle Lee (BA, University of Virginia) grew up all around the United States and was a missionary kid to Kenya throughout high school. He earned his bachelor's in English at the University of Virginia and is a spoken word artist, podcast host, and producer. He has worked for InterVarsity as a media and marketing producer and strategy manager, Hilton Hotels as a complex marketing manager, and now Indigitous US as a director of strategy. Kyle's passion is to inspire the church to think differently and boldly engage the world with the gospel in faith and relevance through digital storytelling, thought leadership, and strategic partnerships, working to catalyze the called and make kingdom work more effective in the digital age.

Michael Hakmin Lee (PhD, Trinity Evangelical Divinity School) serves as associate professor of ministry and leadership and directs MA programs in Ministry Leadership and Evangelism and Leadership within the Litfin Divinity School at Wheaton College. Michael is currently writing a book through Baker Academic on former evangelical ministers leaving the Christian faith. His prior publications include topics related to the theology and philosophy of religions, race and ethnicity, theology of technology, Christian unity, religious mobility, and evangelical deconversions. Michael also serves his community as a certified judo instructor and a travel baseball coach.

Billy McMahan (DMin candidate, Asbury Theological Seminary) is the southwest mobilizer with Africa Inland Mission and also serves as the president of the Great Commission Research Network. He has over fifteen years of experience working with the next generation in church and parachurch ministry and served as a missionary in Indonesia. He also provides missional coaching for churches, organizations, and businesses nationwide on topics such as increasing missional impact, evangelism, developing next generation leaders, creating healthy teams, and more. You can see more of his work at BillyMcMahan.com.

W. Jay Moon (PhD, Asbury Theological Seminary) is a storyteller, strategist, and scholar with a passion for bridging faith, work, and mission. After spending thirteen years as a SIM missionary in Ghana among the Builsa people, he has firsthand experience in church planting, water development, evangelism, and discipleship. Now a professor of evangelism and church planting at Asbury Theological Seminary, he also leads the Office of Faith, Work, and Economics, equipping leaders to integrate faith in everyday life. A prolific author, Jay has written six books—including *Intercultural Discipleship* and *Effective Intercultural Evangelism*—and edited seven more. A sought-after speaker on church planting, marketplace mission, and evangelism, he has served as president of APM and GCRN and is the incoming president of AETE and ASM. Beyond academia, Jay thrives in hands-on creativity, from building treehouses and throwing axes to mentoring small business innovators—always looking for new ways to connect faith and action.

J. D. Payne (PhD, Southern Baptist Theological Seminary) is professor of Christian ministry at Samford University in Birmingham, Alabama and author of sixteen books in the areas of evangelism and missions. He has served as the southeast region vice-president and executive vice-president of administration for the Evangelical Missiological Society. He has been in the academy twenty-six years, including nineteen years in the pastorate.

Marty Shaw Jr. was born and raised in Japan, the son of missionaries. He has served as the vice president of Global Initiatives and the Asia/Pacific Ministry director with WorldVenture. Marty and his wife, Denise, served as missionaries in Japan for twenty years. He has written articles in both English and Japanese on mission strategy and has taught and trained on missiological topics globally. Marty has served on boards in Asia and the US. He and his wife have two adult children.

Contributors

Stephen Stallard (PhD, Southeastern Baptist Theological Seminary) is the assistant professor of pastoral ministry at Western Seminary and the English ministry pastor of the Chinese Evangelical Church of Portland. He is the author of the volume *Missional Preaching: Communicating the Gospel in an Age of Unbelief*. He is married to Sonya, and they have four lovely children.

David Taylor (PhD candidate) is a student in world religions working on his dissertation on folk Islam. His travel among unreached people groups has inspired him to understand the worldviews of those living in folk and animistic religious contexts. David desires to form a biblically grounded missiology in order to help missionaries reach the unreached with the gospel.

Jessica A. Udall (PhD, Columbia International University) is professor of intercultural studies at Evangelical Theological College in Addis Ababa, Ethiopia, and adjunct professor of intercultural studies for Columbia International University. She has authored, co-authored, and co-edited several books on Christian mission, global migration, and diaspora missiology, and she is devoted to mentoring Christian students for wise and effective intercultural partnership in a globalizing world.

Enoch Wan is currently the research professor of intercultural studies and director of the PhD/EdD/DIS programs at Western Seminary, Portland, Oregon. He is a past president of the Evangelical Missiological Society, as well as the founder and advisor of GlobalMissiology.org. He is a board member of the Worldwide Bible Society (USA) and the Tien Dao Christian Media Association.

John E. White (PhD, Biola University) has been a missionary in Ukraine with WorldVenture for over twenty years, teaching cross-cultural and urban mission. He is currently the director of the master's program in urban mission at Ukrainian Evangelical Theological Seminary and serves as the urban initiatives coordinator for WorldVenture. John has authored two books, *Factors Behind the Ukrainian Evangelical Missionary Surge from 1989 to 1999* and *A Stroll Through the Cities of Eurasia: The Flow of Urban History and the Values of Today*.

Joel W. Wright (MDiv, Trinity Evangelical Divinity School) was a career missionary with Converge (1986–2023) serving as a full-time Bible and missions instructor at the Baptist Theological Seminary of São Paulo, Brazil (1991–2007), as well as assuming numerous pastoral roles throughout that time. He now works in diaspora missions through Reliant Mission/ God's Love for the World. He also serves with Lausanne's Global Diaspora Network and Wheaton College Billy Graham Center's Global Diaspora Institute. He also remains active as an associate pastor of the Brazilian Connection Church in the Chicago area. Blessed in marriage for forty-three years, he and his wife have three children and two grandchildren.

Nick Wu (MA candidate, Dallas Theological Seminary) serves as content manager at Indigitous US. He helps lead young adults in digital mission projects and creative media. He is a professional videographer and has produced short documentaries for missions.

Additional Resources

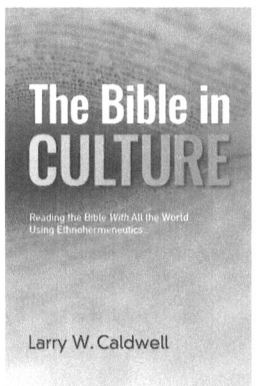

The Bible in Culture: Using Ethnohermeneutics for Reading the Bible With *All the World*

Larry W. Caldwell

Drawing from decades of experience living overseas, Caldwell demonstrates that every culture has its own tools for understanding meaning and shows how God uses these to communicate the truth of his word. This approach is rooted in observing how Jesus, Paul, and others in the early church interpreted Scripture and following their examples. Through real-life illustrations, insights, interactive activities, and case studies, readers will discover how they can also read and interpret God's word in their own cultures.

One New Humanity: Glory, Violence, and the Gospel of Peace

Kristin Caynor and Werner Mischke, authors

One New Humanity offers a vision of glory that confronts the shame and violence of our world. The authors argue that Ephesians 2:13–17 reveals a social and horizontal dimension to the gospel of Christ: In Christ we gain a new peaceable way of being human. Through this extensive look at the gospel of peace, we discover that Scripture speaks more powerfully than we often realize to the problems of polarization, alienation, shame, and violence. This book offers a fresh framework for Jesus-centered reconciliation; we embody Christ's peace, for the world, near and far.

Available at missionbooks.org

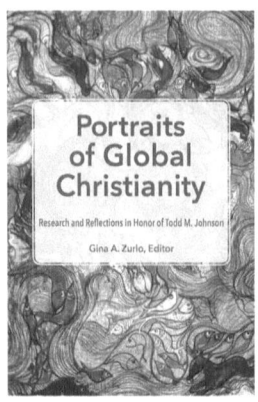

Portraits of Global Christianity: Research and Reflections in Honor of Todd M. Johnson

Gina A. Zurlo, Editor

This book is geared toward a general Christian audience and is written in an accessible style with attractive full-color charts, maps, and graphs to make quantitative data on Christianity and other religions come alive. The reflections and essays in this book in honor of Todd M. Johnson provide readers with concrete examples of how knowledge and experience of Christianity worldwide has fundamentally changed their worldviews, perspectives of the faith, and vocational callings. This book urges readers to seriously consider the growth of Christianity in the global South and its impact on their own lives.

Mobilizing Gen Z: Challenges and Opportunities for the Global Age of Missions

Jolene Erlacher and Katy White

Jolene Erlacher and Katy White blend leading research with the voices of current mission practitioners to unpack the dynamics behind our changing culture and the resulting impact on the church. And perhaps not-so-surprisingly, they reach the conclusion that God has already provided a solution for such a time as this —Gen Z (b. 1996–2010). Through an in-depth profile of this rising cohort—their characteristics, worldview, strengths and weaknesses—the authors illustrate both why Gen Z is sorely needed and why we must seek to engage them differently than previous generations. Encouraging and winsome, *Mobilizing Gen Z* provides practical tools and strategies for engaging, equipping, and retaining Gen Z missionaries.

Available at missionbooks.org